Scoring High

Iowa Tests of Basic Skills®

A Test Prep Program for ITBS®

Book 3
Now with Science

Columbus, OH

The McGraw·Hill Companies

SRAonline.com

 **SRA**

Send all inquiries to:
SRA/McGraw-Hill
8787 Orion Place
Columbus, Ohio 43240-4027

Printed in the United States of America.

ISBN 0-07-604382-7

1 2 3 4 5 6 7 8 9 QPD 09 08 07 06

On Your Way to Scoring High

On the Iowa Tests of Basic Skills®

Book 3

		Page
Family Letter		v
Introduction: Scoring High on ITBS		vii
Scope and Sequence Charts		viii
Orientation Lesson		xii

Unit 1   Vocabulary   1

Lesson 1a	2
Lesson 1b	4
Test Yourself	6

Unit 2   Reading Comprehension   8

Lesson 2a	9
Lesson 2b	16
Test Yourself	22

Unit 3   Spelling   28

Lesson 3a	29
Lesson 3b	31
Test Yourself	33

Unit 4   Capitalization and Punctuation   35

Lesson 4a	36
Lesson 4b	38
Lesson 5a	40
Lesson 5b	42
Test Yourself	44

Unit 5   Usage and Expression   46

Lesson 6a	47
Lesson 6b	49
Lesson 7a	51
Lesson 7b	54
Test Yourself	56

Unit 6   Math Concepts and Estimation   59

Lesson 8a	60
Lesson 8b	63
Lesson 9a	65
Lesson 9b	67
Test Yourself	69

Unit 7   Math Problem Solving   74
           and Data Interpretation

Lesson 10a 75

Lesson 10b 77

Lesson 11a 79

Lesson 11b 81

Test Yourself 83

Unit 8   Math Computation   87

Lesson 12a 88

Lesson 12b 90

Lesson 13a 92

Lesson 13b 94

Test Yourself 96

Unit 9   Maps, Diagrams,   98
              and Reference Materials

Lesson 14a 99

Lesson 14b 101

Lesson 15a 103

Lesson 15b 105

Lesson 16a 107

Lesson 16b 109

Test Yourself 111

Unit 10   Science   118

Lesson 17a 119

Lesson 17b 125

Test Yourself 131

Unit 11   Test Practice   141

Test 1 Vocabulary 146

Test 2 Reading Comprehension 148

Test 3 Spelling 152

Test 4 Capitalization 154

Test 5 Punctuation 156

Test 6 Part 1 Usage 158

Test 6 Part 2 Expression 160

Test 7 Part 1 Math Concepts 162

Test 7 Part 2 Math Estimation 165

Test 8 Part 1 Math Problem 167
         Solving

Test 8 Part 2 Data Interpretation 169

Test 9 Math Computation 171

Test 10 Maps and Diagrams 173

Test 11 Reference Materials 176

Test 12 Science 180

Family Letter

Greetings!

This year, your child, like many students across the country, will be taking a standardized achievement test called the *Iowa Tests of Basic Skills® (ITBS)*. We will be administering this test for several reasons.

- It gives us a snapshot of what your child has learned (achieved). It is one of many ways we assess the skills and knowledge of students because no one test or assessment tool can give an accurate, ongoing picture of your child's development.

- We use ITBS to help us determine where to strengthen our curriculum to better meet the needs of the students. It also helps us see if we are meeting the learning goals we set previously.

In order to give students the best opportunity to show what they know on this standardized achievement test, we will be using SRA/McGraw-Hill's test preparation program, *Scoring High on the Iowa Tests of Basic Skills.* It is designed specifically for the *Iowa Tests of Basic Skills.* Why will we be spending time preparing for this test?

- What happens to your heartbeat when you hear the word *test*? When students hear that word, their anxiety level can rise. However, when they know what to expect, their confidence soars—they are less nervous.

- Test-taking skills can be learned. When preparing, we focus on such skills as reading and listening carefully to directions; budgeting time; answering the easy questions first so more time can be spent on the harder ones; eliminating answer choices that are obviously wrong, and more. These are life skills that students will take with them and use again and again.

- Preparing for the test assures that students won't be surprised by the format of the test. They won't be worried about the type of questions they will see, or how hard the questions will be. They'll know how to fill in answers appropriately. These, and other skills learned ahead of time, will free students to focus on the content of the test and thus give a much more accurate picture of what they know.

How can you help?

- Talk with your child about the purpose of the test. Be positive about the experience.

- Talk to us here at school if you have any questions. Remember, we are a team with the **same** goals in mind—the improvement of your child's educational experience.

- Assure your child that the results of the test are private and won't be used on his or her report card. Remind your child that the test does not measure how smart he or she is, nor does it predict how successful he or she will be in the future.

- Encourage reading at home, and spend time together talking about what you read.

- Be sure your child has plenty of rest on a regular basis, and eats nourishing foods. That's important every day—not just on the day of the test.

Additional information will be provided about the specific subject areas and dates of the tests. Until then, please feel free to contact me if you have any questions about your child's performance or about standardized testing.

Sincerely,

_____

Your child's teacher

Scoring High on the Iowa Tests of Basic Skills
A program that teaches achievement test behaviors

Scoring High on the Iowa Tests of Basic Skills is designed to prepare students for these tests. The program provides instruction and practice in reading, spelling, language, mathematics, study, and science skills. *Scoring High* also familiarizes students with the kinds of test formats and directions that appear on the tests and teaches test-taking strategies that promote success.

Students who are used to a comfortable learning environment are often unaccustomed to the structured setting in which achievement tests are given. Even good students who are used to working independently may have difficulty maintaining a silent, sustained effort or following directions that are read to a large group. *Scoring High*, with its emphasis on group instruction, teaches these test-taking skills systematically.

Using *Scoring High* to help prepare students for the Iowa Tests of Basic Skills will increase the probability of your students doing their best. Students' self-confidence will be at a maximum, and their proficiency in the skills tested will be higher as a result of the newly learned test-taking strategies and increased familiarity with test formats.

Scoring High can be used effectively along with your regular reading, language, mathematics, and science curriculums. By applying subject-area skills in the context of the test-taking situation, students will not only strengthen their skills, but will accumulate a reserve of test-taking strategies.

Eight Student Books for Grades 1–8

To choose the most appropriate book for each student, match the level of the Iowa Tests of Basic Skills that the student will take to the corresponding Scoring High book.

Grade Levels	Test Levels
Book 1	Level 7
Book 2	Level 8
Book 3	Level 9
Book 4	Level 10
Book 5	Level 11
Book 6	Level 12
Book 7	Level 13
Book 8	Level 14

Sequential Skill Development

Each student book is organized into units reflecting the subject areas covered on the corresponding levels of the Iowa Tests of Basic Skills. This book covers reading, spelling, language, mathematics, study, and science skills. Each lesson within a unit focuses on one or two of the subject-area skills and the test-taking strategies that complement the skills. The last lesson in each unit is designed to give students experience in taking an achievement test in that subject area.

The Test Practice section at the end of each book also provides practice in taking achievement tests and will increase students' confidence in their test-taking skills.

Features of the Student Lessons

Each student lesson in subject-area skills contains:

- A Sample(s) section including directions and one or more teacher-directed sample questions
- A Tips section providing test-taking strategies
- A Practice section

Each Test Yourself lesson at the end of a unit is designed like an achievement test in the unit's subject area.

How the Teacher's Edition Works

Since a program that teaches test-taking skills as well as subject-area skills may be new to your students, the Teacher's Edition makes a special effort to provide detailed lesson plans. Each lesson lists subject-area and test-taking skills. In addition, teaching suggestions are provided for handling each part of the lesson—Sample(s), Tips, and Practice. The text for the subject-area and Test Yourself lessons is designed to help students become familiar with following oral directions and with the terminology used on the tests.

Before you begin Lesson 1, you should use the Orientation Lesson on pages xii–xv to acquaint students with the program organization and the procedure for using the student book.

Scope and Sequence: Test-taking Skills

	UNIT										
	1	2	3	4	5	6	7	8	9	10	11
Analyzing questions or answer choices		✓		✓	✓		✓		✓		✓
Avoiding attractive distractors							✓				✓
Checking items by the opposite operation								✓			✓
Comparing or evaluating answer choices						✓	✓		✓		✓
Computing carefully							✓	✓			✓
Considering every answer choice	✓										✓
Converting items to a workable format							✓	✓			✓
Finding the answer without computing						✓	✓				✓
Following printed directions	✓			✓	✓					✓	✓
Identifying and using key words, numbers, and pictures		✓				✓			✓	✓	✓
Indicating that an item has no mistakes			✓	✓	✓						✓
Indicating that the correct answer is not given							✓	✓			✓
Managing time effectively	✓	✓	✓	✓	✓	✓	✓	✓	✓	✓	✓
Marking the right answer as soon as it is found					✓						✓
Noting the lettering of answer choices	✓										✓
Performing the correct operation							✓	✓			✓
Prioritizing questions	✓									✓	✓
Reasoning from facts and evidence		✓									✓
Recalling error types			✓	✓	✓						✓
Referring to a graphic						✓				✓	✓
Referring to a passage to answer questions		✓									✓
Referring to a reference source									✓		✓
Rephrasing a question						✓					✓
Rereading a question									✓	✓	✓
Reworking a problem								✓			✓
Skimming a passage		✓									✓
Skimming a reference source							✓		✓		✓
Skimming questions or answer choices	✓				✓					✓	✓
Skipping difficult items and returning to them later			✓	✓	✓						✓
Subvocalizing answer choices					✓						✓
Taking the best guess when unsure of the answer	✓							✓	✓		✓
Transferring numbers accurately							✓	✓			✓
Understanding unusual item formats				✓	✓						✓
Using charts, diagrams, and graphs								✓			✓
Using context to find an answer					✓						✓
Working methodically	✓	✓	✓	✓	✓	✓	✓	✓	✓	✓	✓

Scope and Sequence: Reading Skills

	UNIT										
	1	2	3	4	5	6	7	8	9	10	11
Identifying synonyms	✓										✓
Analyzing characters		✓									✓
Comparing and contrasting		✓									
Deriving word meanings		✓									✓
Drawing conclusions		✓									✓
Identifying feelings		✓									
Making inferences		✓									✓
Making predictions		✓									✓
Recognizing an author's technique		✓									✓
Recognizing details		✓									✓
Recognizing the narrator		✓									
Understanding literary devices											✓
Understanding reasons		✓									✓
Understanding the author's purpose		✓									
Understanding the main idea		✓									

Scope and Sequence: Language Skills

	UNIT										
	1	2	3	4	5	6	7	8	9	10	11
Identifying spelling errors			✓								✓
Choosing the best paragraph for a given purpose					✓						✓
Choosing the best word to complete a sentence					✓						✓
Identifying capitalization errors				✓							✓
Identifying correctly formed sentences					✓						✓
Identifying mistakes in usage					✓						✓
Identifying punctuation errors				✓							✓
Identifying the best closing sentence for a paragraph					✓						✓
Identifying the best location for a sentence in a paragraph					✓						✓
Identifying the best opening sentence for a paragraph					✓						✓
Identifying the sentence that does not fit in a paragraph					✓						✓

Scope and Sequence: Mathematics Skills

	UNIT										
	1	2	3	4	5	6	7	8	9	10	11
Adding, subtracting, multiplying, and dividing whole numbers, fractions, and decimals								✓			✓
Comparing metric and standard units						✓					
Comparing and ordering whole numbers						✓					✓
Estimating and rounding						✓					✓
Estimating measurement						✓					✓
Finding area						✓					✓
Identifying a line of symmetry						✓					
Identifying parts of a figure						✓					✓
Identifying problem solving strategies						✓					✓
Identifying the best measurement unit						✓					✓
Interpreting tables, diagrams, and graphs							✓				✓
Recognizing alternate forms of a number						✓					✓
Recognizing fractional parts						✓					✓
Recognizing odd and even numbers						✓					✓
Recognizing plane figures						✓					✓
Recognizing value of coins or bills						✓					✓
Sequencing numbers						✓					
Solving word problems							✓				✓
Telling time						✓					✓
Understanding average (mean)						✓					
Understanding characteristics of related numbers						✓					✓
Understanding factors and remainders						✓					
Understanding mathematical language						✓					
Understanding number sentences						✓					✓
Understanding permutations and combinations						✓					✓
Understanding place value						✓					✓
Understanding regrouping						✓					✓
Understanding simple probability						✓					
Understanding special properties of zero						✓					
Understanding transformations						✓					
Using a calendar						✓					
Using a number line						✓					✓

Scoring High on the Iowa Tests of Basic Skills

Scope and Sequence: Study Skills

	UNIT										
	1	2	3	4	5	6	7	8	9	10	11
Alphabetizing words or names									✓		✓
Differentiating among reference sources									✓		✓
Identifying key words									✓		
Understanding a diagram									✓		
Understanding a map									✓		✓
Using a calendar									✓		✓
Using a chart											✓
Using a dictionary									✓		✓
Using a table of contents									✓		✓

Scope and Sequence: Science Skills

	UNIT										
	1	2	3	4	5	6	7	8	9	10	11
Classifying things based on characteristics										✓	✓
Differentiating plants and animals											✓
Recalling characteristics and functions of the human body										✓	✓
Recalling characteristics of Earth and bodies in space										✓	✓
Recognizing characteristics of a habitat										✓	✓
Recognizing forms, sources, and principles of energy										✓	✓
Recognizing health and safety practices											✓
Recognizing importance of environmentally sound practices										✓	✓
Recognizing moon phases										✓	
Recognizing states and properties of matter										✓	✓
Understanding diseases and their sources										✓	✓
Understanding electricity and circuits											✓
Understanding fossilization										✓	✓
Understanding gravity, inertia, and friction										✓	✓
Understanding life cycles and reproduction										✓	✓
Understanding magnetism										✓	✓
Understanding plant and animal behaviors and characteristics										✓	✓
Understanding properties of light										✓	
Understanding scientific instruments, measurement, and processes										✓	✓
Understanding the water cycle										✓	
Understanding weather, climate, and seasons										✓	✓
Using illustrations, charts, and graphs										✓	✓

Orientation Lesson

Focus
Understanding the purpose and structure of *Scoring High on the Iowa Tests of Basic Skills*

Note: Before you begin Lesson 1, use this introductory lesson to acquaint the students with the program orientation and procedures for using this book.

Say Taking a test is something that you do many times during each school year. What kind of tests have you taken? *(math tests, reading tests, spelling tests, daily quizzes, etc.)* Have you ever taken an achievement test that covers many subjects? An achievement test shows how well you are doing in these subjects compared to other students in your grade. How are achievement tests different from the regular tests you take in class? *(many students take them on the same day; special pencils, books, and answer sheets are used; etc.)* Some students get nervous when they take achievement tests. Has this ever happened to you?

Encourage the students to discuss their feelings about test taking. Point out that almost everyone feels anxious or worried when facing a test-taking situation.

Display the cover of Scoring High on the Iowa Tests of Basic Skills.

Say Here is a new book that you'll be using for the next several weeks. The Book is called *Scoring High on the Iowa Tests of Basic Skills.*

Distribute the books to the students.

Say This book will help you improve your reading, language, mathematics, study, and science skills. It will also help you gain the confidence and skills you need to do well on achievement

Scoring High

Iowa Tests of Basic Skills®
A Test Prep Program for ITBS®

Book 3
Now with Science

SRA

tests. What does the title say you will be doing when you finish this book? *(scoring high)* Scoring high on achievement tests is what this program is all about. If you learn the skills taught in this book, you will be ready to do your best on the *Iowa Tests of Basic Skills.*

Share this information with the students if you know when they will be taking the *Iowa Tests of Basic Skills*. Then make sure the students understand that the goal of their *Scoring High* books is to improve their test-taking skills.

Tell the students to turn to the table of contents at the front of their books.

Say This page is a progress chart. It shows the contents of the book. How many units are there? *(11)* Let's read the names of the units together. In these units you will learn reading, spelling, language, mathematics, study skills, science, and test-taking skills. The last lesson in each unit is called Test Yourself. It reviews what you have learned in the unit. In Unit 11, the Test Practice section, you will have a chance to use all the skills you have learned on tests that are somewhat like real achievement tests. This page will also help you keep track of the lessons you have completed. Do you see the box beside each lesson number? When you finish a lesson, you will write your score in the box to show your progress.

Make sure the students understand the information presented on this page. Ask questions such as, "On what page does Lesson 10a start?" *(61)* "What is Lesson 2a called?" *(Reading Comprehension)* "What do you think Lesson 10a is about?" *(solving mathematics problems)*

On Your Way to Scoring High

On the **Iowa Tests of Basic Skills®**

Book 3

Name _____

Unit 1   **Vocabulary**

My Score   Lesson   Page

☐   1a Vocabulary 1
☐   1b Vocabulary 2
☐   Test Yourself 3

Unit 2   **Reading Comprehension**

My Score   Lesson   Page

☐   2a Reading Comprehension 5
☐   2b Reading Comprehension 12
☐   Test Yourself 18

Unit 3   **Spelling**

My Score   Lesson   Page

☐   3a Spelling 24
☐   3b Spelling 26
☐   Test Yourself 28

Unit 4   **Capitalization and Punctuation**

My Score   Lesson   Page

☐   4a Capitalization 31
☐   4b Capitalization 32
☐   5a Punctuation 33
☐   5b Punctuation 34
☐   Test Yourself 35

Unit 5   **Usage and Expression**

My Score   Lesson   Page

☐   6a Usage 37
☐   6b Usage 39
☐   7a Expression 40
☐   7b Expression 43
☐   Test Yourself 45

Unit 6   **Math Concepts and Estimation**

My Score   Lesson   Page

☐   8a Math Concepts 48
☐   8b Math Concepts 51
☐   9a Math Estimation 53
☐   9b Math Estimation 55
☐   Test Yourself 56

Unit 7   **Math Problem Solving and Data Interpretation**

My Score	Lesson	Page
☐	10a Math Problem Solving	61
☐	10b Math Problem Solving	63
☐	11a Data Interpretation	64
☐	11b Data Interpretation	66
☐	Test Yourself	67

Unit 8   **Math Computation**

My Score	Lesson	Page
☐	12a Computation	71
☐	12b Computation	72
☐	13a Computation	73
☐	13b Computation	74
☐	Test Yourself	75

Unit 9   **Maps, Diagrams, and Reference Materials**

My Score	Lesson	Page
☐	14a Maps and Diagrams	76
☐	14b Maps and Diagrams	78
☐	15a Reference Materials	80
☐	15b Reference Materials	81
☐	16a Reference Materials	82
☐	16b Reference Materials	84
☐	Test Yourself	85

Unit 10   **Science**

My Score	Lesson	Page
☐	17a Science Skills	92
☐	17b Science Skills	98
☐	Test Yourself	104

Unit 11   **Test Practice**

		Page
Name and Answer Sheet		115

My Score	Test	
☐	1 Vocabulary	119
☐	2 Reading Comprehension	121
☐	3 Spelling	125
☐	4 Capitalization	127
☐	5 Punctuation	128
☐	6 Part 1 Usage	129
☐	6 Part 2 Expression	130
☐	7 Part 1 Math Concepts	131
☐	7 Part 2 Math Estimation	134
☐	8 Part 1 Math Problem Solving	135
☐	8 Part 2 Data Interpretation	136
☐	9 Math Computation	137
☐	10 Maps and Diagrams	138
☐	11 Reference Materials	141
☐	12 Science	145

Say Now let's look at two of the lessons. Turn to Lesson 1a on page 1. Where is the lesson number and title? *(at the top of the page, beside the unit number)* What is the title of the lesson? *(Vocabulary)*

Familiarize the students with the lesson layout and sequence of instruction. Have them locate the directions and sample items. Explain that you will work through the Samples section together. Then have the students find the STOP sign in the lower right-hand corner of the page. Explain that when they come to the STOP sign at the bottom of a page, they should not continue on to the next page. They may check their work on the present lesson.

Have the students locate the Tips sign below the Samples section.

Say What does the sign point out to you? *(the tips)* Each lesson has tips that suggest new ways to work through the items. Tests can be tricky. The tips will tell you what to watch out for. They will help you find the best answer quickly.

Have the students locate the Practice section below the tips. Explain that they will do the practice items by themselves. Tell the students they will have an opportunity to discuss any problems they had when they complete the Practice section.

Ask the students to turn to the Test Yourself lesson on page 3 of their books. Tell the students the Test Yourself lessons may seem like real tests, but they are not. The Test Yourself lessons are designed to give them opportunities to apply the skills and tips they have learned in timed, trial-run situations. Then have the students find the GO sign in the lower right-hand corner of the page. Explain that when they come to the GO sign at the bottom of a page, they should turn to the next page and continue working.

Explain that you will go over the answers together after the students complete each lesson. Then they will figure out their scores and record the number of correct answers in the boxes on the progress chart. Be sure to point out that the students' scores are only for them to see how well they are doing.

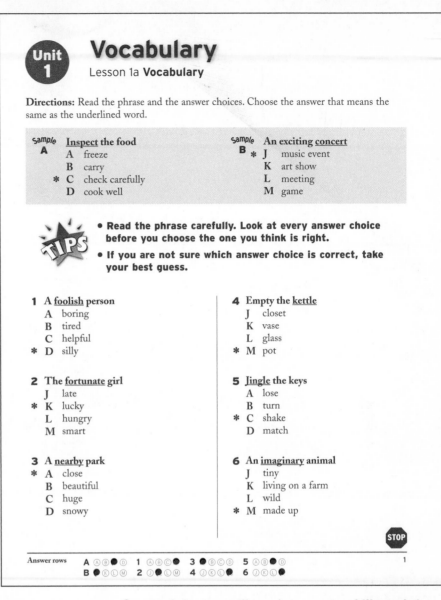

Say Each lesson will teach you new skills and tips. What will you have learned when you finish this book? *(vocabulary, reading, spelling, language arts, mathematics, study skills, science, and test-taking skills; how to do my best on an achievement test)* When you know you can do your best, how do you think you will feel on test day? You may be a little nervous, but you should also feel confident that you are ready to do your best.

Unit 1

Background

This unit contains three lessons that deal with vocabulary skills. Students are asked to identify words with similar meanings.

• **In Lesson 1a,** students identify words that have the same meaning as target words in phrases. Students are encouraged to follow printed directions. They note the lettering of answer choices, consider every answer choice, and take their best guess when unsure of the answer.

• **In Lesson 1b,** students identify words that have the same meaning as target words in phrases. In addition to reviewing the test-taking skills introduced in Lesson 1a, students learn how to skim and prioritize answer choices.

• **In the Test Yourself lesson,** the vocabulary skills and test-taking skills introduced in Lessons 1a and 1b are reinforced and presented in a format that gives students the experience of taking an achievement test. Techniques for managing time effectively when taking a standardized test are reinforced.

Instructional **Objectives**

Lesson 1a **Vocabulary** Lesson 1b **Vocabulary**	Given a phrase with a target word, students identify which of four answer choices means the same as the target word.
Test Yourself	Given questions similar to those in Lessons 1a and 1b, students utilize vocabulary skills and test-taking strategies on achievement test formats.

Focus

Reading Skill
- identifying synonyms

Test-taking Skills
- following printed directions
- noting lettering of answer choices
- considering every answer choice
- taking the best guess when unsure of the answer

Samples A and B

Say Turn to Lesson 1a on page 1. The page number is at the bottom of the page on the right.

Check to see that the students have found the right page.

Say In this lesson you will find words that have the same or nearly the same meaning as another word used in a phrase. Read the directions at the top of the page to yourself while I read them aloud to you.

Read the directions to the students.

Say Let's do Sample A. Listen carefully. Read the phrase with the underlined word. Think about what the word means as it is used in the phrase. Now, look at the four answer choices below the phrase. Which of the four answers means about the same as the underlined word? *(pause)* The answer is C because *inspect* and *check carefully* mean about the same thing. Fill in the circle for answer C in the answer rows at the bottom of the page. Be sure your answer circle is completely filled in with a dark mark and that you have marked the correct answer circle.

Check to see that the students have marked the correct circle.

Say Now do Sample B by yourself. Read the phrase and fill in the circle for the word or words that means the same as the underlined word. *(pause)* Which answer choice is correct? *(answer J)* Yes, a *concert* is a *music event*.

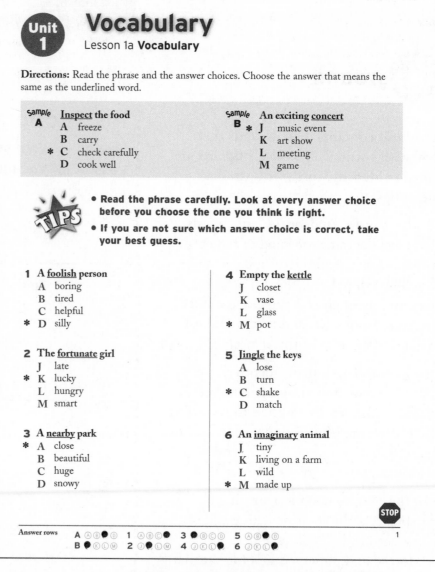

Make sure that circle J for Sample B is completely filled in. Press your pencil firmly so your mark comes out dark.

Check to see that the students have marked the correct circle.

★TIPS

Say Now let's look at the tips.

Read the tips aloud to the students.

Say Be sure to take your time and work carefully. Read the phrase with the underlined word and all of the answer choices. If you are not sure which answer choice is correct, take your best guess. It is better to guess than to leave an answer blank.

Practice

Say We are ready for the Practice items. Remember, the letters for the answer choices change from question to question. For odd-numbered questions, they are A-B-C-D. For even-numbered questions, they are J-K-L-M. You must pay careful attention to the letters for the answer choices and the circles in the answer rows at the bottom of the page. It's a good idea to double-check to be sure that you have filled in the circle for the answer choice you think is correct. Check both the item number and the answer letter. If you make a mistake when you fill in the answer circle, your answer will still be counted wrong, even if you knew what the correct answer was.

Work until you come to the STOP sign at the bottom of the page. Fill in your answer circles with dark marks and completely erase any marks for answers that you change. Do you have any questions? Start working now.

Allow time for the students to do Numbers 1 through 6.

Say It's time to stop. You have finished Lesson 1a.

Review the answers with the students. Ask them whether they remembered to look at all the answer choices and to take the best guess when they were unsure of the correct answer. Did they have any difficulty marking the circles in the answer rows? If any questions caused particular difficulty, work through each of the answer choices.

Have the students indicate completion of the lesson by entering their score for this activity on the progress chart at the beginning of the book.

 Unit 1

Vocabulary
Lesson 1a **Vocabulary**

Directions: Read the phrase and the answer choices. Choose the answer that means the same as the underlined word.

Sample A	<u>Inspect</u> the food		Sample B	An exciting <u>concert</u>
	A freeze		*	J music event
	B carry			K art show
* C	check carefully			L meeting
	D cook well			M game

TIPS
- Read the phrase carefully. Look at every answer choice before you choose the one you think is right.
- If you are not sure which answer choice is correct, take your best guess.

1 A <u>foolish</u> person
 A boring
 B tired
 C helpful
* D silly

2 The <u>fortunate</u> girl
 J late
* K lucky
 L hungry
 M smart

3 A <u>nearby</u> park
* A close
 B beautiful
 C huge
 D snowy

4 Empty the <u>kettle</u>
 J closet
 K vase
 L glass
* M pot

5 <u>Jingle</u> the keys
 A lose
 B turn
* C shake
 D match

6 An <u>imaginary</u> animal
 J tiny
 K living on a farm
 L wild
* M made up

STOP

Answer rows   A ⒶⒷ●Ⓓ   1 ⒶⒷⒸ●   3 ●ⒷⒸⒹ   5 ⒶⒷ●Ⓓ   1
      B ●ⓀⓁⓂ   2 Ⓙ●ⓁⓂ   4 ⒿⓀⓁ●   6 ⒿⓀⓁ●

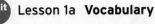

Focus

Reading Skill
• identifying synonyms

Test-taking Skills
• working methodically
• following printed directions
• noting lettering of answer choices
• considering every answer choice
• skimming answer choices
• prioritizing questions

Samples A and B

Say Turn to Lesson 1b on page 2. The page number is at the bottom of the page on the left.

Check to see that the students have found the right page.

Say In this lesson you will do more vocabulary items. Read the directions at the top of the page to yourself.

Allow time for the students to read the directions.

Say Read the phrase with the underlined word for Sample A. Think about what the word means as it is used in the phrase. Now, look at the four answer choices below the phrase. Which of the four answers means about the same as the underlined word? *(pause)* The answer is B, *hat*. In this phrase, *cap* and *hat* mean the same thing. Fill in the circle for answer B in the answer rows at the bottom of the page. Be sure your answer circle is completely filled in with a dark mark and that you have marked the correct answer circle.

Check to see that the students have marked the correct circle.

Say Now do Sample B by yourself. Read the phrase and fill in the circle for the answer that means the same as the underlined word. You may find it helpful to substitute each answer for the underlined word. *(pause)* Which answer choice is correct? *(answer M)* Yes, *cut* and *chop* mean about the same thing. Make sure that circle M for Sample B is completely filled in.

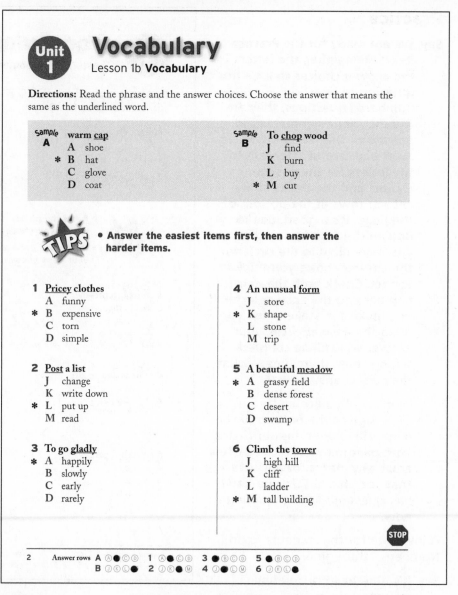

Press your pencil firmly so your mark comes out dark.

Check to see that the students have marked the correct circle.

★TIPS

Say Let's review the tip.

Read the tip aloud to the students.

Say One strategy you can use is to skim all of the items and do the easiest ones first. This will save you time and make it more likely that you will be able to answer all of the items you know.

Review as necessary the process of reviewing items and doing the easiest ones first.

Practice

Say We are ready for the Practice items. Remember, the letters for the answer choices change from question to question. For odd-numbered questions, they are A-B-C-D. For even-numbered questions, they are J-K-L-M. You must pay careful attention to the letters for the answer choices and the circles in the answer rows at the bottom of the page. It's a good idea to double-check to be sure that you have filled in the circle for the answer choice you think is correct. Check both the item number and the answer letter. If you make a mistake when you fill in the answer circle, your answer will still be counted wrong, even if you knew what the correct answer was. And remember, you should skim the items and do the easiest ones first.

Work until you come to the STOP sign at the bottom of the page. Fill in your answer circles with dark marks and completely erase any marks for answers that you change. Do you have any questions? Start working now.

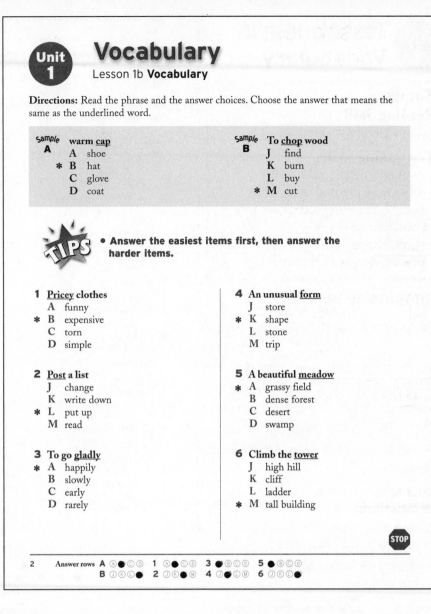

Allow time for the students to do Numbers 1 through 6.

Say It's time to stop. You have finished Lesson 1b.

Review the answers with the students. Ask them whether they remembered to skim the items and to do the easiest ones first. If any questions caused particular difficulty, work through each of the answer choices.

Have the students indicate completion of the lesson by entering their score for this activity on the progress chart at the beginning of the book.

Focus

Reading Skill
• identifying synonyms

Test-taking Skills
• managing time effectively
• following printed directions
• noting the lettering of answer choices
• considering every answer choice
• taking the best guess when unsure of the answer
• working methodically
• skimming answer choices
• prioritizing questions

This lesson simulates an actual test-taking experience. Therefore, it is recommended that the directions be read verbatim and the suggested procedures and time allowances be followed.

Directions

Administration Time: approximately 15 minutes

Say Turn to the Test Yourself lesson on page 3.

Check to be sure the students have found the right page. Point out to the students that this Test Yourself lesson is timed like a real test, but that they will score it themselves to see how well they are doing. Explain that it is important to work quickly and to answer as many questions as possible.

Say This lesson will check how well you understand word meanings. Remember to make sure that the circles for your answer choices are completely filled in. Press your pencil firmly so that your marks come out dark. Completely erase any marks for answers that you change. Do not write anything except your answer choices in your books.

Read the phrase with the underlined word for Sample A. Think about what the word means as it is used in the phrase. Now, look at the four answer choices below the phrase. Which of the four answers means about the same as

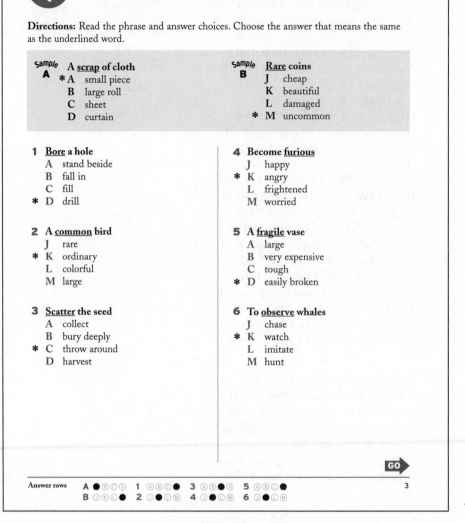

the underlined word? *(pause)* **The answer is A,** *small piece.* **Fill in the circle for answer A in the answer rows at the bottom of the page. Be sure your answer circle is completely filled in with a dark mark and that you have marked the correct answer circle.**

Check to see that the students have marked the correct circle.

Say Now do Sample B by yourself. Read the phrase and fill in the circle for the answer that means the same as the underlined word. *(pause)* **Which answer choice is correct?** *(answer M)* **Yes,** *rare* **and** *uncommon* **mean about the same thing. Make sure that circle M for Sample B is completely filled in. Press your pencil firmly so your mark comes out dark.**

Check to see that the students have marked the correct circle.

Say Now you will answer more questions. Fill in the spaces for your answers in the rows at the bottom of the page. When you come to the GO sign at the bottom of the page, turn to the next page and continue working. Work until you come to the STOP sign at the bottom of page 4. When you have finished, you can check over your answers to this test. Then wait for the rest of the group to finish. Any questions?

Answer any questions that the students have.

Say Start working now. You have 10 minutes.

Allow 10 minutes. Most students should finish in a shorter time.

Say It's time to stop. You have completed the Test Yourself lesson. Check to see that you have completely filled in your answer circles with dark marks. Make sure that any marks for answers that you changed have been completely erased. Now you may close your books.

Have the students indicate completion of the lesson by entering their score for this activity on the progress chart at the beginning of the book. Collect the students' books if this is the end of the testing session.

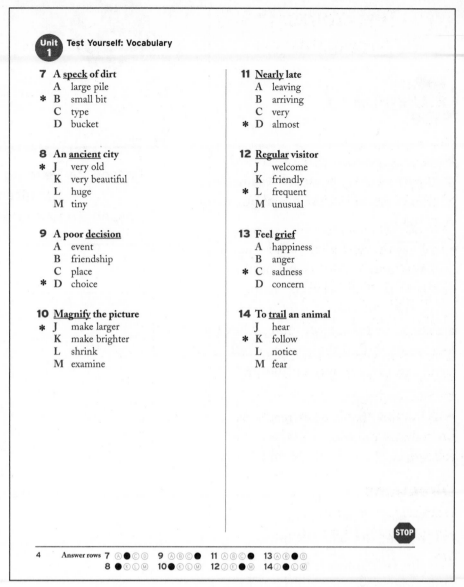

Unit 1 Test Yourself: Vocabulary

7 A <u>speck</u> of dirt
   A   large pile
 * B   small bit
   C   type
   D   bucket

8 An <u>ancient</u> city
 * J   very old
   K   very beautiful
   L   huge
   M   tiny

9 A poor <u>decision</u>
   A   event
   B   friendship
   C   place
 * D   choice

10 <u>Magnify</u> the picture
 * J   make larger
   K   make brighter
   L   shrink
   M   examine

11 <u>Nearly</u> late
   A   leaving
   B   arriving
   C   very
 * D   almost

12 <u>Regular</u> visitor
   J   welcome
   K   friendly
 * L   frequent
   M   unusual

13 Feel <u>grief</u>
   A   happiness
   B   anger
 * C   sadness
   D   concern

14 To <u>trail</u> an animal
   J   hear
 * K   follow
   L   notice
   M   fear

STOP

4   Answer rows   7 Ⓐ●ⒸⒹ   9 ⒶⒷⒸ●   11 ⒶⒷⒸ●   13 ⒶⒷ●Ⓓ
                   8 ●ⓀⓁⓂ   10 ●ⓀⓁⓂ   12 ⒿⓀ●Ⓜ   14 Ⓙ●ⓁⓂ

Background

This unit contains three lessons that deal with reading comprehension skills. Students answer questions about stories they read.

• **In Lesson 2a**, students read a passage and answer questions based on the content of the passage. Students are encouraged to skim a passage and refer to a passage to answer questions. They use key words to find the answer, work methodically, and reason from facts and evidence.

• **In Lesson 2b,** students read a passage and answer questions based on the content of the passage. In addition to reviewing the test-taking skills introduced in Lesson 2a, students learn the importance of analyzing answer choices and reading between the lines.

• **In the Test Yourself lesson,** the reading skills and test-taking skills introduced in Lessons 2a and 2b are reinforced and presented in a format that gives students the experience of taking an achievement test. Techniques for managing time effectively when taking a standardized test are reinforced.

Instructional **Objectives**

Lesson 2a **Reading Comprehension** Lesson 2b **Reading Comprehension**	Given a written passage and a literal or inferential question based on the passage, students identify which of four answer choices is correct.
Test Yourself	Given questions similar to those in Lessons 2a and 2b, students utilize reading comprehension and test-taking strategies on achievement test formats.

Focus

Reading Skills
- identifying feelings
- understanding the main idea
- deriving word meanings
- recognizing details
- analyzing characters
- drawing conclusions
- making inferences
- recognizing an author's technique
- understanding reasons

Test-taking Skills
- skimming a passage
- referring to a passage to answer questions
- using key words to find the answer
- working methodically
- reasoning from facts and evidence

Sample A

Say Turn to Lesson 2a on page 5. In this lesson you will answer questions about passages that you read. Begin by reading the directions at the top of the page to yourself while I read them out loud.

Read the directions to the students.

Say Let's begin by doing Sample A. Skim the passage to yourself. *(pause)* Now, read the question next to the passage. To find the correct answer, look back at the passage. What is the correct answer? *(answer C)* You can tell from the story that Robbie probably feels excited. Fill in answer circle C for Sample A in the answer rows at the bottom of the page. Make sure the circle is completely filled in. Press your pencil firmly so that your mark comes out dark.

Check to see that the students have marked the correct answer circle. Discuss with them how to tell from the story that Robbie is excited.

Reading Comprehension
Lesson 2a **Reading Comprehension**

Directions: Read the passage and the answer choices. Choose the best answer.

Sample A

Robbie got up early without anyone waking him. Today he and the rest of the family were going fishing at Parker Lake. Robbie loved fishing, and Parker Lake had the best fishing around. They were going to rent a boat and spend the whole day on the lake. He was sure he would catch a big one.

How do you think Robbie feels?
- A Worried
- B Proud
- * C Excited
- D Disappointed

TIPS
- Skim the passage quickly, then read the questions.
- Look back to the passage to find the answers to the questions. Key words in the question will tell you where to look.

A horse and a dog sat talking one day. The dog said, "I have found a tree full of apples on the other side of the road. We will have all the food we need from the tree. We can leave our owners and be free to roam as we please."

The horse said to the dog, "My owner gives me an apple every day. When he runs out of apples, he feeds me other tasty food. Why would I leave my owner when he feeds me well and takes good care of me?"

The dog decided to leave without the horse. He crossed the road and sat under the tree, but he could not reach the apples there. He waited for the apples to fall. The only apples that fell from the tree were the rotten ones that tasted bad, so the dog returned to his owner.

1 What is the main point of this fable?
- * A Be sure a change doesn't make things worse.
- B Don't listen to close friends.
- C Don't be afraid to try new things.
- D Think before you stay where you are.

2 In the first paragraph, what does the word "roam" mean?
- J To hop up and down
- K To watch closely
- * L To run freely
- M To stay in one place

GO

Answer rows   A ⒶⒷ●Ⓓ   1 ●ⒷⒸⒹ   2 ⒥Ⓚ●Ⓜ   5

★ TIPS

Say Now let's look at the tips. Who will read them?

Have a volunteer read the tips aloud.

Say The best way to answer reading comprehension questions is to skim the passage quickly and then read the questions. Refer back to the passage to answer the questions, but don't re-read the story for each question. Key words in the question will tell you where in the passage to look for the correct answer. If you can find the same key words in the passage, you can usually find the correct answer nearby.

Practice

Say Now we are ready for Practice. You will read more passages and answer questions about them in the same way that we did the sample. Work as quickly as you can. Skim the passage and then read the questions. Use the meaning of the passage to find the answers. Use key words in the question to find the part of the passage that contains the answer. Fill in your answers in the circles at the bottom of the page. When you see a GO sign, turn the page and continue working. Work until you come to the STOP sign at the bottom of page 11. Remember to make sure that your answer circles are filled in with dark marks. Completely erase any marks for answers that you change. Do you have any questions? Start working now.

Allow time for the students to read the stories and answer the questions.

Amanda walked with her friend, Ineta, to the park. Every day after school, the friends would spend a few minutes on the swings. They loved to swing high in the air. They sang as they rocked back and forth, back and forth.

"I wonder if this is what a bird feels like," said Ineta. Amanda smiled and wondered, too.

"You know," said Amanda, "I think I'd like to be a bird. They can go high in the air and live in the trees and build nests. I could feel like we do when we swing all the time."

"If I were a bird, I think I'd miss swimming and walking and playing ball and riding bikes," said Ineta. She looked over at Amanda to see what she thought.

"You're right. Flying is for the birds. I think I'd miss playing on the swings with you, Ineta," said Amanda. "We do a lot of things that birds can't."

Ineta and Amanda slid their feet on the dirt to slow down their swinging. It was time to go home. The girls walked together for a while, then headed in different directions. They waved at each other as they walked toward their own houses.

GO →

6

3 **What did the girls do to stop swinging?**
   A Held very still
   B Just waited for the swing to stop
 ∗ C Dragged their feet
   D Asked friends for help

4 **Which of these best describes Ineta?**
   J She likes to tease Amanda.
 ∗ K She likes to swing.
   L She is very tall.
   M She wants to be a bird.

5 **What does Amanda mean when she says, "Flying is for the birds"?**
   A She wants to jump out of the swing.
   B Ineta should fly a plane.
   C Only birds can fly in the air.
 ∗ D She doesn't really want to fly.

6 **The way that Ineta and Amanda talk to each other shows that they are**
   J gym partners.
   K sisters.
 ∗ L good friends.
   M classmates.

7 **At the end of the story, how does Amanda feel about flying?**
 ∗ A Uninterested
   B Excited
   C Helpless
   D Silly

8 **What did Ineta and Amanda like to do after school?**
 ∗ J Swing at the park
   K Visit the zoo
   L Walk to the store
   M Run home quickly

GO

Answer rows **3** Ⓐ Ⓑ ● Ⓓ   **4** Ⓙ ● Ⓛ Ⓜ   **5** Ⓐ Ⓑ Ⓒ ●   **6** Ⓙ Ⓚ ● Ⓜ   **7** ● Ⓑ Ⓒ Ⓓ   **8** ● Ⓚ Ⓛ Ⓜ **7**

"Mom, there's nothing to do. I'm bored."

"Why don't you walk down to the park?"

"That's really boring. Can I go over to Alida's? Aunt Millie said it's okay."

"That's a good idea. Don't stop in the video arcade like you usually do. I'll call Aunt Millie in about twenty minutes to check up on you."

Reggie grabbed his coat and hat and ran out the door and down the steps. He waited for the light to change, looked both ways, and crossed the street. There was always a lot of traffic on the street outside his apartment building, and he didn't want to get hit by a car.

He ran into the park and followed the path that went by the lake. Alida and her family lived on the other side of the park. Their apartment was almost a mile away, and he didn't want to waste time and worry his mother.

As Reggie passed the lake, he saw the strangest thing. A crowd of people was gathered around watching pirates row an old-fashioned boat on the lake! Although he knew he should go right over to Alida's apartment, Reggie couldn't resist joining the crowd of people by the lake. When he got closer, he saw lots of lights, some cameras, and some people shouting orders at the pirates. It was very exciting, especially when the pirates got into a sword fight. None of them got hurt, of course, but one of them fell into the lake. Everyone got a good laugh at that.

After about ten minutes, Reggie suddenly remembered what he was supposed to be doing. He turned away from the crowd and started running down the path. If he hurried, he would still get to Alida's apartment before his mother called.

GO ▶

8

9 What do you think Reggie will do if he is late getting to Alida's?

   A   Make up a story explaining why he was late

* B   Explain what happened in the park

   C   Not care that he is late

   D   Say that there was so much traffic he couldn't cross the street

10 Where do you think Reggie lives?

   J   On a quiet street

   K   Near a river

* L   On a busy street

   M   Near the ocean

11 Which of these statements is probably true about Reggie?

   A   He never does what his mother says.

   B   His sister's name is Alida.

   C   He often jogs in the park.

* D   He likes to play video games.

12 What do you think happened at the lake?

   J   Students were practicing for a school play.

* K   Some people were making a movie.

   L   Real pirates were in the park.

   M   Some people were getting ready for Halloween.

13 About how long does it usually take to get to Alida's apartment?

* A   Less than twenty minutes

   B   More than twenty minutes

   C   About five minutes

   D   About thirty minutes

14 How will Reggie probably feel when he gets to Alida's house?

   J   Sad

   K   Angry

   L   Disappointed

* M   Excited

GO

Answer rows **9** Ⓐ ● Ⓒ Ⓓ   **11** Ⓐ Ⓑ Ⓒ ●   **13** ● Ⓑ Ⓒ Ⓓ   9

          10 Ⓙ Ⓚ ● Ⓜ   **12** Ⓙ ● Ⓛ Ⓜ   **14** Ⓙ Ⓚ Ⓛ ●

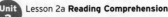

A group of ten children, a spotted beagle, and a yellow bird have become well known to children and adults for over fifty years. The comic strip "Peanuts" was the work of just one man, Charles Schulz.

Schulz loved drawing. His kindergarten teacher even told him he would become an artist some day. Schulz knew that he wanted to make his own comic strip. His father signed him up for a drawing class by mail. The artist had a hard time in the class, though. He received low marks in the class called "Drawing of Children."

After finishing the class, he became a soldier in World War II. Though he couldn't draw much in the war, he did sketch cartoons from the war on letters soldiers wrote to friends and family back home.

When he returned home from the war, Schulz began teaching at the art school where he took his class by mail. There he made friends that would later be found in his comic strips. One friend was named Charlie Brown, the character that is most famous.

The first national comic strip Charles Schulz made was called "L'il Folks." Because other cartoon strips had names like this already, someone suggested renaming the comic "Peanuts." Schulz didn't like the name because it made his work sound unimportant. Luckily, the name stayed.

Through the years, the "Peanuts" gang has been popular in the United States and around the world. "Peanuts" has been printed in 2,600 newspapers, and the comic strip has been translated into seventy-five different languages. In May 2001, the "Peanuts" gang appeared on United States stamps as well. Though Charles Schulz died in 2000, "Peanuts" will live forever in the memory of his readers.

GO ▶

10

Say It's time to stop. You have finished Lesson 2a.

Review the answers with the students. Ask them if they remembered to look back at the passage to find the answers to the questions. If any questions caused particular difficulty, work through the story, questions, and answer choices. Ask the students which key words helped them find the answers and discuss any strategies they used.

Have the students indicate completion of the lesson by entering their score for this activity on the progress chart at the beginning of the book.

15 What does the author tell us by describing Schulz's class in the second paragraph?

* **A** That Schulz was a success even after receiving a low mark
  B That Schulz wasn't very good at drawing children
  C That Schulz's kindergarten teacher was wrong
  D That Schulz should have stopped drawing after the class

16 What does the author mean by saying that some of Schulz's friends were "found" in his comic strips?

  J Charlie Brown was a boy who was lost.
  K Schulz wrote stories about real people.
* **L** Schulz's characters were like the friends he met.
  M Charlie Brown was a name Schulz made up.

17 How did Schulz find ways to draw during the war?

  A He practiced sketching at night.
  B He drew maps for his boss.
  C He worked as a teacher at an art school.
* **D** He sketched cartoons on letters others wrote.

18 In the last paragraph, what does "translated" mean?

  J Explained more clearly
* **K** Written in a different language
  L Drawn in different colors
  M Made into a book

19 Why did Schulz not like the name "Peanuts"?

  A He thought the name was silly.
* **B** He thought it made his work sound unimportant.
  C He didn't like to eat peanuts.
  D He didn't think children would like the name.

20 What is the main idea of this passage?

* **J** Charles Schulz's comic strips were a great success.
  K Charles Schulz fought in World War II.
  L The "Peanuts" comic strip was first named "L'il Folks."
  M Drawing was Charles Schulz's hobby.

STOP

Answer rows 15 ⏺ⒷⒸⒹ 17 ⒶⒷⒸ⏺ 19 Ⓐ⏺ⒸⒹ
16 ⒿⓀ⏺Ⓜ 18 Ⓙ⏺ⓁⓂ 20 ⏺ⓀⓁⓂ

11

Focus

Reading Skills
- making inferences
- recognizing details
- understanding the author's purpose
- comparing and contrasting
- understanding reasons
- drawing conclusions
- making predictions
- analyzing characters
- understanding the main idea

Test-taking Skills
- analyzing answer choices
- working methodically
- reasoning from facts and evidence

Sample A

Say Turn to Lesson 2b on page 12. In this lesson you will answer questions about passages that you read. Begin by reading the directions at the top of the page to yourself while I read them out loud.

Read the directions to the students.

Say Now we'll do Sample A. Read the passage to yourself. *(pause)* Now, read the question next to the passage. What is the correct answer to the question? *(answer D)* Fill in answer circle D for Sample A in the answer rows at the bottom of the page. Make sure the circle is completely filled in. Press your pencil firmly so that your mark comes out dark.

Check to see that the students have marked the correct answer circle.

★TIPS

Say Now let's look at the tip. Who will read it?

Have a volunteer read the tip aloud.

Reading Comprehension
Lesson 2b **Reading Comprehension**

Directions: Read the passage and the answer choices. Choose the best answer.

Sample A Mr. and Mrs. Romero couldn't believe what they saw. A pony was standing in the middle of their lawn eating the grass. It seemed quite at home and wasn't afraid at all when some children walked up to it. The pony looked at the children and then walked over to them and nudged them with its nose.

The pony in this story
A belongs to the Romero family.
B is afraid of children.
C was eating flowers.
∗ D is probably lost.

TIPS
- For some items, you have to "read between the lines." This means you can't answer the question with words from the story.

The paper clip looks like a simple invention that has been around for centuries. Surprisingly, paper clips have been around only since the end of the 1800s.

Before the invention of the paper clip, people kept papers together in all kinds of interesting ways. Most people would poke a hole through the papers and tie ribbon through the hole. Later, straight pins were used. Both of these ways of holding paper together left holes in the paper.

With the invention of steel wire came the idea of the paper clip. Steel wire is bendable. It also stays in place after it is bent.

In the early 1900s the Gem Company in Great Britain designed paper clips with rounded tops. These are the ones we see most often today.

1 How did people keep papers together before the paper clip?
A With bendable steel wire
B With tape
C With a rubber band
∗ D With a ribbon

2 What is the author trying to do in this passage?
∗ J Tell us about something we use often
K Make readers think about inventions
L Give advice about inventing things
M Explain how to make something

GO

12   Answer rows A Ⓐ Ⓑ ● Ⓓ   1 Ⓐ Ⓑ Ⓒ ●   2 ● Ⓚ Ⓛ Ⓜ

Say Sometimes an answer won't be stated directly in the passage. You have to "read between the lines" to find the answer. This means that you use the information and your own thinking to find the answer.

Explain the tip further, if necessary. Explain how it was necessary to "read between the lines" to answer Sample A.

Practice

Say Now we are ready for Practice. You will read more passages and answer questions about them in the same way that we did the sample. Work as quickly as you can. Skim the passage and then read the questions. Use the meaning of the passage to find the answers. If necessary, "read between the lines" to find the answers. Fill in your answers in the circles at the bottom of the page. When you see a GO sign, turn the page and continue working. Work until you come to the STOP sign at the bottom of page 17. Remember to make sure that your answer circles are filled in with dark marks. Completely erase any marks for answers that you change. Do you have any questions? Start working now.

Allow time for the students to read the stories and answer the questions.

3 Why was the paper clip better than other things that held papers?
A   Paper clips used wire that was hard to bend.
B   Ribbon was very expensive to use.
* C Paper clips left no holes in the paper.
D   Straight pins slipped out of the paper easily.

4 What is probably the reason people once used straight pins to hold papers?
J   Straight pins could poke through cloth.
* K People had straight pins in their homes.
L   Straight pins were cheaper than paper clips.
M   Some straight pins had heads that were colored.

Slink, slink, slink goes the inchworm. Its body loops as it slowly moves forward. Its back legs scurry to catch up to its front legs. Then its front legs run far in front, leaving its back legs behind.

Inchworms do not have different parts or segments like some other worms. Because of this, inchworms cannot wiggle as most worms do. Their bodies must move all at once. This is why their bodies loop when they walk.

Sometimes inchworms can stand straight up in the air, very still. This makes them look like the sticks they crawl on. They want to look like sticks so other animals do not catch them.

5 How does an inchworm crawl?
A   By twisting and wiggling the parts of its body
* B By moving its back legs and then its front legs
C   By using its tail to move it forward
D   By rolling from one side to the other

6 What do inchworms look like when they stand up straight?
J   Flowers
K   Trees
L   Leaves
* M Sticks

7 How is an inchworm different from other worms?
* A It has no segments like other worms.
B   It is longer than other worms.
C   It is shorter than other worms.
D   It tastes better than other worms.

8 According to the author, in what way does the above difference change the inchworm?
J   How big it is
K   Where it rests
* L How it moves
M   What color it is

GO

Answer rows 3 Ⓐ Ⓑ ● Ⓓ   4 Ⓙ ● Ⓛ Ⓜ   5 Ⓐ ● Ⓒ Ⓓ   6 Ⓙ Ⓚ Ⓛ ●   7 ● Ⓑ Ⓒ Ⓓ   8 Ⓙ Ⓚ ● Ⓜ   13

Lucy sat very still as the plane took off. She liked flying, but always felt a little funny when the plane took off and landed. This plane was smaller than any other she ever had been on, and she didn't know what it would be like.

The take-off was smooth, and in a few minutes, they were flying high above the ground. All around them, Lucy could see the ocean.

The plane headed south from Miami toward Key West. Lucy, her mother, and her two brothers were going there to visit her father. He was in the Coast Guard and was stationed in Key West.

Lucy looked out the window and saw a chain of islands. Her mother said they were the Florida Keys. A road and a series of bridges connected the islands. Key West was the last island in the chain.

"Mom, why are they called keys?"

"It's from the Spanish word *cayo,* which means "island" or "reef." The first European explorers here were from Spain."

The water below had lots of different colors. The deepest water was dark blue, and along the shore, it was very light. In between, there were many shades of blue. On this background of blue were lots of boats, some with sails and some with motors. As the boats moved across the surface, they left streaks of white in their wake.

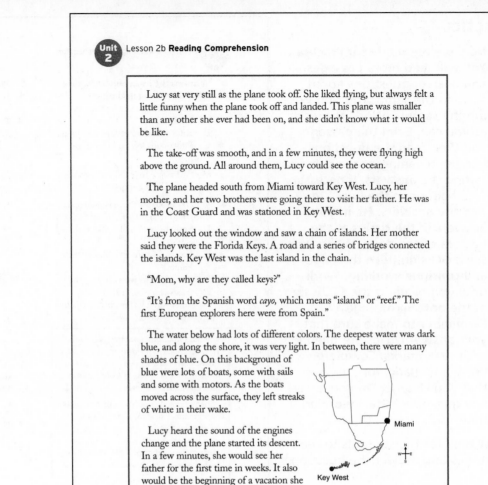

Lucy heard the sound of the engines change and the plane started its descent. In a few minutes, she would see her father for the first time in weeks. It also would be the beginning of a vacation she would remember forever.

GO

14

9 When Lucy flies back to Miami, in which direction will she travel?

* **A** Northeast

B South

C Southeast

D West

10 How did Lucy first know the plane was about to land?

J She saw the airport.

K The pilot turned the plane toward the airport.

* **L** The sound of the engines changed.

M The pilot made an announcement over the intercom.

11 What can you conclude about the water around the Florida Keys?

A Deeper water is lighter in color than shallow water.

* **B** Deeper water is darker in color than shallow water.

C It seems to be very rough.

D It seems to be very calm.

12 Why was Lucy going to Key West?

* **J** To visit her father

K To visit her mother

L To move there

M To go to school there

13 What kinds of things do you think Lucy will do in Key West?

A Climb mountains, ski, and go ice skating

B Stay inside and watch television because it is cold

* **C** Swim, ride in a boat, and lie on the beach

D Visit farms and ride on a tractor

14 Which of these is true about Lucy?

J She had never flown on a plane before.

K She was afraid of flying.

L She often flies on small planes.

* **M** She had never flown on a plane this small before.

Answer rows **9** ●ⒷⒸⒹ   **11** Ⓐ●ⒸⒹ   **13** ⒶⒷ●Ⓓ   15
10 ⒿⓀ●Ⓜ   **12** ●ⓀⓁⓂ   **14** ⒿⓀⓁ●

If you think your town is crowded, listen to this. Almost one fourth of the people on Earth live in one country—China. It has a population of more than one billion people and is growing by thousands of people every day!

China is located in the eastern part of Asia. It has the third-largest area in the world, just behind Russia and Canada. China has many neighbors, including North Korea, Russia, Pakistan, India, and other countries.

The official name of China is the People's Republic of China. The people of China call their country "The Middle Kingdom." This name came from long ago. The early Chinese believed that their country was the center of the world. They kept the name even after they found out this was not true.

Instead of states, China is divided into twenty-three provinces. These provinces are very different from one another. Some have very high mountains, but others are close to the sea and are very flat. One part of China is so high up in the mountains that people from the lowlands have trouble breathing there.

Because it has so many people, China must produce a lot of food. Fortunately, China has rich soil in many places. The most important food grown in China is rice. It is grown in paddies, which are fields that can be covered with water. This is necessary because rice is a swamp plant.

Many different languages are spoken by the Chinese people. The most common is Mandarin. It is considered to be the national language. Mandarin and the other Chinese languages are written with characters. A character is a symbol that has a special meaning. For example, there are characters for common words like *woman, man, house,* and so on. In our language, each letter of the alphabet stands for one or more sounds.

GO ➤

16

Say It's time to stop. You have finished Lesson 2b.

Review the answers with the students. Ask them if they remembered to look back at the passage to find the answers to the questions. If any questions caused particular difficulty, work through the story, questions, and answer choices. Ask the students which items they had to answer by "reading between the lines."

Have the students indicate completion of the lesson by entering their score for this activity on the progress chart at the beginning of the book.

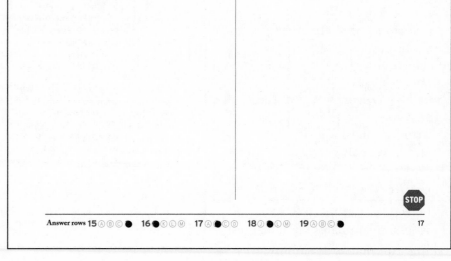

15 What is this passage mainly about?
   A   Provinces
   B   Language
   C   Asia
 * D   China

16 Which of these is true about provinces in China?
 * J   They are like states.
   K   They are all the same size.
   L   People in each province speak different languages.
   M   They are very mountainous.

17 If farmers want to raise rice, which of these would they need?
   A   Chinese workers
 * B   Lots of water
   C   Large, dry areas
   D   Heavy tractors

18 How are Chinese characters and letters of the alphabet different?
   J   Letters stand for words, and characters stand for characters.
 * K   Letters stand for sounds, and characters stand for words.
   L   Letters are written, and characters are spoken.
   M   Letters are in Chinese, and characters are in English.

19 Which of these is true about China?
   A   It has more land than Russia.
   B   It has fewer people than Canada.
   C   It has more land than Canada.
 * D   It has less land than Russia.

STOP

Answer rows **15** Ⓐ Ⓑ Ⓒ ●   **16** ● Ⓚ Ⓛ Ⓜ   **17** Ⓐ ● Ⓒ Ⓓ   **18** Ⓙ ● Ⓛ Ⓜ   **19** Ⓐ Ⓑ Ⓒ ●   17

Focus

Reading Skills
- understanding the main idea
- making predictions
- making inferences
- deriving word meanings
- understanding reasons
- recognizing details
- drawing conclusions
- recognizing the narrator
- identifying feelings
- analyzing characters

Test-taking Skills
- managing time effectively
- skimming a passage
- referring to a passage to answer questions
- using key words to find the answer
- working methodically
- reasoning from facts and evidence
- analyzing answer choices

Test Yourself: Reading Comprehension

Directions: Read the passage and the answer choices. Choose the best answer.

Sample A

Americans love to eat with their hands. Some of our most popular foods, including sandwiches, apples, and corn, are finger foods. To this list can be added pizza, tacos, and fried chicken. People in other countries like to make fun of this habit, but when they visit here, they eat the same way.

What is this story mostly about?
A Food
B Fast-food restaurants
C Customs in foreign countries
* D An unusual American habit

Deep in the rain forests of Central and South America lives an unusual animal called the tree sloth. What makes this animal so unusual is how it lives. The sloth spends most of its life hanging upside down in trees! High in the branches of tall trees, the sloth is protected from enemies and can enjoy a diet of leaves and fruit. On the ground, the sloth is awkward and can be caught easily. Its arms are perfect for holding onto branches, but they are not designed for walking.

Tree sloths have grayish-brown fur, but they often appear to be green. The green color comes from microscopic plants called algae that often grow on the sloth's fur. This happens because of the warm, moist places in which the sloth lives and because tree sloths move so slowly. In fact, tree sloths move so slowly that they often appear to be doing nothing at all.

1 Where do you think the sloth is most likely to be attacked by its enemies?
A In the air
B In the water
C In trees
* D On the ground

2 Which of these would be the best place for algae to grow?
J High in trees
* K In warm, moist places
L In cool, dry places
M On grayish-brown fur

3 The word "slothful" has the same root as the word "sloth." What do you think "slothful" means?
* A Lazy
B Active
C Hungry
D Fast

GO

18   Answer rows   A Ⓐ Ⓑ Ⓒ ●   1 Ⓐ Ⓑ Ⓒ ●   2 Ⓙ ● Ⓛ Ⓜ   3 ● Ⓑ Ⓒ Ⓓ

This lesson simulates an actual test-taking experience. Therefore, it is recommended that the directions be read verbatim and the suggested procedures and time allowances be followed.

Directions

Administration Time: approximately 35 minutes

Say Turn to the Test Yourself lesson on page 18.

Check to be sure the students have found the right page. Point out to the students that this Test Yourself lesson is timed like a real test, but that they will score it themselves to see how well they are doing. Explain that it is important to work quickly and to answer as many questions as possible.

Say This lesson will check how well you understand what you read. Remember to make sure that the circles for your answer choices are completely filled in. Press your

pencil firmly so that your marks come out dark. Completely erase any marks for answers that you change. Do not write anything except your answer choices in your books.

Look at Sample A. Read the passage and answer the question about it. The answer rows are at the bottom of the page.

Allow time for the students to fill in their answers.

Say The correct answer is D. The story is about an unusual American habit. If you chose another answer, erase yours and fill in answer D now.

Check to see that the students have correctly filled in their answer circles with a dark mark.

Say Now you will do more items like Sample A. There are four different passages in this lesson. When you come to the GO sign at the bottom of a page, turn the page and continue working. Work until you come to the STOP sign at the bottom of page 23. Fill in your answers in the rows at the bottom of the page. Make sure you fill in the circles completely with dark marks. Completely erase any marks for answers you change. You will have 30 minutes. You may begin.

Allow 30 minutes.

When the car stopped, Juan didn't get out right away. He looked at the river that flowed beside the parking lot. He had dreamed about this day for years.

At that moment, another car pulled up beside them. It pulled a boat on a trailer. Juan's father got out, along with his sister and their guide. Today, the four of them and the guide would float the Snake River in Idaho.

The guide backed the trailer into the water and slid the boat off. Carefully, he pulled the boat against the current up to a sandy beach. He then drove the car up the ramp and into the parking lot.

Following the guide's directions, the family put their supplies in the boat. They climbed into the boat and sat still as the guide expertly pushed the boat from the beach and jumped in. He moved quickly from the front of the boat to the rear, started the motor, and pulled into the current of the river. The guide cut the motor and the boat started drifting, steered by a long pole the guide held.

"You have the honor," said Juan's father. Juan picked up his fishing rod as if in a daze. He looked carefully at the fly he had tied on the end of the almost invisible line. Juan let some line out, made a slight movement with his arm, and his fly floated through the air and landed softly. The artificial fly drifted for just a few seconds when it was taken with a slurp by a large trout. Juan's dream had come true.

4 Why didn't Juan get out of the car right away?
J He was a little nervous.
K He wanted to wait for his father, sister, and the guide.
L He didn't know where the boat was.
✱ M He wanted to enjoy looking at the river.

5 What does it mean to say the family would "float the Snake River"?
✱ A They would fish from a boat that was floating down the river.
B They would float down the river with inner tubes.
C They would watch the guide float the boat into the water.
D They would fish with flies that floated on the water.

6 Why didn't the family help the guide push the boat?
J They were unloading the car.
K They were too excited.
✱ L He didn't need their help.
M It was too dangerous.

7 What was Juan's dream?
A To meet a fishing guide
✱ B To fish in the Snake River
C To go to Idaho
D To have a family vacation

GO

Answer rows 4 ⓙⓀⓁ● 5 ●ⒷⒸⒹ 6 ⓙⓀ●Ⓜ 7 Ⓐ●ⒸⒹ   19

In 1558, Elizabeth I became queen of England. For the next forty years, she was a strong ruler who helped England become a major world power.

The future queen of England was born on September 7, 1533. Elizabeth was the daughter of Henry VIII and his wife, Anne Boleyn. She became queen when her half-sister, Mary I, died. Mary was queen from 1553 to 1558.

While she was a child and even during her reign, Elizabeth's life was always in danger. Her opponents wanted to take control of England, and one way to do this was to murder the queen. Fortunately for England, no attempt on Elizabeth's life succeeded.

Elizabeth was well educated, which was unusual for a woman at that time. She could speak and read several foreign languages, she loved music, and she was a musician. During her reign, called the Elizabethan Period, the arts blossomed in England. The most famous writer in the English language, William Shakespeare, lived during the reign of Queen Elizabeth. Many other writers, artists, musicians, and architects also were active.

Although she was much loved by the people of England, Elizabeth was threatened by Philip I, the ruler of Spain. He wanted to rule England. He sent a large fleet called the Spanish Armada to make war on England. The English navy defeated the Spanish fleet, which was damaged by a great storm. After the defeat, Philip gave up his efforts to control England.

Queen Elizabeth never married and had no children. Her father, Henry VIII, had no other descendants. This meant that the rule of her family, the Tudors, ended with her. The next ruler of England was James I, a member of the Stuart family.

GO

20

8 What does the phrase "the arts blossomed" mean?

* J People were more interested in art, writing, and music.
 K People were more interested in gardening.
 L People painted lots of flowers.
 M The arts were a lot like flowers.

9 What can you say about women during the Elizabethan Period?

 A Most of them were well educated.
 B None of them were rulers of England.
* C Most of them were not well educated.
 D None of them could go to school.

10 What do you think an "armada" is?

 J A group of sailors
 K A Spanish ship
 L An English ship
* M A group of ships

11 Who was Mary I?

 A The mother of Elizabeth
* B The half-sister of Elizabeth
 C The queen after Elizabeth died
 D A famous writer

12 What is this passage mainly about?

 J England
 K The Elizabethan Period
 L Politics
* M A queen of England

GO

Answer rows 8 ● Ⓚ Ⓛ Ⓜ   9 Ⓐ Ⓑ ● Ⓓ   10 Ⓙ Ⓚ Ⓛ ●   11 Ⓐ ● Ⓒ Ⓓ   12 Ⓙ Ⓚ Ⓛ ●   21

Last Sunday, my dog Buddy started scratching his face. Pretty soon, it was red and sore. I was really worried.

"Mom, something is wrong with Buddy. Look at his face."

"This doesn't look very good, Lucas. Let's put some medicine on it and see what happens. If it doesn't get any better, we'll have to take him to the doctor."

I rubbed the medicine on Buddy's face and was very careful not to get it into his eyes. He didn't like it very much, but he held still for me.

The next day, he was even worse, so Dad stayed home from work and we took Buddy to the veterinarian. The doctor examined Buddy and gave us some pills. We had to give them to Buddy three times a day. The doctor said it would be easiest if we mixed it into food or a treat. The doctor also gave us a special collar that would keep Buddy from scratching his face. When we put the collar on Buddy, he looked like a clown. I felt bad for him.

I gave Buddy his medicine every day just like the doctor said. For a day or two it didn't seem to help. Then Buddy stopped trying to scratch his face. Pretty soon, his face started to get better.

A week later, my Aunt Janelle and I took Buddy back to the doctor. He examined Buddy again and said he was okay. The veterinarian thought that Buddy had an allergy, kind of like when I start to sneeze when Dad cuts the lawn. He said we should keep an eye on Buddy to see if we could find out what he was allergic to. If we found out, we could avoid it in the future.

GO

22

Say It's time to stop. You have completed the Test Yourself lesson.

Check to see that the students have correctly filled in their answer circles. At this point, go over the answers with the students. Did they have enough time to complete the lesson? Did they remember to skim the passage and to look for key words in the questions? Did they take the best guess when they were unsure of the answer?

Work through any questions that caused difficulty. It may be helpful to discuss the strategies students used to answer the comprehension items. You may also want to have the students identify the specific part of a passage that helped them find the right answer.

Have the students indicate completion of the lesson by entering their score for this activity on the progress chart at the beginning of the book.

---

13 Who is telling this story?
* **A** Lucas
  B Buddy
  C Aunt Janelle
  D The doctor

14 What made Buddy look like a clown?
  J Scratches on his nose
  K The medicine on his face
* **L** A special collar
  M The pills

15 How do you think Lucas felt at the end of the story?
  A Worried because Buddy had an allergy
  B Happy because Buddy had an allergy
  C Disappointed because the doctor couldn't fix the problem
* **D** Relieved because Buddy was getting better

16 How long did it take for the medicine to begin to work?
* **J** A few days
  K Right away
  L More than a week
  M It didn't work.

17 What shows that Lucas was responsible?
  A He rode in the car to the doctor with Aunt Janelle.
* **B** He gave Buddy his medicine every day.
  C He tried to get to school on time.
  D He felt bad because Buddy had to wear a funny collar.

STOP

Answer rows **13** ● Ⓑ Ⓒ Ⓓ   **14** Ⓙ Ⓚ ● Ⓜ   **15** Ⓐ Ⓑ Ⓒ ●   **16** ● Ⓚ Ⓛ Ⓜ   **17** Ⓐ ● Ⓒ Ⓓ   23

Unit 3

This unit contains three lessons that deal with spelling skills. Students are asked to identify a misspelled word in isolation.

• **In Lesson 3a,** students identify an incorrectly spelled word. Students work methodically, skip difficult items and return to them later, and indicate that an item has no mistakes.

• **In Lesson 3b,** students identify an incorrectly spelled word. In addition to reviewing the test-taking skills introduced in Lesson 3a, students learn about subvocalizing answer choices and recalling error types.

• **In the Test Yourself lesson,** the spelling skills and test-taking skills introduced in Lessons 3a and 3b are reinforced and presented in a format that gives students the experience of taking an achievement test. Techniques for managing time effectively when taking a standardized test are reinforced.

Instructional **Objectives**

Lesson 3a **Spelling** Lesson 3b **Spelling**	Given four words, students identify which of the four is misspelled or indicates that there are no mistakes.
Test Yourself	Given questions similar to those in Lessons 3a and 3b, students utilize spelling skills and test-taking strategies on achievement test formats.

Lesson 3a
Spelling

Focus

Spelling Skill
• identifying spelling errors

Test-taking Skills
• working methodically
• skipping difficult items and returning to them later
• indicating that an item has no mistakes

Samples A and B

Say Turn to Lesson 3a on page 24. In this lesson you will find misspelled words. Read the directions at the top of the page to yourself while I read them out loud.

Read the directions out loud to the students.

Say Let's look at Sample A. Look at the answer choices. Find the word that has a spelling mistake. If none of the words has a mistake, choose the last answer, No mistakes. Which answer did you choose? *(answer A, f-r-e-c-h)* Mark circle A for Sample A in the answer rows at the bottom of the page. Make sure the circle is completely filled in. Press your pencil firmly so that your mark comes out dark.

Check to see that the students have filled in the correct answer circle. Review the correct spelling of the word <u>fresh</u>.

Say Do Sample B yourself. Find the word that has a spelling mistake. If none of the words has a mistake, choose the last answer. *(pause)* Which answer should you choose? *(answer N, No mistakes)* What should you do now? *(mark the circle for answer N in the answer rows)* Make sure the circle is completely filled in with a dark mark.

Check to see that the students have filled in the correct answer circle.

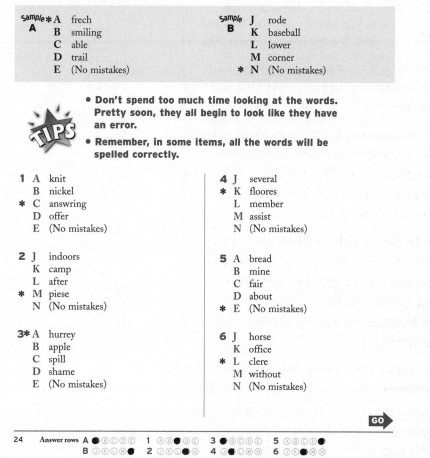

Spelling
Lesson 3a Spelling

Directions: Fill in the space for any word that has a spelling mistake. If there is no mistake, fill in the last answer space.

Sample *A frech
A   B smiling
      C able
      D trail
      E (No mistakes)

Sample   J rode
B   K baseball
         L lower
         M corner
       * N (No mistakes)

TIPS
• Don't spend too much time looking at the words. Pretty soon, they all begin to look like they have an error.
• Remember, in some items, all the words will be spelled correctly.

1 A knit
   B nickel
 * C answring
   D offer
   E (No mistakes)

2 J indoors
   K camp
   L after
 * M piese
   N (No mistakes)

3* A hurrey
   B apple
   C spill
   D shame
   E (No mistakes)

4 J several
 * K floores
   L member
   M assist
   N (No mistakes)

5 A bread
   B mine
   C fair
   D about
 * E (No mistakes)

6 J horse
   K office
 * L clere
   M without
   N (No mistakes)

GO

24 Answer rows A ●ⒷⒸⒹⒺ 1 Ⓐ●ⒸⒹⒺ 3 ●ⒷⒸⒹⒺ 5 ⒶⒷⒸⒹ●
                 B ⒿⓀⓁⓂ● 2 ⒿⓀⓁ●Ⓝ 4 ⒿⓀⓁⓂⓃ 6 ⒿⓀ●ⓂⓃ

★TIPS

Say Now let's look at the tips.

Have a volunteer read the tips aloud.

Say Look at each word letter by letter and think about what the word means. Try to remember where you have seen the word before. Don't spend too much time looking at the words, however. This will waste time and make you think all the words have an error. If you are having trouble finding the misspelled word, skip the item and come back to it later. And don't forget that in some items, all of the words are spelled correctly.

Practice

Say Now we are ready for Practice. Work as quickly as you can, and if an item seems difficult, skip it and return to it after you have done the other items. Don't forget, if all of the words are spelled correctly, choose the last answer, No mistakes. When you come the the GO sign at the bottom of the page, continue working. Work until you come to the STOP sign at the bottom of page 25. Remember to make sure that your answer circles are completely filled in with dark marks. Completely erase any marks for answers that you change. Any questions? Start working now.

Allow time for the students to mark their answers.

Say It's time to stop. You have finished Lesson 3a.

Review the answers with the students. If any items caused particular difficulty, work through each of the answer choices. Do an informal item analysis to determine which items were most difficult. Discuss with the students the words that gave them the most difficulty, including the misspelled words and the distractors that are spelled correctly and that the students identify as wrong.

Have the students indicate completion of the lesson by entering their score for this activity on the progress chart at the beginning of the book.

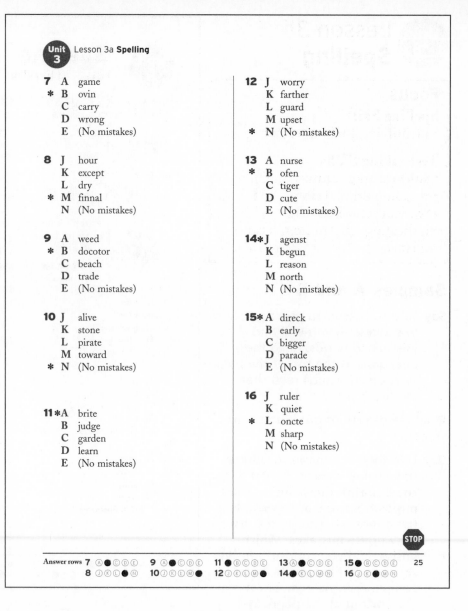

Unit 3   Lesson 3a **Spelling**

7   A   game
* B   ovin
  C   carry
  D   wrong
  E   (No mistakes)

8   J   hour
  K   except
  L   dry
* M   finnal
  N   (No mistakes)

9   A   weed
* B   docotor
  C   beach
  D   trade
  E   (No mistakes)

10   J   alive
  K   stone
  L   pirate
  M   toward
* N   (No mistakes)

11 * A   brite
  B   judge
  C   garden
  D   learn
  E   (No mistakes)

12   J   worry
  K   farther
  L   guard
  M   upset
* N   (No mistakes)

13   A   nurse
* B   ofen
  C   tiger
  D   cute
  E   (No mistakes)

14 * J   agenst
  K   begun
  L   reason
  M   north
  N   (No mistakes)

15 * A   direck
  B   early
  C   bigger
  D   parade
  E   (No mistakes)

16   J   ruler
  K   quiet
* L   oncte
  M   sharp
  N   (No mistakes)

STOP

Answer rows   7 Ⓐ●ⒸⒹⒺ   9 Ⓐ●ⒸⒹⒺ   11 ●ⒷⒸⒹⒺ   13 Ⓐ●ⒸⒹⒺ   15 ●ⒷⒸⒹⒺ   25
  8 ⒿⓀⓁ●Ⓝ   10 ⒿⓀⓁⓂ●   12 ⒿⓀⓁⓂ●   14 ●ⓀⓁⓂⓃ   16 ⒿⓀ●ⓂⓃ

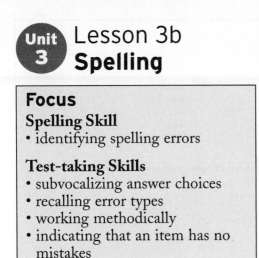

Lesson 3b
Spelling

Focus

Spelling Skill
• identifying spelling errors

Test-taking Skills
• subvocalizing answer choices
• recalling error types
• working methodically
• indicating that an item has no mistakes

Samples A and B

Say Turn to Lesson 3b on page 26. In this lesson you will find more misspelled words. Read the directions at the top of the page to yourself while I read them out loud.

Read the directions out loud to the students.

Say Find Sample A at the top of the page. Look at the answer choices. Find the word that has a spelling mistake. If none of the words has a mistake, choose the last answer. Which answer should you choose? *(answer E, No mistakes)* All the words are correct, so you should mark circle E for Sample A in the answer rows at the bottom of the page. Make sure the circle is completely filled in. Press your pencil firmly so that your mark comes out dark.

Check to see that the students have filled in the correct answer circle.

Say Do Sample B yourself. Find the word that has a spelling mistake. If none of the words has a mistake, choose the last answer. *(pause)* Which answer is correct? *(answer J, l-a-t-e-l-e-y)* What should you do now? *(mark the circle for answer J in the answer rows)* Make sure the circle is completely filled in with a dark mark.

Check to see that the students have filled in the correct answer circle. Review the correct spelling of the word <u>lately</u>.

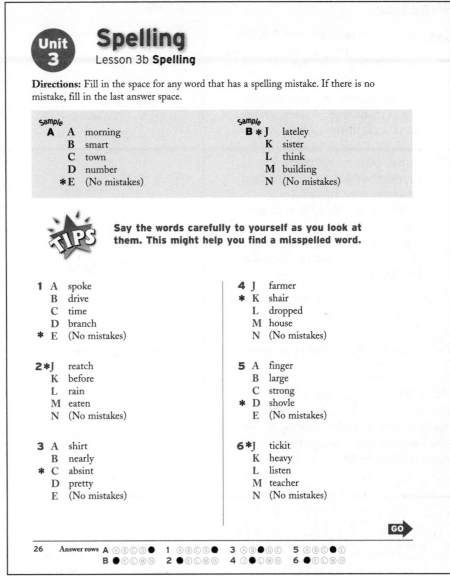

★**TIPS**

Say Now let's look at the tip.

Have a volunteer read the tip aloud.

Say Say the words carefully to yourself. If you pronounce them correctly, you can often find the word that is spelled wrong. Look at the word as you say it to yourself. Look for wrong letters, extra letters, and missing letters.

Lesson 3b **Spelling**   31

Practice

Say Now we are ready for Practice. Work as quickly as you can and remember that there are different kinds of spelling errors. When you come to the GO sign at the bottom of the page, continue working. Work until you come to the STOP sign at the bottom of page 27. Remember to make sure that your answer circles are completely filled in with dark marks. Completely erase any marks for answers that you change. Any questions? Start working now.

Allow time for the students to mark their answers.

Say It's time to stop. You have finished Lesson 3b.

Review the answers with the students. If any items caused particular difficulty, work through each of the answer choices. Review the various types of spelling errors in each of the items.

Have the students indicate completion of the lesson by entering their score for this activity on the progress chart at the beginning of the book.

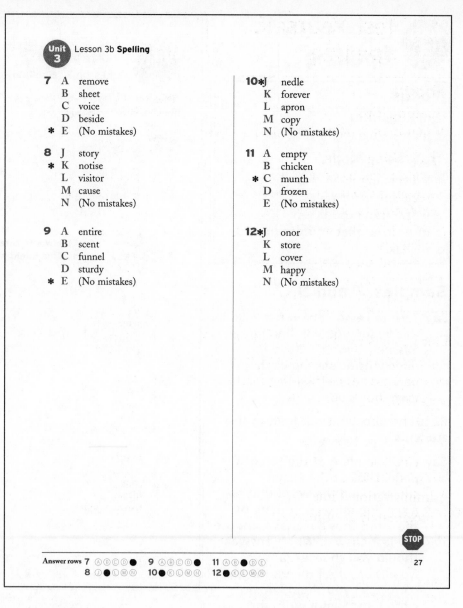

Unit 3 Lesson 3b **Spelling**

7 A remove
   B sheet
   C voice
   D beside
 * E (No mistakes)

8 J story
 * K notise
   L visitor
   M cause
   N (No mistakes)

9 A entire
   B scent
   C funnel
   D sturdy
 * E (No mistakes)

10 *J nedle
   K forever
   L apron
   M copy
   N (No mistakes)

11 A empty
   B chicken
 * C munth
   D frozen
   E (No mistakes)

12 *J onor
   K store
   L cover
   M happy
   N (No mistakes)

STOP

Answer rows 7 Ⓐ Ⓑ Ⓒ Ⓓ ●   9 Ⓐ Ⓑ Ⓒ Ⓓ ●   11 Ⓐ Ⓑ ● Ⓓ Ⓔ   27
             8 Ⓙ ● Ⓛ Ⓜ Ⓝ   10 ● Ⓚ Ⓛ Ⓜ Ⓝ   12 ● Ⓚ Ⓛ Ⓜ Ⓝ

Focus

Spelling Skill
• identifying spelling errors

Test-taking Skills
• working methodically
• skipping difficult items and returning to them later
• indicating that an item has no mistakes
• subvocalizing answer choices
• recalling error types
• managing time effectively

This lesson simulates an actual test-taking experience. Therefore it is recommended that the directions be read verbatim and that the suggested procedures and time allowances be followed.

Directions

Administration Time:
approximately 20 minutes

Say Turn to the Test Yourself lesson on page 28.

Point out to the students that this Test Yourself lesson is timed like a real test, but that they will score it themselves to see how well they are doing. Remind the students to work quickly and to mark the answer as soon as they are sure which word is misspelled.

Say This lesson will check how well you can find words with spelling errors. Remember to make sure that the circles for your answer choices are completely filled in. Press your pencil firmly so that your marks come out dark. Completely erase any answers that you change. Do not write anything except your answer choices in your books.

Look at the answer choices for Sample A. Find the answer choice that has a spelling error. If there is no error, choose the last answer choice. Mark the circle for your answer.

Allow time for the students to mark their answers.

Unit 3 **Test Yourself: Spelling**

Directions: Fill in the space for any word that has a spelling mistake. If there is no mistake, fill in the last answer space.

Sample A
  ＊ A straw
  B easey
  C study
  D pretend
  E (No mistakes)

Sample B
  J crust
  K law
  L seventh
  M dusty
  ＊ N (No mistakes)

1
  A dinner
  B garden
  C ready
  ＊ D senter
  E (No mistakes)

2 ＊ J lisden
  K silly
  L warm
  M unless
  N (No mistakes)

3
  A strange
  B beside
  C button
  D asleep
  ＊ E (No mistakes)

4 J prize
  ＊ K awache
  L phone
  M friend
  N (No mistakes)

5
  A hidden
  B around
  C short
  ＊ D pouder
  E (No mistakes)

6 J father
  K lasted
  L rainy
  M turkey
  ＊ N (No mistakes)

7
  A aboard
  B weakest
  C bench
  ＊ D thirstey
  E (No mistakes)

8 ＊ J fireing
  K valley
  L iron
  M cherry
  N (No mistakes)

GO

28   Answer rows   A Ⓐ●ⒸⒹⒺ   1 ⒶⒷⒸ●Ⓔ   3 ⒶⒷⒸⒹ●   5 ⒶⒷⒸ●Ⓔ   7 ⒶⒷⒸ●Ⓔ
                   B ⒿⓀⓁⓂ●   2 ●ⓀⓁⓂⓃ   4 ⒿⓀ●ⓂⓃ   6 ⒿⓀⓁⓂ●   8 ●ⓀⓁⓂⓃ

Say The circle for answer B should have been marked because it is the incorrect spelling of *e-a-s-y*. If you chose another answer, erase yours and fill in circle B now.

Check to see that the students have correctly marked their answer circles for Sample A.

Say Do Sample B yourself. Mark the circle for the answer choice that has a spelling mistake. If there is no error, choose the last answer choice. Mark the circle for your answer.

Allow time for the students to fill in their answers.

Say You should have filled in the circle for answer N because none of the words has a spelling error. If you chose another answer, erase yours and fill in circle N now.

Check to see that the students have correctly marked their answer circles for Sample B.

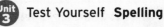

Say Now you will do Numbers 1 through 18 in the same way that we did the samples. When you come to the GO sign at the bottom of the page, continue working. Work until you come to the STOP sign at the bottom of page 29. When you have finished, you can check over your answers to this lesson. Then wait for the rest of the group to finish. Any questions? You will have 15 minutes. Begin working now.

Allow 15 minutes.

Say It's time to stop. You have completed the Test Yourself lesson. Check to see that you have completely filled in your answer circles with dark marks. Make sure that any marks for answers that you changed have been completely erased.

Go over the lesson with the students. Ask them if they had enough time to finish the lesson. Ask for volunteers to identify the spelling errors in each item.

Work through any questions that caused difficulty. Discuss any rules the students used to determine whether or not a word is spelled correctly. If necessary, provide additional practice questions similar to the ones in this unit.

Have the students indicate completion of the lesson by entering their score for this activity on the progress chart at the beginning of the book.

Unit 3 Test Yourself: Spelling

9 A driving
B birth
* C leeder
D covering
E (No mistakes)

10 J purple
K tight
L boil
* M gentel
N (No mistakes)

11 A guard
B meeting
C railroad
D probably
* E (No mistakes)

12 *J travle
K fence
L prepare
M machine
N (No mistakes)

13 A cattle
B tunnel
C done
D brook
* E (No mistakes)

14 J marry
K cake
L kneel
* M wellcome
N (No mistakes)

15 A tape
B mirror
* C puzzel
D jacket
E (No mistakes)

16 J beard
* K sunnie
L glove
M every
N (No mistakes)

17 A float
B juice
C tower
D arrive
* E (No mistakes)

18 *J wonderfull
K lose
L harm
M cardboard
N (No mistakes)

STOP

Answer rows **9** (A)(B)●(D)(E) **11** (A)(B)(C)(D)● **13** (A)(B)(C)(D)● **15** (A)(B)●(D)(E) **17** (A)(B)(C)(D)● 29
10 (J)(K)(L)●(N) **12** ●(K)(L)(M)(N) **14** (J)(K)(L)●(N) **16** (J)●(L)(M)(N) **18** ●(K)(L)(M)(N)

Unit 4

Background

This unit contains five lessons that deal with capitalization and punctuation skills.

• **In Lessons 4a and 4b,** students identify mistakes in capitalization in written text. Students work methodically and practice understanding unusual item formats. They analyze answer choices, recall error types, and indicate that an item has no mistakes.

• **In Lessons 5a and 5b,** students identify mistakes in punctuation in written text. In addition to reviewing the test-taking skills introduced in the two previous lessons, students learn the importance of skipping difficult items and returning to them later and recalling special punctuation rules.

• **In the Test Yourself lesson,** the capitalization and punctuation skills and test-taking skills introduced in Lessons 4a through 5b are reinforced and presented in a format that gives students the experience of taking an achievement test. Techniques for managing time effectively when taking a standardized test are reinforced.

Instructional **Objectives**

Lesson 4a **Capitalization** Lesson 4b **Capitalization**	Given text that is divided into three parts, students identifiy which part has a capitalization mistake or indicate that there is no mistake.
Lesson 5a **Punctuation** Lesson 5b **Punctuation**	Given text that is divided into three parts, students identify which part has a punctuation mistake or indicate that there is no mistake.
Test Yourself	Given questions that are similar to those in Lessons 4a through 5b, students utilize capitalization, punctuation, and test-taking strategies on achievement test formats.

Focus

Language Skill
• identifying capitalization errors

Test-taking Skills
• working methodically
• understanding unusual item formats
• analyzing answer choices
• recalling error types
• indicating that an item has no mistakes

Samples A and B

Say Turn to Lesson 4a on page 31. In this lesson you will look for capitalization in sentences. Read the directions at the top of the page to yourself while I read them out loud.

Read the directions out loud to the students.

Say Let's begin with Sample A. It is one sentence divided into three parts. You are to find the part that has a mistake in capitalization. If there is no mistake, choose the last answer, No mistakes. Read the answer choices to yourself. Does one of them have a mistake in capitalization? *(yes, answer B)* Answer B has a mistake because *Sandy* should begin with a capital letter. Fill in circle B for Sample A in the answer rows at the bottom of the page. Check to make sure your answer circle is completely filled in with a dark mark.

Check to see that the students have filled in the correct answer circle.

Say Do Sample B yourself. Mark the circle for the answer choice that has a capitalization mistake. If there is no error, choose the last answer choice. Mark the circle for your answer.

Allow time for the students to fill in their answers.

Say You should have filled in the circle for answer M, No mistakes. If you chose another answer, erase yours and fill in circle M now.

Directions: Fill in the space for the answer that has a capitalization mistake. Fill in the last answer space if there is no mistake.

Sample A *	A B C D	Did you ask sandy and Ted if they wanted to go? (No mistakes)
Sample B *	J K L M	My school is having a picnic next week for all the students. (No mistakes)

TIPS
• Read each answer choice word by word.
• Sentences and important words should begin with capital letters. Look for missing capital letters in these words.

1
A The light in my
B room is broken. May
C I read in your room?
* D (No mistakes)

2
J This rock is from
* K oregon. I found it
L near Crater Lake.
M (No mistakes)

3 * A We met dr. Harkins
B at the museum and
C spent the afternoon there.
D (No mistakes)

4
J My older sister lives
K in Chicago. She is a
L teacher in a high school.
* M (No mistakes)

5
A Our dog loves the
* B water. she jumps in
C if we go to the lake.
D (No mistakes)

6
J The store is closed.
K We'll have to drive to
* L the one on central avenue.
M (No mistakes)

STOP

Answer rows
A Ⓐ●ⒸⒹ   1 ⒶⒷⒸ●   3 ●ⒷⒸⒹ   5 Ⓐ●ⒸⒹ
B ⒿⓀⓁ●   2 Ⓙ●ⓁⓂ   4 ⒿⓀⓁ●   6 ⒿⓀ●Ⓜ

31

Check to see that the students have filled in the correct answer circle.

TIPS

Say Now let's look at the tips.

Have a volunteer read the tips aloud.

Say Look at each word in the sentence. Be sure the first word in a sentence and important words in a sentence are capitalized. And don't forget, sometimes the mistake will be a word that begins with a capital letter when it should not.

Discuss with the students the error types they should be looking for. Be sure to review the different types of proper nouns with which the students have had experience.

Practice

Say Now you will do the Practice items. Remember to look carefully at all of the answer choices for a capitalization mistake. Make sure you fill in the circles in the answer rows with dark marks. Do not write anything except your answer choices in your books. Completely erase any marks for answers that you change. Work until you come to the STOP sign at the bottom of the page. Any questions? Start working now.

Allow time for the students to fill in their answers.

Say It's time to stop. You have finished Lesson 4a.

Review the answers with the students. It will be helpful to discuss the errors in the items and the capitalization rules with which the errors are associated. If any questions caused particular difficulty, work through each of the answer choices.

Have the students indicate completion of the lesson by entering their score for this activity on the progress chart at the beginning of the book.

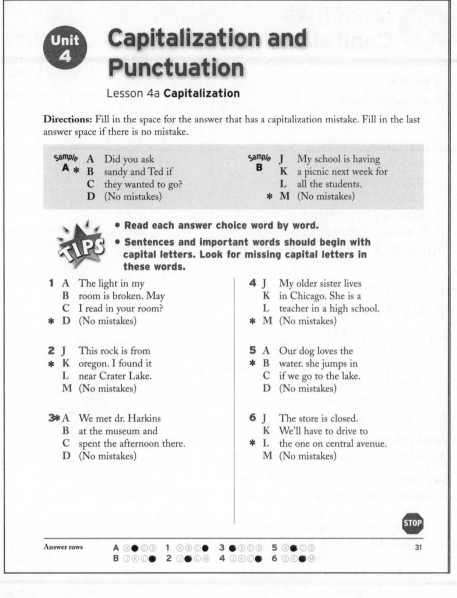

Unit 4 Capitalization and Punctuation

Lesson 4a **Capitalization**

Directions: Fill in the space for the answer that has a capitalization mistake. Fill in the last answer space if there is no mistake.

Sample **A**
* A Did you ask
* B sandy and Ted if
  C they wanted to go?
  D (No mistakes)

Sample **B**
  J My school is having
  K a picnic next week for
  L all the students.
* M (No mistakes)

TIPS
- Read each answer choice word by word.
- Sentences and important words should begin with capital letters. Look for missing capital letters in these words.

1
  A The light in my
  B room is broken. May
  C I read in your room?
* D (No mistakes)

2
  J This rock is from
* K oregon. I found it
  L near Crater Lake.
  M (No mistakes)

3 *
  A We met dr. Harkins
  B at the museum and
  C spent the afternoon there.
  D (No mistakes)

4
  J My older sister lives
  K in Chicago. She is a
  L teacher in a high school.
* M (No mistakes)

5
  A Our dog loves the
* B water. she jumps in
  C if we go to the lake.
  D (No mistakes)

6
  J The store is closed.
  K We'll have to drive to
* L the one on central avenue.
  M (No mistakes)

STOP

Answer rows   A Ⓐ●ⒸⒹ 1 ⒶⒷⒸ● 3 ●ⒷⒸⒹ 5 Ⓐ●ⒸⒹ   31
             B ⒿⓀⓁ● 2 Ⓙ●ⓁⓂ 4 ⒿⓀⓁ● 6 ⒿⓀ●Ⓜ

Lesson 4b
Capitalization

Unit 4

Focus

Language Skill
• identifying capitalization errors

Test-taking Skills
• working methodically
• understanding unusual item formats
• recalling error types
• indicating that an item has no mistakes

Samples A and B

Say Turn to Lesson 4b on page 32. This is another lesson about capitalization. Read the directions at the top of the page to yourself while I read them out loud.

Read the directions out loud to the students.

Say Let's do Sample A. It is two sentences divided into three parts. You are to find the part that has a mistake in capitalization. If there is no mistake, choose the last answer, No mistakes. Does one of the answer choices have a mistake in capitalization? *(yes, answer C)* Answer C has a mistake because the nickname *Red* should begin with a capital letter. Fill in circle C for Sample A in the answer rows at the bottom of the page. Check to make sure your answer circle is completely filled in with a dark mark.

Check to see that the students have filled in the correct answer circle.

Say Do Sample B yourself. Mark the circle for the answer choice that has a capitalization mistake. If there is no error, choose the last answer choice. Mark the circle for your answer.

Allow time for the students to fill in their answers.

Say You should have filled in the circle for answer J. The word *street* is capitalized, and it should not be. If you chose another answer, erase yours and fill in circle J now.

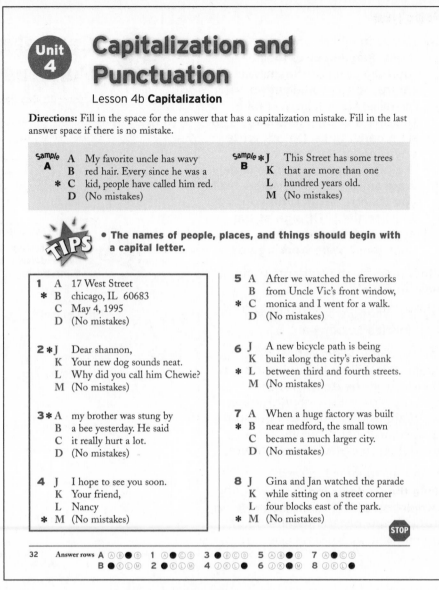

Unit 4
Capitalization and Punctuation

Lesson 4b **Capitalization**

Directions: Fill in the space for the answer that has a capitalization mistake. Fill in the last answer space if there is no mistake.

Sample A
A My favorite uncle has wavy
B red hair. Every since he was a
* C kid, people have called him red.
D (No mistakes)

Sample B
* J This Street has some trees
K that are more than one
L hundred years old.
M (No mistakes)

TIPS
• The names of people, places, and things should begin with a capital letter.

1
A 17 West Street
* B chicago, IL 60683
C May 4, 1995
D (No mistakes)

2
* J Dear shannon,
K Your new dog sounds neat.
L Why did you call him Chewie?
M (No mistakes)

3
* A my brother was stung by
B a bee yesterday. He said
C it really hurt a lot.
D (No mistakes)

4
J I hope to see you soon.
K Your friend,
L Nancy
* M (No mistakes)

5
A After we watched the fireworks
B from Uncle Vic's front window,
* C monica and I went for a walk.
D (No mistakes)

6
J A new bicycle path is being
K built along the city's riverbank
* L between third and fourth streets.
M (No mistakes)

7
A When a huge factory was built
* B near medford, the small town
C became a much larger city.
D (No mistakes)

8
J Gina and Jan watched the parade
K while sitting on a street corner
L four blocks east of the park.
* M (No mistakes)

STOP

32   Answer rows   A Ⓐ Ⓑ ● Ⓓ   1 Ⓐ ● Ⓒ Ⓓ   3 ● Ⓑ Ⓒ Ⓓ   5 Ⓐ Ⓑ ● Ⓓ   7 Ⓐ ● Ⓒ Ⓓ
                   B ● Ⓚ Ⓛ Ⓜ   2 ● Ⓚ Ⓛ Ⓜ   4 Ⓙ Ⓚ Ⓛ ●   6 Ⓙ Ⓚ ● Ⓜ   8 Ⓙ Ⓚ Ⓛ ●

Check to see that the students have filled in the correct answer circle.

TIPS

Say Now let's look at the tip.

Have a volunteer read the tip aloud.

Say Proper nouns should be capitalized. These are the names of people, places, and things. Some of the items in this lesson form a letter. You have to be careful because there are special rules for capitalizing a letter.

Remind the students about the capitalization rules for the parts of a letter.

Practice

Say Now you will do the Practice items. Remember to look carefully at all of the answer choices for a capitalization mistake, especially the items that involve parts of a letter. Make sure you fill in the circles in the answer rows with dark marks. Do not write anything except your answer choices in your books. Completely erase any marks for answers that you change. Work until you come to the STOP sign at the bottom of the page. Any questions? Start working now.

Allow time for the students to fill in their answers.

Say It's time to stop. You have finished Lesson 4b.

Review the answers with the students. It will be helpful to discuss the errors in the items and the rules for capitalization. If any questions caused particular difficulty, work through each of the answer choices.

Have the students indicate completion of the lesson by entering their score for this activity on the progress chart at the beginning of the book.

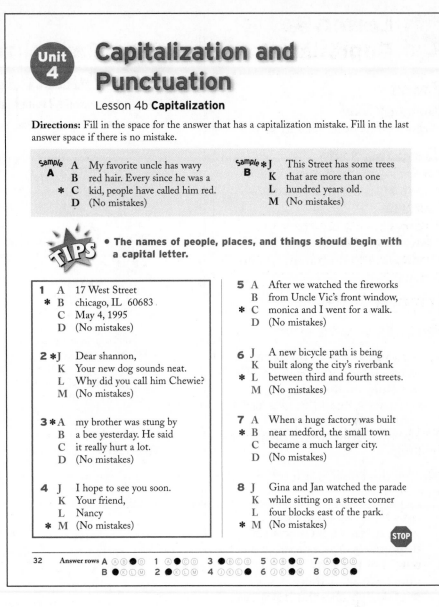

Unit 4 — Capitalization and Punctuation

Lesson 4b **Capitalization**

Directions: Fill in the space for the answer that has a capitalization mistake. Fill in the last answer space if there is no mistake.

Sample A
A My favorite uncle has wavy
B red hair. Every since he was a
* C kid, people have called him red.
D (No mistakes)

Sample B
* J This Street has some trees
K that are more than one
L hundred years old.
M (No mistakes)

TIPS
• The names of people, places, and things should begin with a capital letter.

1 A 17 West Street
* B chicago, IL 60683
C May 4, 1995
D (No mistakes)

2 * J Dear shannon,
K Your new dog sounds neat.
L Why did you call him Chewie?
M (No mistakes)

3 * A my brother was stung by
B a bee yesterday. He said
C it really hurt a lot.
D (No mistakes)

4 J I hope to see you soon.
K Your friend,
L Nancy
* M (No mistakes)

5 A After we watched the fireworks
B from Uncle Vic's front window,
* C monica and I went for a walk.
D (No mistakes)

6 J A new bicycle path is being
K built along the city's riverbank
* L between third and fourth streets.
M (No mistakes)

7 A When a huge factory was built
* B near medford, the small town
C became a much larger city.
D (No mistakes)

8 J Gina and Jan watched the parade
K while sitting on a street corner
L four blocks east of the park.
* M (No mistakes)

STOP

32 Answer rows A ⓐⓑ●ⓓ 1 ⓐ●ⓒⓓ 3 ●ⓑⓒⓓ 5 ⓐⓑ●ⓓ 7 ⓐ●ⓒⓓ
B ●ⓚⓛⓜ 2 ●ⓚⓛⓜ 4 ⓙⓚⓛ● 6 ⓙⓚ●ⓜ 8 ⓙⓚⓛ●

Lesson 5a
Punctuation

Focus

Language Skill
• identifying punctuation errors

Test-taking Skills
• working methodically
• understanding unusual item formats
• skipping difficult items and returning to them later
• indicating that an item has no mistakes
• recalling error types

Samples A and B

Say Turn to Lesson 5a on page 33. In this lesson you will look for punctuation mistakes in sentences. Read the directions at the top of the page to yourself while I read them out loud.

Read the directions out loud to the students.

Say Let's begin with Sample A. It is two sentences divided into three parts. You are to find the part that has a mistake in punctuation. If there is no mistake, choose the last answer. Read the answer choices to yourself. Does one of them have a mistake in punctuation? (yes, answer B) Answer B has a mistake because there should be a period after the word *meal*. Fill in circle B for Sample A in the answer rows at the bottom of the page. Check to make sure your answer circle is completely filled in with a dark mark.

Check to see that the students have filled in the correct answer circle.

Say Now do Sample B by yourself. Read the answer choices and look for a mistake in punctuation. Choose the last answer if the punctuation is correct. (pause) Which answer did you choose? (the last one, M) Yes, the punctuation in this item is correct. Fill in circle M for Sample B in the answer rows at the bottom of the page.

Unit 4

Capitalization and Punctuation

Lesson 5a **Punctuation**

Directions: Fill in the space for the answer that has a punctuation mistake. Fill in the last answer space if there is no mistake.

Sample A	A	This is a wonderful
*	B	meal Thank you for
	C	inviting me to dinner.
	D	(No mistakes)

Sample B	J	Where is the hose?
	K	I will need it to
	L	wash the car today.
*	M	(No mistakes)

TIPS
• Sentences must end with a punctuation mark. Abbreviations and dates are punctuated. Look for missing punctuation marks in these places.
• Look carefully at each punctuation mark to be sure it is correct.

1 *A Whose hat is this
  B I found it on the
  C bench under the tree.
  D (No mistakes)

2 J The beach was as quiet
  * K as the empty sky above
  L Not a single bird was singing.
  M (No mistakes)

3 A The train to Boston leaves
  * B at 235 P.M. on Track 7. We should
  C be at the station a little early.
  D (No mistakes)

4 *J Rocks bricks and cement can be
  K used to make stepping stones.
  L What material do you like best?
  M (No mistakes)

5 A The wind blew
  B the door closed. It
  C made a loud noise.
  * D (No mistakes)

6 J Susanne found an
  K old picture of our school
  * L dated August 3 1928.
  M (No mistakes)

STOP

Answer rows   A Ⓐ●ⒸⒹ 1 ●ⒷⒸⒹ 3 Ⓐ●ⒸⒹ 5 ⒶⒷⒸ●   33
              B ⒿⓀⓁ● 2 Ⓙ●ⓁⓂ 4 ●ⓀⓁⓂ 6 ⒿⓀ●Ⓜ

---

bottom of the page. Check to make sure that answer circle M is completely filled in with a dark mark.

Check to see that the students have filled in the correct answer circle.

★TIPS

Say Now let's look at the tips.

Have a volunteer read the tips aloud.

Say Always begin by looking for missing or wrong end punctuation. Then read the sentence again and look for missing or wrong punctuation inside the sentence. Be sure to work carefully. It is easy to miss a punctuation mistake.

Review with the students the punctuation rules with which they should be familiar.

Practice

Say Now you will do some Practice items. Look carefully at each answer choice for missing, extra, or wrong punctuation. Make sure you fill in the circles in the answer rows with dark marks. Do not write anything except your answer choices in your books. Completely erase any marks for answers that you change. Work until you come to the STOP sign at the bottom of the page. Any questions? Start working now.

Allow time for the students to fill in their answers.

Say It's time to stop. You have finished Lesson 5a.

Review the answers with the students. It will be helpful to discuss the punctuation errors in the items. If any questions caused particular difficulty, work through each of the answer choices.

Have the students indicate completion of the lesson by entering their score for this activity on the progress chart at the beginning of the book.

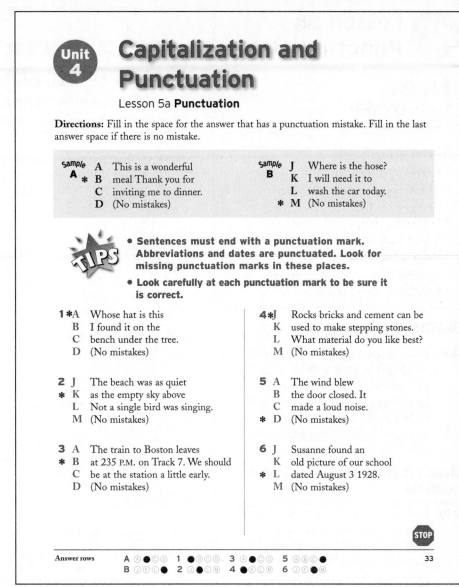

Unit 4 — Capitalization and Punctuation

Lesson 5a **Punctuation**

Directions: Fill in the space for the answer that has a punctuation mistake. Fill in the last answer space if there is no mistake.

Sample A
A   This is a wonderful
* B   meal Thank you for
C   inviting me to dinner.
D   (No mistakes)

Sample B
J   Where is the hose?
K   I will need it to
L   wash the car today.
* M   (No mistakes)

TIPS
• Sentences must end with a punctuation mark. Abbreviations and dates are punctuated. Look for missing punctuation marks in these places.
• Look carefully at each punctuation mark to be sure it is correct.

1 * A   Whose hat is this
B   I found it on the
C   bench under the tree.
D   (No mistakes)

2 J   The beach was as quiet
* K   as the empty sky above
L   Not a single bird was singing.
M   (No mistakes)

3 A   The train to Boston leaves
* B   at 235 P.M. on Track 7. We should
C   be at the station a little early.
D   (No mistakes)

4 * J   Rocks bricks and cement can be
K   used to make stepping stones.
L   What material do you like best?
M   (No mistakes)

5 A   The wind blew
B   the door closed. It
C   made a loud noise.
* D   (No mistakes)

6 J   Susanne found an
K   old picture of our school
* L   dated August 3 1928.
M   (No mistakes)

STOP

Answer rows   A Ⓐ●ⒸⒹ 1 ●ⒷⒸⒹ 3 Ⓐ●ⒸⒹ 5 ⒶⒷⒸ●
　　　　　　 B ⒿⓀⓁ● 2 Ⓙ●ⓁⓂ 4 ●ⓀⓁⓂ 6 ⒿⓀ●Ⓜ   33

Lesson 5b
Punctuation

Focus

Language Skill
- identifying punctuation errors

Test-taking Skills
- working methodically
- analyzing answer choices
- understanding unusual item formats
- indicating that an item has no mistakes
- recalling special punctuation rules

Samples A and B

Say Turn to Lesson 5b on page 34. In this lesson you will look for punctuation mistakes in sentences. Read the directions at the top of the page to yourself while I read them out loud.

Read the directions out loud to the students.

Say Find Sample A at the top of the page. Read the answer choices and look for a mistake in punctuation. Choose the last answer if the punctuation is correct. *(pause)* Which answer did you choose? *(the third one, C)* There should be a period after *Mr* because it is an abbreviation. Fill in circle C for Sample A in the answer rows at the bottom of the page. Check to make sure that answer circle C is completely filled in with a dark mark.

Check to see that the students have filled in the correct answer circle.

Say Now do Sample B yourself. Fill in the space for the answer that has a mistake in punctuation. Choose the last answer if the punctuation is correct. *(pause)* The last answer is correct because none of the answer choices has a punctuation mistake. Fill in circle M for Sample B in the answer rows at the bottom of the page. Check to make sure your answer circle is completely filled in with a dark mark.

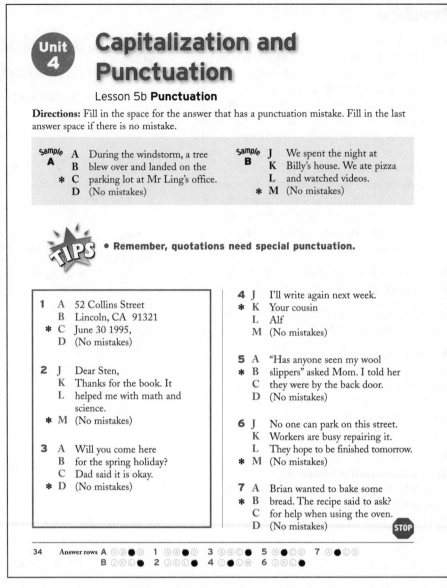

Unit 4
Capitalization and Punctuation

Lesson 5b Punctuation

Directions: Fill in the space for the answer that has a punctuation mistake. Fill in the last answer space if there is no mistake.

Sample A
- A During the windstorm, a tree
- B blew over and landed on the
- *C parking lot at Mr Ling's office.
- D (No mistakes)

Sample B
- J We spent the night at
- K Billy's house. We ate pizza
- L and watched videos.
- *M (No mistakes)

TIPS • Remember, quotations need special punctuation.

1
- A 52 Collins Street
- B Lincoln, CA 91321
- *C June 30 1995,
- D (No mistakes)

2
- J Dear Sten,
- K Thanks for the book. It
- L helped me with math and science.
- *M (No mistakes)

3
- A Will you come here
- B for the spring holiday?
- C Dad said it is okay.
- *D (No mistakes)

4
- J I'll write again next week.
- *K Your cousin
- L Alf
- M (No mistakes)

5
- A "Has anyone seen my wool
- *B slippers" asked Mom. I told her
- C they were by the back door.
- D (No mistakes)

6
- J No one can park on this street.
- K Workers are busy repairing it.
- L They hope to be finished tomorrow.
- *M (No mistakes)

7
- A Brian wanted to bake some
- *B bread. The recipe said to ask?
- C for help when using the oven.
- D (No mistakes)

STOP

34   Answer rows A Ⓐ Ⓑ ● Ⓓ   1 Ⓐ Ⓑ ● Ⓓ   3 Ⓐ Ⓑ Ⓒ ●   5 Ⓐ ● Ⓒ Ⓓ   7 Ⓐ ● Ⓒ Ⓓ
         B Ⓙ Ⓚ Ⓛ ●   2 Ⓙ Ⓚ Ⓛ ●   4 Ⓙ ● Ⓛ Ⓜ   6 Ⓙ Ⓚ Ⓛ ●

Check to see that the students have filled in the correct answer circle.

★ TIPS

Say Now let's look at the tip.

Have a volunteer read the tip aloud.

Say Quotations require special punctuation. So do letters. Both of these forms of writing are in this lesson, so you should pay close attention to them.

Review the punctuation rules for quotations and letters with the students.

Practice

Say Now you will do some Practice items. Remember to look carefully at all of the answer choices, especially those involving quotations or a letter. Make sure you fill in the circles in the answer rows with dark marks. Do not write anything except your answer choices in your books. Completely erase any marks for answers that you change. Work until you come to the STOP sign at the bottom of the page. Any questions? Start working now.

Allow time for the students to fill in their answers.

Say It's time to stop. You have finished Lesson 5b.

Review the answers with the students. It will be helpful to discuss the punctuation errors in the items. If any questions caused particular difficulty, work through each of the answer choices.

Have the students indicate completion of the lesson by entering their score for this activity on the progress chart at the beginning of the book.

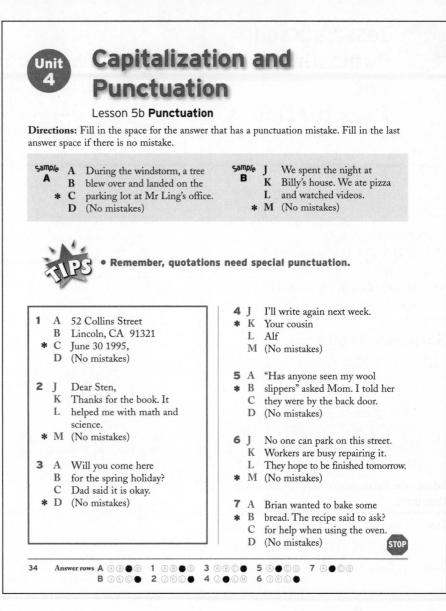

Unit 4 — Capitalization and Punctuation

Lesson 5b **Punctuation**

Directions: Fill in the space for the answer that has a punctuation mistake. Fill in the last answer space if there is no mistake.

Sample A
A   During the windstorm, a tree
B   blew over and landed on the
* C   parking lot at Mr Ling's office.
D   (No mistakes)

Sample B
J   We spent the night at
K   Billy's house. We ate pizza
L   and watched videos.
* M   (No mistakes)

TIPS • Remember, quotations need special punctuation.

1
A   52 Collins Street
B   Lincoln, CA 91321
* C   June 30 1995,
D   (No mistakes)

2
J   Dear Sten,
K   Thanks for the book. It
L   helped me with math and science.
* M   (No mistakes)

3
A   Will you come here
B   for the spring holiday?
C   Dad said it is okay.
* D   (No mistakes)

4
J   I'll write again next week.
* K   Your cousin
L   Alf
M   (No mistakes)

5
A   "Has anyone seen my wool
* B   slippers" asked Mom. I told her
C   they were by the back door.
D   (No mistakes)

6
J   No one can park on this street.
K   Workers are busy repairing it.
L   They hope to be finished tomorrow.
* M   (No mistakes)

7
A   Brian wanted to bake some
* B   bread. The recipe said to ask?
C   for help when using the oven.
D   (No mistakes)

STOP

34   Answer rows   A Ⓐ Ⓑ ● Ⓓ   1 Ⓐ Ⓑ ● Ⓓ   3 Ⓐ Ⓑ Ⓒ ●   5 Ⓐ ● Ⓒ Ⓓ   7 Ⓐ ● Ⓒ Ⓓ
              B Ⓙ Ⓚ Ⓛ ●   2 Ⓙ Ⓚ Ⓛ ●   4 Ⓙ ● Ⓛ Ⓜ   6 Ⓙ Ⓚ Ⓛ ●

Capitalization and Punctuation

Focus

Language Skills
• identifying capitalization errors
• identifying punctuation errors

Test-taking Skills
• managing time effectively
• following printed directions
• working methodically
• understanding unusual item formats
• analyzing answer choices
• recalling error types
• indicating that an item has no mistakes
• recalling special punctuation rules
• skipping difficult items and returning to them later

This lesson simulates an actual test-taking experience. Therefore, it is recommended that the directions be read verbatim and the suggested procedures and time allowances be followed.

Directions
Administration Time: approximately 20 minutes

Say Turn to the Test Yourself lesson on page 35.

Point out to the students that this Test Yourself lesson is timed like a real test, but that they will score it themselves to see how well they are doing. Remind the students to pace themselves and to check the clock after they have finished the capitalization items to see how much time is left. Encourage the students to avoid spending too much time on any one item and to take the best guess if they are unsure of the answer.

Say There are two types of items in the Test Yourself lesson, so you will have to read the directions for each section and pay close attention to what you are doing. Remember to make sure that the circles in the answer rows

are completely filled in. Press your pencil firmly so that your marks come out dark. Completely erase any marks for answers that you change. Do not write anything except your answer choices in your books.

Look at Sample A and listen carefully. Read the answer choices to yourself. Mark the circle for the answer that has a mistake in capitalization. Choose the last answer, No mistakes, if none of the answer choices has a mistake. Mark the circle for your answer.

Allow time for the students to fill in their answers.

Say The circle for answer B should be filled in because *Chipper* should begin with a capital letter. It is a nickname. If you chose another answer, erase yours and fill in the circle for answer B now.

Sample A ✳
A The bird in the pet store is
B named chipper because it
C is always in a good mood.
D (No mistakes)

Sample B
J Here is an easy treat. Pour
K milk into a glass and add
L cocoa. Stir it together.
✳ M (No mistakes)

Directions: For questions 1–9, fill in the space for the answer that has a capitalization mistake. Fill in the last answer space if there is no mistake.

1 A My sister was a good swimmer
B who won lots of awards, but
✳ C i was always better with music.
D (No mistakes)

2 J Noodles are tasty. My
K favorite kind is chinese
L noodles made of rice.
✳ M (No mistakes)

3 A Mud from the Missouri River
B mixes with the Mississippi, giving
C the water a brownish color.
✳ D (No mistakes)

4 J Dogs and cats are the most
✳ K common household pets. fish
L are also fairly common.
M (No mistakes)

5 A Kirkpatrick Macmillan added
B pedals to a scooter in 1839
✳ C and created the first Bicycle.
D (No mistakes)

6 J Chef Julia Child admits that
✳ K as a young child in california
L she made plenty of mud pies.
M (No mistakes)

7 A 4389 Ginger Lane
B Santa Rosa, CA 95401
✳ C may 23, 2001
D (No mistakes)

8 ✳ J dear Mom,
K Today Lisa and I saw blue
L dragonflies for the first time.
M (No mistakes)

9 A We're having a great time.
B all my love,
✳ C Lori
D (No mistakes)

GO

Answer rows A Ⓐ●ⒸⒹ   1 Ⓐ●●Ⓓ   3 ⒶⒷⒸ●   5 ⒶⒷ●Ⓓ   7 Ⓐ●●Ⓓ   9 ⒶⒷ●Ⓓ   35
              B ⒿⓀⓁ●   2 ⒿⓀⓁ●   4 Ⓙ●ⓁⓂ   6 Ⓙ●ⓁⓂ   8 ●ⓀⓁⓂ

Check to see that the students have filled in the correct answer circle.

Say Now do Sample B. Read the answer choices to yourself. Mark the circle for the answer that has a mistake in punctuation. Choose the last answer, No mistakes, if none of the answer choices has a mistake in punctuation. Mark the circle for your answer.

Allow time for the students to fill in their answers.

Say The circle for answer M should be filled in. There are no punctuation mistakes in any of the answer choices. If you chose another answer, erase yours and fill in the circle for answer M now.

Check to see that the students have filled in the correct answer circle.

Say Now you will do more items. Read the directions for each section. When you come to the GO sign at the bottom of the page, turn the page and continue working. Work until you come to the STOP sign on page 36. If you are not sure of an answer, fill in the circle for the answer you think might be right. Do you have any questions?

Answer any questions the students have.

Say You may begin working. You will have 15 minutes.

Allow 15 minutes.

Say It's time to stop. You have finished the Test Yourself lesson. Check to see that you have completely filled in your answer circles with dark marks. Make sure that any marks for answers that you changed have been completely erased.

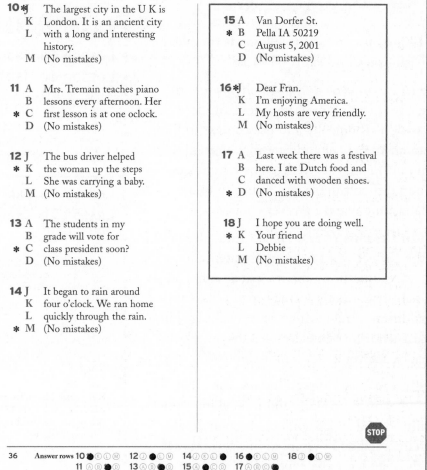

Directions: For questions 10–18, fill in the space for the answer that has a punctuation mistake. Fill in the last answer space if there is no mistake.

10 * J   The largest city in the U K is
   K   London. It is an ancient city
   L   with a long and interesting history.
   M   (No mistakes)

11 A   Mrs. Tremain teaches piano
   B   lessons every afternoon. Her
* C   first lesson is at one oclock.
   D   (No mistakes)

12 J   The bus driver helped
* K   the woman up the steps
   L   She was carrying a baby.
   M   (No mistakes)

13 A   The students in my
   B   grade will vote for
* C   class president soon?
   D   (No mistakes)

14 J   It began to rain around
   K   four o'clock. We ran home
   L   quickly through the rain.
* M   (No mistakes)

15 A   Van Dorfer St.
* B   Pella IA 50219
   C   August 5, 2001
   D   (No mistakes)

16 * J   Dear Fran.
   K   I'm enjoying America.
   L   My hosts are very friendly.
   M   (No mistakes)

17 A   Last week there was a festival
   B   here. I ate Dutch food and
   C   danced with wooden shoes.
* D   (No mistakes)

18 J   I hope you are doing well.
* K   Your friend
   L   Debbie
   M   (No mistakes)

STOP

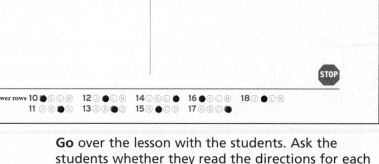

36   Answer rows 10 ● K L M   12 J ● L M   14 J K L ●   16 ● K L M   18 J ● L M
            11 A B ● D   13 A B ● D   15 A ● C D   17 A B C ●

Go over the lesson with the students. Ask the students whether they read the directions for each section. Did they have enough time to finish all of the items? Which items were most difficult?

Work through any questions that caused difficulty. Have the students indicate completion of the lesson by entering their score for this activity on the progress chart at the beginning of the book.

Unit 5

Background

This unit contains five lessons that deal with usage and expression skills.

• **In Lessons 6a and 6b,** students identify usage mistakes in written text. Students work methodically and use context to find an answer. They indicate that an item has no mistakes, subvocalize answer choices, skip difficult items and return to them later, and analyze answer choices.

• **In Lessons 7a and 7b,** students identify the correct word to fit in a sentence, answer questions about a paragraph, and identify correctly formed sentences. In addition to reviewing the test-taking skills learned in previous lessons, they mark the right answer as soon as it is found.

• **In the Test Yourself lesson,** the usage and expression skills and test-taking skills introduced in Lessons 6a through 7b are reinforced and presented in a format that gives students the experience of taking an achievement test. Techniques for managing time effectively when taking a standardized test are reinforced.

Instructional Objectives

Lesson 6a **Usage** Lesson 6b **Usage**	Given text divided into three parts, students identify which part has a usage mistake or indicate that there is no mistake.
Lesson 7a **Expression** Lesson 7b **Expression**	Given a sentence with an underlined word or words, students identify which of three answer choices should replace the word or words or indicate that there should be no change. Given a paragraph and questions about it, students identify which of four answer choices is correct. Given four sentences, students identify the best way to express the underlying idea.
Test Yourself	Given questions similar to those in Lessons 6a through 7b, students utilize English skills and test-taking strategies on achievement test formats.

Lesson 6a
Usage

Focus

Language Skill
• identifying mistakes in usage

Test-taking Skills
• using context to find an answer
• indicating that an item has no mistakes
• subvocalizing answer choices
• skipping difficult items and returning to them later

Samples A and B

Say Turn to Lesson 6a on page 37. In this lesson you will look for mistakes in the correct use of English. Read the directions at the top of the page to yourself while I read them out loud.

Read the directions out loud to the students.

Say Let's begin with Sample A. It is a sentence divided into three parts. You are to find the part that has a mistake in English. If there is no mistake, choose the last answer, No mistakes. Read the answer choices to yourself. Does one of them have a mistake? *(no)* None of the answer choices has a mistake, so answer D is correct. Fill in circle D for Sample A in the answer rows at the bottom of the page. Check to make sure the answer circle is completely filled in with a dark mark.

Check to see that the students have filled in the correct answer circle.

Say Now do Sample B. Read the answer choices and look for a mistake in English. Choose the last answer if there is no mistake. *(pause)* Which answer did you choose? *(answer K)* Answer K has a mistake. It contains two negatives. Fill in circle K for Sample B in the answer rows at the bottom of the page. Check to make sure the answer circle is completely filled in with a dark mark.

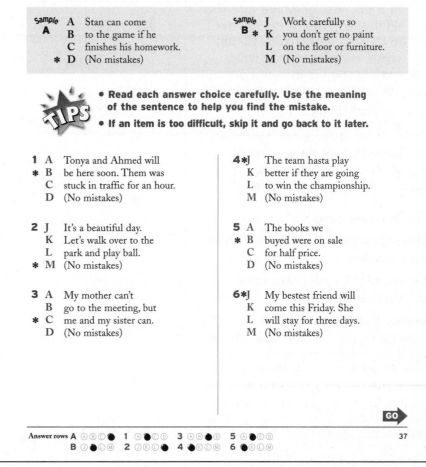

Check to see that the students have filled in the correct answer circle. Review the correct way to write answer choice K.

⭐**TIPS**

Say Now let's look at the tips.

Have a volunteer read the tips aloud.

Say Read each answer choice and think about what each means. The meaning will help you choose the correct answer. And remember, if an item seems difficult, skip it and move on to another item. After you have tried all the other items, come back and do the ones you skipped.

Practice

Say Let's do the Practice items now. Say the answer choices to yourself and listen for the one that sounds incorrect. Use the meaning of the sentences to find the answer. Make sure you fill in the circles in the answer rows with dark marks. Do not write anything except your answer choices in your books. Completely erase any marks for answers that you change. When you come to the GO sign at the bottom of the page, turn the page and continue working. Work until you come to the STOP sign at the bottom of page 38. Any questions? Start working now.

Allow time for the students to fill in their answers.

Say It's time to stop. You have finished Lesson 6a.

Review the answers with the students. It will be helpful to discuss the error types that appear in the lesson and have the students read aloud the correct form of the sentences. If any questions caused particular difficulty, work through each of the answer choices.

Have the students indicate completion of the lesson by entering their score for this activity on the progress chart at the beginning of the book.

Unit 5 Lesson 6a **Usage**

7   A   Last summer, all Joey did
    B   was read every day. In three
   * C   months he readed fifty books.
    D   (No mistakes)

8 * J   Nan borrowed me her bike.
    K   Mine was broken, and I wanted
    L   to ride with some of my friends.
    M   (No mistakes)

9 * A   Them plants are banana trees.
    B   My mother planted them last
    C   year, and they are doing well.
    D   (No mistakes)

10   J   Mom and Dad gave each of us
    K   money for our day at the fair, but
   * L   Stu spended it all in the first hour.
    M   (No mistakes)

11 * A   Troy hasn't been to no other
    B   state except Arizona. He said
    C   he wants to travel more.
    D   (No mistakes)

12   J   Ann Bancroft made history when
    K   she became the first woman to
    L   cross the ice to the North Pole.
   * M   (No mistakes)

13 * A   My mother singed in a choir
    B   when she was younger. She thinks
    C   singing in one might be fun now.
    D   (No mistakes)

14   J   I just met a preschooler who
    K   already knows how to speak
   * L   two languages and doing math.
    M   (No mistakes)

STOP

38   Answer rows   7 (A)(B)●(D)   9 ●(B)(C)(D)   11 ●(B)(C)(D)   13 ●(B)(C)(D)
             8 ●(K)(L)(M)   10 (J)(K)●(M)   12 (J)(K)(L)●   14 (J)(K)●(M)

Lesson 6b
Unit 5 Usage

Focus

Language Skill
• identifying mistakes in usage

Test-taking Skills
• working methodically
• recalling usage errors
• indicating that an item has no mistakes
• analyzing answer choices

Samples A and B

Say Turn to Lesson 6b on page 39. This is another lesson in which you will look for mistakes in the correct use of English. Read the directions at the top of the page to yourself while I read them out loud.

Read the directions out loud to the students.

Say Sample A is a sentence divided into three parts. You are to find the part that has a mistake in English. If there is no mistake, choose the last answer, No mistakes. (pause) Answer B is correct because the word *were* should be *was*. Fill in answer circle B for Sample A in the answer rows at the bottom of the page. Check to make sure that the answer circle is completely filled in with a dark mark.

Check to see that the students have filled in the correct answer circle. Explain that the subject of the sentence is *box,* so the verb should be *was.* This item type is especially difficult for many students.

Say Now do Sample B. Read the answer choices and look for a mistake in English usage. Choose the last answer if there is no mistake. (pause) Which answer did you choose? (answer M) Yes, there are no mistakes in Sample B. Fill in circle M for Sample B in the answer rows at the bottom of the page. Make sure the circle is completely filled in with a dark mark.

Check to see that the students have filled in the correct answer circle.

Unit 5 Usage and Expression

Lesson 6b **Usage**

Directions: Fill in the space for the answer that has a mistake in usage. Fill in the last answer space if there is no mistake.

Sample A
* A   A box of old books
* B   were in the attic. Gail
  C   took them to the library.
  D   (No mistakes)

Sample B
  J   Collecting coins is a
  K   hobby that is enjoyed by
  L   many people.
* M   (No mistakes)

TIPS
• Look carefully to see if the answer choices make up one or two sentences. This will help you find the usage error.

1 *A   There isn't nothing
   B   good on television. Let's
   C   play a board game.
   D   (No mistakes)

2 J   My uncle is building
   K   a deck in the backyard.
 * L   I and Wendy will help.
   M   (No mistakes)

3 A   If we had practiced more,
 * B   we mighta won the game.
   C   We'll play again next week.
   D   (No mistakes)

4 J   My sister and I
 * K   teached my little brother
   L   how to build a snowman.
   M   (No mistakes)

5 A   Miller Lake is
 * B   nowheres near as
   C   big as Lake Jarvis.
   D   (No mistakes)

6 *J   This juice cost lesser
   K   than the one we usually
   L   buy. We should try some.
   M   (No mistakes)

7 A   Let's go to the mall today.
   B   Call Ben and Jerry and ask
 * C   if them wants to go.
   D   (No mistakes)

8 J   The weather has been
   K   good all week. I hope the
   L   weekend is just as nice.
 * M   (No mistakes)

STOP

Answer rows
A Ⓐ●ⒸⒹ   1 ●ⒷⒸⒹ   3 Ⓐ●ⒸⒹ   5 Ⓐ●ⒸⒹ   7 ⒶⒷ●Ⓓ   39
B ⒿⓀⓁ●   2 ⒿⓀ●Ⓜ   4 Ⓙ●ⓁⓂ   6 ●ⓀⓁⓂ   8 ⒿⓀⓁ●

★ TIPS

Say Now let's look at the tip.

Have a volunteer read the tip aloud.

Say One of the first things you should do is see if the answer choices make up one or two sentences. This will help you find the right answer.

Have the students identify the number of sentences in the Samples.

Practice

Say Let's do the Practice items now. Look for the answer that has a mistake in English usage, and pay attention to the number of sentences in the answer choices. Mark your answers in the rows at the bottom of the page. Make sure you fill in the circles in the answer rows with dark marks. Do not write anything except your answer choices in your books. Completely erase any marks for answers that you change. Work until you come to the STOP sign at the bottom of the page. Any questions? Start working now.

Allow time for the students to fill in their answers.

Say It's time to stop. You have finished Lesson 6b.

Review the answers with the students. It will be helpful to discuss the error types that appear in the lesson and have the students read aloud the correct form of the sentences. If any questions caused particular difficulty, work through each of the answer choices.

Have the students indicate completion of the lesson by entering their score for this activity on the progress chart at the beginning of the book.

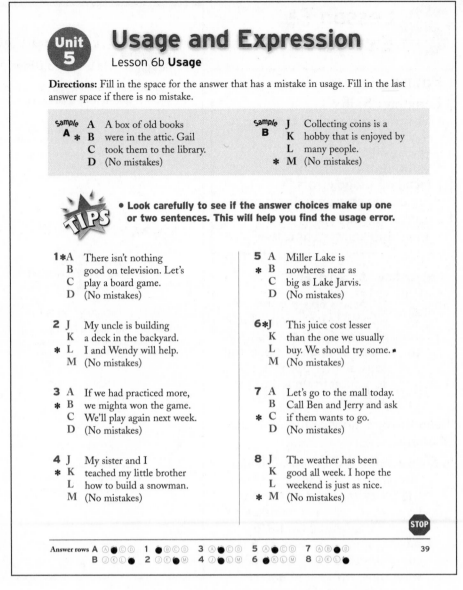

Unit 5 — Usage and Expression
Lesson 6b Usage

Directions: Fill in the space for the answer that has a mistake in usage. Fill in the last answer space if there is no mistake.

Sample A
* A   A box of old books
* B   were in the attic. Gail
* C   took them to the library.
* D   (No mistakes)

Sample B
* J   Collecting coins is a
* K   hobby that is enjoyed by
* L   many people.
* M   (No mistakes)

• Look carefully to see if the answer choices make up one or two sentences. This will help you find the usage error.

1 *A There isn't nothing
   B good on television. Let's
   C play a board game.
   D (No mistakes)

2 J My uncle is building
   K a deck in the backyard.
   *L I and Wendy will help.
   M (No mistakes)

3 A If we had practiced more,
   *B we mighta won the game.
   C We'll play again next week.
   D (No mistakes)

4 J My sister and I
   *K teached my little brother
   L how to build a snowman.
   M (No mistakes)

5 A Miller Lake is
   *B nowheres near as
   C big as Lake Jarvis.
   D (No mistakes)

6 *J This juice cost lesser
   K than the one we usually
   L buy. We should try some.
   M (No mistakes)

7 A Let's go to the mall today.
   B Call Ben and Jerry and ask
   *C if them wants to go.
   D (No mistakes)

8 J The weather has been
   K good all week. I hope the
   L weekend is just as nice.
   *M (No mistakes)

STOP

Answer rows A Ⓐ●ⒸⒹ 1 ●ⒷⒸⒹ 3 Ⓐ●ⒸⒹ 5 Ⓐ●ⒸⒹ 7 ⒶⒷ●Ⓓ   39
            B ⒿⓀⓁ● 2 ⒿⓀ●Ⓜ 4 Ⓙ●ⓁⓂ 6 ●ⓀⓁⓂ 8 ⒿⓀⓁ●

Lesson 7a
Expression

Focus

Language Skills
- choosing the best word to complete a sentence
- identifying correctly formed sentences
- identifying the best opening sentence for a paragraph
- identifying the sentence that does not fit in a paragraph
- identifying the best location for a sentence in a paragraph
- identifying the best closing sentence for a paragraph

Test-taking Skills
- following printed directions
- understanding unusual item formats
- skimming answer choices
- marking the right answer as soon as it is found
- skipping difficult items and returning to them later

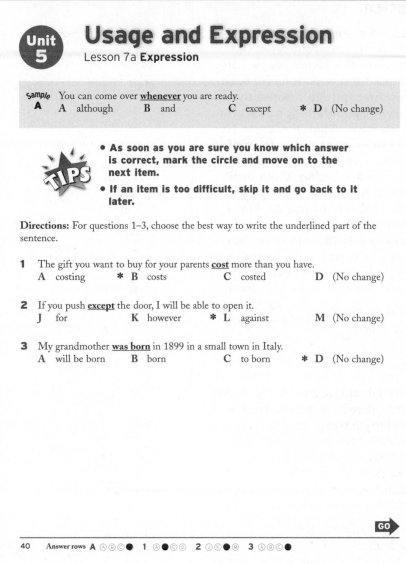

Usage and Expression
Lesson 7a **Expression**

Sample A You can come over **whenever** you are ready.
   A   although   B   and   C   except   * D   (No change)

TIPS
- As soon as you are sure you know which answer is correct, mark the circle and move on to the next item.
- If an item is too difficult, skip it and go back to it later.

Directions: For questions 1–3, choose the best way to write the underlined part of the sentence.

1 The gift you want to buy for your parents **cost** more than you have.
   A   costing   * B   costs   C   costed   D   (No change)

2 If you push **except** the door, I will be able to open it.
   J   for   K   however   * L   against   M   (No change)

3 My grandmother **was born** in 1899 in a small town in Italy.
   A   will be born   B   born   C   to born   * D   (No change)

GO

40   Answer rows   A ⒶⒷⒸ●   1 Ⓐ●ⒸⒹ   2 ⒿⓀ●Ⓜ   3 ⒶⒷⒸ●

Sample A

Say Turn to Lesson 7a on page 40. In this lesson you will work with sentences and paragraphs. There are directions for each section of this lesson, so read them carefully before you answer questions.

Look at Sample A. Read the sentence with the underlined word. Then read each of the answer choices. Find the answer choice that is the best way to write the underlined part of the sentence. If the underlined part is already correct, choose answer D, No change. *(pause)* Which answer choice is correct? *(D, No change)* The underlined part is correct as it is. Mark answer circle D for Sample A in the answer rows at the bottom of the page. Make sure the circle is completely filled in with a dark mark.

Check to see that the students have filled in the correct answer circle. Review the Sample so students understand the correct answer.

TIPS

Say Who will read the tips for us?

Have a volunteer read the tips aloud.

Say When you are sure you know which answer choice is correct, mark it and move on to the next item. If an item seems difficult, skip it and move on to the next item. You can come back to any item you skipped. These two strategies will save you time on a test.

Practice

Say Now we are ready for Practice. There are different types of items in this lesson, so be sure to read the directions for each section carefully. Choose the answer you think is correct for each item. When you come to the GO sign at the bottom of a page, turn the page and continue working. Work until you come to the STOP sign at the bottom of page 42. Make sure your answer circles are completely filled in with dark marks. Do not write anything except your answer choices in your books. Completely erase any marks for answers that you change. Any questions? Start working now.

Allow time for the students to fill in their answers. Walk around the room to be sure the students know how to answer the different item types in the lesson.

Unit 5 Lesson 7a **Expression**

Directions: For questions 4–9, choose the best way to express the idea.

4 *J   A work crew is beginning to build a bridge across the river.
    K   A work crew across the river is to beginning build a bridge.
    L   Across the river a work crew a bridge is beginning to build.
    M   Across the river is beginning a work crew to build a bridge.

5   A   Please before you go to school turn off the radio.
    B   Before you go to school turn off the radio please.
    C   Turn the radio off before you go to school please.
 * D   Please turn the radio off before you go to school.

6 *J   Alvin's mother works out at the gym almost every night.
    K   Alvin's mother almost every night. Works out at the gym.
    L   At the gym, Alvin's mother almost every night works out.
    M   Almost every night, at the gym Alvin's mother works out.

7   A   A group of children on the corner for the school bus waited.
    B   On the corner for the school bus waited a group of children.
    C   On the corner waited for the school bus a group of children.
 * D   A group of children waited on the corner for the school bus.

8   J   Parked near the corner is our car.
    K   Near the corner is parked our car.
 * L   Our car is parked near the corner.
    M   Is parked our car near the corner.

9   A   Getting up early in the morning Steve doesn't like.
    B   Early in the morning doesn't like Steve getting up.
 * C   Steve doesn't like getting up early in the morning.
    D   In the morning early getting up Steve doesn't like.

GO

Answer rows   4 ●ⓀⓁⓂ   6 ●ⓀⓁⓂ   8 ⒿⓀ●Ⓜ   41
               5 ⒶⒷⒸ●   7 ⒶⒷⒸ●   9 Ⓐ●ⒸⒹ

Say It's time to stop. You have finished Lesson 7a.

Review the answers with the students. If any questions caused particular difficulty, work through each of the answer choices. It will be helpful to have the students read the items aloud in order to give them practice listening for the one that sounds best.

Have the students indicate completion of the lesson by entering their score for this activity on the progress chart at the beginning of the book.

Directions: Use this paragraph to answer questions 10–13.

> ¹Once we found a box of old postcards. ²We kneeled down on the ground and started looking at all of them. ³Most people send postcards when they travel. ⁴We didn't have enough money to buy them all. ⁵Tilda and I wanted to buy all of them. ⁶We asked how much the box would cost. ⁷We chose our favorites instead.

10 Choose the best first sentence to add to this paragraph.
J   I love postcards.
K   Let me tell you about some different postcards.
L   There are a lot of yard sales in our neighborhood.
* M   Tilda and I find interesting things at yard sales.

11 Which sentence should be left out of this paragraph?
A   Sentence 1
B   Sentence 2
* C   Sentence 3
D   Sentence 4

12 Where is the best place for sentence 4?
J   Where it is now
K   Between sentences 5 and 6
* L   Between sentence 6 and 7
M   After sentence 7

13 Choose the best last sentence to add to this paragraph.
A   Collecting postcards is a great hobby.
* B   After we paid for them, we took our treasures home.
C   One postcard had some writing on the back of it.
D   If a postcard is in good shape, it is worth more money.

STOP

42   Answer rows   **10** ⓙⓀⓁ●   **11** ⒶⒷ●Ⓓ   **12** ⒿⓀ●Ⓜ   **13** Ⓐ●ⒸⒹ

Unit 5 Lesson 7b Expression

Focus

Language Skills
- choosing the best word to complete a sentence
- identifying correctly formed sentences
- identifying the best opening sentence for a paragraph
- identifying the sentence that does not fit in a paragraph
- identifying the best location for a sentence in a paragraph
- identifying the best closing sentence for a paragraph

Test-taking Skills
- following printed directions
- understanding unusual item formats
- working methodically

Sample A

Say Turn to Lesson 7b on page 43. In this lesson you will work with sentences and paragraphs. There are directions for each section of this lesson, so read them carefully before you answer questions.

Look at Sample A. Read the directions. Then read each of the answer choices. Find the answer choice that is the best way to express the idea. *(pause)* Which answer choice is correct? *(answer B)* Answer B is the best way to express the idea. Mark circle B for Sample A in the answer rows at the bottom of the page. Make sure the circle is completely filled in with a dark mark.

Check to see that the students have filled in the correct answer circle. If necessary, elaborate on the correct answer to the sample item.

Unit 5 Usage and Expression
Lesson 7b Expression

Directions: Choose the best way to express the idea.

> **Sample A** ✳
> A In our yard on top of the tree landed a large bird.
> B A large bird landed on top of the tree in our yard.
> C A large bird on top of the tree landed in our yard.
> D In our yard landed a large bird on top of the tree.

TIPS
- Read the directions and items carefully so you know what you are supposed to do.

> ¹Last weekend we did something different. ²The beach is in the southern part of New Jersey. ³We went for a hike on the beach. ⁴The ocean and the bay come together there. ⁵There are lots of sand dunes and very few people ever go there. ⁶New Jersey is next to Pennsylvania. ⁷During the hike, we found lots of interesting shells and rocks.

Directions: Use this paragraph to answer questions 1–4.

1 Choose the best first sentence to add to this paragraph.
  A What does your family like to do?
  B Beaches are more interesting than many people think.
  C Hiking is one of the best exercises.
  ✳ D My family likes to do lots of things outdoors.

2 Which sentence should be left out of this paragraph?
  J Sentence 4
  K Sentence 5
  ✳ L Sentence 6
  M Sentence 7

3 What is the best place for sentence 3?
  A Where it is
  ✳ B Between sentences 1 and 2
  C Between sentences 4 and 5
  D After sentence 7

4 Choose the best last sentence to add to this paragraph.
  J Last year we went for a hike in the mountains in Maine.
  ✳ K After we finished, we had a cookout on the beach.
  L My hiking shoes are comfortable.
  M It took us about two hours to drive from home to the beach.

GO

Answer rows A Ⓐ●ⒸⒹ 1 ⒶⒷⒸ● 2 ⒿⓀ●Ⓜ 3 Ⓐ●ⒸⒹ 4 Ⓙ●ⓁⓂ   43

★ TIPS

Say Who will read the tip for us?

Have a volunteer read the tip aloud.

Say Mark the answer when you are sure it is correct. Remember that if an item seems difficult, skip it and come back to it later.

There are different kinds of items in this lesson. Be sure to read the directions for each part and to pay attention to what you are doing. This is especially important on an achievement test.

Practice

Unit 5   Lesson 7b **Expression**

Directions: For questions 5–7, choose the best way to write the underlined part of the sentence.

5 All the children **except** Kyle remembered to do their homework.
   A and   B or   C though   **✱ D** (No change)

6 Some trees **were blowed** over in the storm last night.
   J blowing   **✱ K** were blown   L has blowed   M (No change)

7 It's cold today, **or** it is supposed to warm up tomorrow.
✱ A but   B then   C however   D (No change)

Directions: For questions 8 and 9, choose the best way to express the idea.

8 ✱ J My shoes always seem to be untied.
   K Untied my shoes always seem to be.
   L To be untied my shoes always seem.
   M Always my untied shoes seem to be.

9 A A black olive put Calvin on each finger.
   B A black olive on Calvin put each finger.
✱ C Calvin put a black olive on each finger.
   D On each finger, a black olive Calvin put.

44   **Answer rows**   5 Ⓐ Ⓑ Ⓒ ●   6 Ⓙ ● Ⓛ Ⓜ   7 ● Ⓑ Ⓒ Ⓓ   8 ● Ⓚ Ⓛ Ⓜ   9 Ⓐ Ⓑ ● Ⓓ

Unit 5 Test Yourself: Usage and Expression

Focus

Language Skills
- identifying mistakes in usage
- choosing the best word to complete a sentence
- identifying correctly formed sentences

Test-taking Skills
- managing time effectively
- following printed directions
- using context to find an answer
- indicating that an item has no mistakes
- subvocalizing answer choices
- skipping difficult items and returning to them later
- working methodically
- recalling usage errors
- analyzing answer choices
- understanding unusual item formats
- skimming answer choices
- marking the right answer as soon as it is found

This lesson simulates an actual test-taking experience. Therefore, it is recommended that the directions be read verbatim and the suggested procedures and time allowances be followed.

Directions

Administration Time: approximately 20 minutes

Say Turn to the Test Yourself lesson on page 45.

Point out to the students that this Test Yourself lesson is timed like a real test, but that they will score it themselves to see how well they are doing. Remind the students to pace themselves and to check the clock after they have finished Number 11 to see how much time is left. This is about the halfway point in the lesson. Encourage the students to avoid spending too much time on any one item and to take the best guess if they are unsure of the answer.

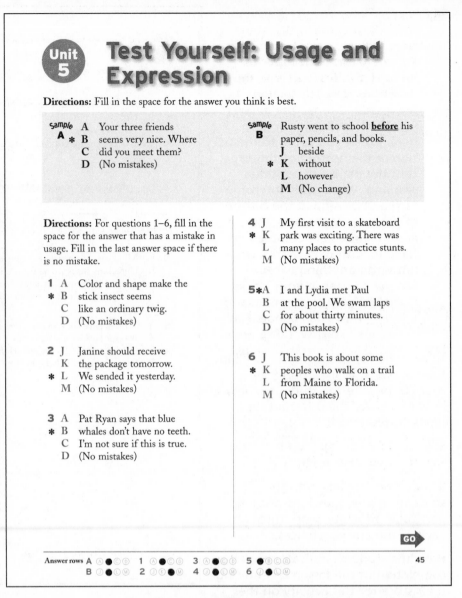

Unit 5 Test Yourself: Usage and Expression

Directions: Fill in the space for the answer you think is best.

Sample A
- A Your three friends
- *B seems very nice. Where
- C did you meet them?
- D (No mistakes)

Sample B
Rusty went to school **before** his paper, pencils, and books.
- J beside
- *K without
- L however
- M (No change)

Directions: For questions 1–6, fill in the space for the answer that has a mistake in usage. Fill in the last answer space if there is no mistake.

1
- A Color and shape make the
- *B stick insect seems
- C like an ordinary twig.
- D (No mistakes)

2
- J Janine should receive
- K the package tomorrow.
- *L We sended it yesterday.
- M (No mistakes)

3
- A Pat Ryan says that blue
- *B whales don't have no teeth.
- C I'm not sure if this is true.
- D (No mistakes)

4
- J My first visit to a skateboard
- *K park was exciting. There was
- L many places to practice stunts.
- M (No mistakes)

5
- *A I and Lydia met Paul
- B at the pool. We swam laps
- C for about thirty minutes.
- D (No mistakes)

6
- J This book is about some
- *K peoples who walk on a trail
- L from Maine to Florida.
- M (No mistakes)

Answer rows   A Ⓐ●ⒸⒹ   1 Ⓐ●ⒸⒹ   3 Ⓐ●ⒸⒹ   5 ●ⒷⒸⒹ
　　　　　　　　　B Ⓙ●ⓁⓂ   2 ⒿⓀ●Ⓜ   4 Ⓙ●ⓁⓂ   6 Ⓙ●ⓁⓂ

GO

45

Say There are different types of items in the Test Yourself lesson, so you will have to read the directions for each section and pay close attention to what you are doing. Remember to make sure that the circles in the answer rows are completely filled in. Press your pencil firmly so that your marks come out dark. Completely erase any marks for answers that you change. Do not write anything except your answer choices in your books.

Look at Sample A and listen carefully. Read the answer choices to yourself. Mark the circle for the answer that has a mistake in English usage. Choose the last answer, No mistakes, if none of the answer choices has a mistake. Mark the circle for your answer.

Allow time for the students to fill in their answers.

Say The circle for answer B should be filled in because the word *seems* should be *seem*. If you chose another answer, erase yours and fill in the circle for answer B now.

Check to see that the students have filled in the correct answer circle.

Say Now do Sample B. Read the sentence with the underlined part and each of the answer choices. Fill in the circle for the answer that is the best way to write the underlined part. If the underlined part is correct, choose the last answer, No change.

Allow time for the students to fill in their answers.

Say The circle for answer K should be filled in. If you chose another answer, erase yours and fill in the circle for answer K now.

Check to see that the students have filled in the correct answer circle.

Say Now you will do more items. Read the directions for each section. When you come to the GO sign at the bottom of a page, turn the page and continue working. Work until you come to the STOP sign on page 47. If you are not sure of an answer, fill in the circle for the answer you think might be right. Do you have any questions?

Answer any questions the students have.

Say You may begin working. You will have 15 minutes.

Allow 15 minutes.

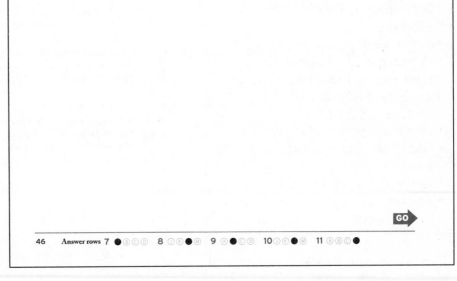

Unit 5 Test Yourself: Usage and Expression

Directions: For questions 7–11, choose the best way to write the underlined part of the sentence.

7 We will wait under the awning **still** it has stopped raining.
* A until   B then   C maybe   D (No change)

8 Cheryl **playing** in every basketball game except one.
J have played   K to play   * L has played   M (No change)

9 They **saw** the circus perform next week.
A seen   * B will see   C had seen   D (No change)

10 The general knew **so** the soldiers needed to rest.
J yet   K as   * L when   M (No change)

11 My sister put the map **where** she would remember it.
A if   B unless   C how   * D (No change)

GO

46   Answer rows   7 ●Ⓑ©Ⓓ   8 ⒿⓀ●Ⓜ   9 Ⓐ●©Ⓓ   10 ⒿⓀ●Ⓜ   11 Ⓐ Ⓑ©●

Say It's time to stop. You have finished the Test Yourself lesson. Check to see that you have completely filled in your answer circles with dark marks. Make sure that any marks for answers that you changed have been completely erased.

Go over the lesson with the students. Ask the students if they read the directions for each section. Did they have enough time to finish all the items? Which items were most difficult? Work through any questions that caused difficulty.

Have the students indicate completion of the lesson by entering their score for this activity on the progress chart at the beginning of the book.

Directions: For questions 12–17, choose the best way to express the idea.

12 J For five years my father was almost in the Coast Guard.
 K In the Coast Guard was my father for almost five years.
 L Almost in the Coast Guard my father was for five years.
✱ **M** My father was in the Coast Guard for almost five years.

13 A On a flower landing, I watched a butterfly.
✱ **B** I watched a butterfly landing on a flower.
 C Landing on a flower, I watched a butterfly.
 D I watched landing, on a flower, a butterfly.

14 J Hiro tried one spoonful, which the spicy soup smelled.
 K Although Hiro tried one, the spoonful smelled spicy soup.
 L Hiro tried one soup spoon even though it smelled spicy.
✱ **M** Although the soup smelled spicy, Hiro tried one spoonful of it.

15 ✱**A** A dog named Rudy dug a big hole in our front yard.
 B A dog named Rudy digging a big hole. In our front yard.
 C Our front yard. A dog named Rudy dug a big hole in it.
 D A big hole. A dog named Rudy dug it in our front yard.

16 J For the first time this year froze the pond.
 K This year the pond for the first time froze.
✱ **L** The pond froze for the first time this year.
 M The first time for the pond this year froze.

17 A That bad movie was not very good.
✱ **B** That movie was not very good.
 C That movie was pretty bad but not very good.
 D That movie, which was not very good, was pretty bad.

STOP

Answer rows 12 ⓙⓀⓁ● 14 ⓙⓀⓁ● 16 ⓙⓀ●ⓜ
13 Ⓐ●ⓒⒹ 15 ●ⒷⒸⒹ 17 Ⓐ●ⒸⒹ

47

Unit 6

Background

This unit contains five lessons that deal with math concepts and estimation skills.

• **In Lessons 8a and 8b,** students solve problems involving math concepts. Students identify and use key words, numbers, and pictures. They refer to a graphic, find the answer without computing, work methodically, evaluate answer choices, and rephrase questions.

• **In Lessons 9a and 9b,** students solve problems involving estimation. In addition to reviewing the test-taking skills introduced in the two previous lessons, students learn the importance of working carefully on scratch paper.

• **In the Test Yourself lesson,** the math concepts and estimation skills and test-taking skills introduced in Lessons 8a through 9b are reinforced and presented in a format that gives students the experience of taking an achievement test. Techniques for managing time effectively when taking a standardized test are reinforced.

Instructional Objectives

Lesson 8a **Math Concepts** Lesson 8b **Math Concepts**	Given a problem involving math concepts, students identify which of four answer choices is correct.
Lesson 9a **Math Estimation** Lesson 9b **Math Estimation**	Given a problem involving estimation, students identify which of four answer choices is correct.
Test Yourself	Given questions similar to those in Lessons 8a through 9b, students utilize math concepts, estimation, and test-taking strategies on achievement test formats.

Unit 6 Lesson 8a
Math Concepts

Focus

Mathematics Skills
- recognizing odd and even numbers
- recognizing value of coins or bills
- using a number line
- identifying parts of a figure
- identifying the best measurement unit
- understanding number sentences
- recognizing plane figures
- estimating measurement
- using a calendar
- finding area
- recognizing fractional parts
- understanding mathematical language
- understanding regrouping
- understanding permutations and combinations

Test-taking Skills
- identifying and using key words, numbers, and pictures
- referring to a graphic
- finding the answer without computing
- working methodically
- evaluating answer choices

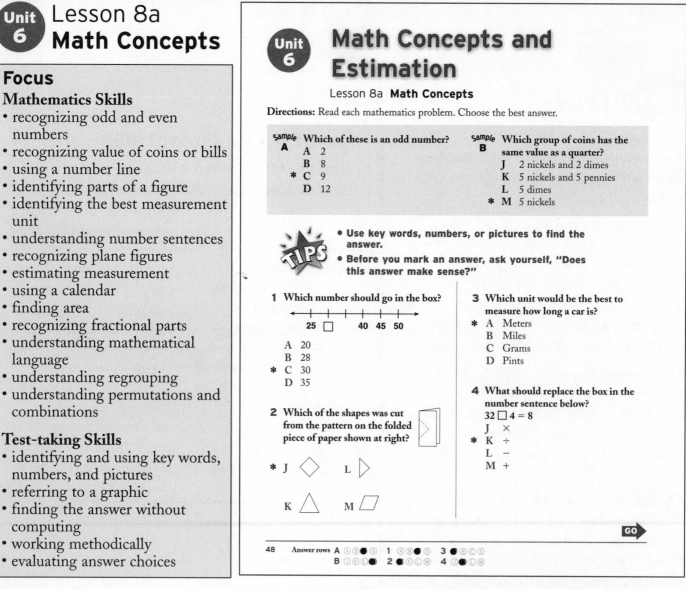

Unit 6 Math Concepts and Estimation

Lesson 8a **Math Concepts**

Directions: Read each mathematics problem. Choose the best answer.

Sample A Which of these is an odd number?
  A 2
  B 8
  * C 9
  D 12

Sample B Which group of coins has the same value as a quarter?
  J 2 nickels and 2 dimes
  K 5 nickels and 5 pennies
  L 5 dimes
  * M 5 nickels

TIPS
- Use key words, numbers, or pictures to find the answer.
- Before you mark an answer, ask yourself, "Does this answer make sense?"

1 Which number should go in the box?
  25 ☐ 40 45 50
  A 20
  B 28
  * C 30
  D 35

2 Which of the shapes was cut from the pattern on the folded piece of paper shown at right?
  * J ◇ L ▷
  K △ M ▱

3 Which unit would be the best to measure how long a car is?
  * A Meters
  B Miles
  C Grams
  D Pints

4 What should replace the box in the number sentence below?
  32 ☐ 4 = 8
  J ×
  * K ÷
  L −
  M +

48   Answer rows A Ⓐ Ⓑ ● Ⓓ 1 Ⓐ Ⓑ ● Ⓓ 3 ● Ⓑ Ⓒ Ⓓ
                 B Ⓙ Ⓚ Ⓛ ● 2 ● Ⓚ Ⓛ Ⓜ 4 Ⓙ ● Ⓛ Ⓜ

Samples A and B

Distribute scratch paper to the students.

Say Turn to Lesson 8a on page 48. In this lesson you will work on math problems. Read the directions at the top of the page to yourself.

Allow time for the students to read the directions.

Say Find Sample A. Read the question to yourselves. Think about the important words in the question. *(pause)* Which answer choice is correct? *(answer C, 9)* Yes, answer C is correct because *9* is an odd number. Mark answer C for Sample A in the answer rows. Make sure the circle is completely filled in with a dark mark.

Check to see that the students have filled in the correct answer circle.

Say Now we'll do Sample B. Read the question to yourself. Which answer is correct? *(answer M)* Fill in answer M for Sample B in the answer rows at the bottom of the page. Be sure you fill in the circle with a dark mark.

Check to see that the students have filled in the correct answer circle. If necessary, elaborate on the solutions to the sample items.

⭐TIPS

Say Now let's look at the tips.

Have a volunteer read the tips aloud to the group.

Say You should look for key words, numbers, and pictures in a problem. They will help you find the answer. And before you mark your answer, be sure it makes sense. Compare it with the question and any graphic that is part of the question.

Practice

Say We are ready for Practice. You are going to do more problems in the same way that we did the samples. Do not write anything except your answer choices in your book. If you think it will help, you may do your work on the scratch paper I gave you. Remember to look for key words, numbers, and pictures in the problems. You should also remember that you don't have to compute to find some of the answers in this lesson. When you have finished working a problem, fill in the circle for your answer in the answer rows at the bottom of the page. Make sure that the circles for your answer choices are completely filled in with dark marks. Completely erase any marks for answers that you change. When you come to the GO sign at the bottom of a page, turn the page and continue working. Work until you come to the STOP sign at the bottom of page 50. Do you have any questions? Start working now.

Allow time for the students to fill in their answers.

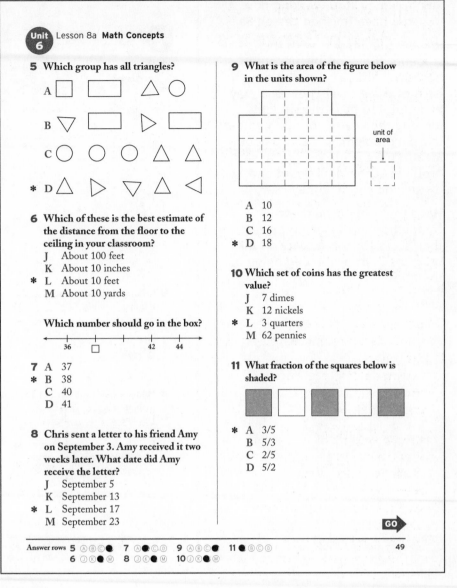

Say You may stop working now.
You have finished Lesson 8a.

Review the answers with the students. If any problems caused particular difficulty, work through each of the answer choices. It may be helpful to have the students identify the key words and numbers in each problem. It is also a good idea to have volunteers solve each problem at the chalkboard and discuss the strategy they used.

Have the students indicate completion of the lesson by entering their score for this activity on the progress chart at the beginning of the book.

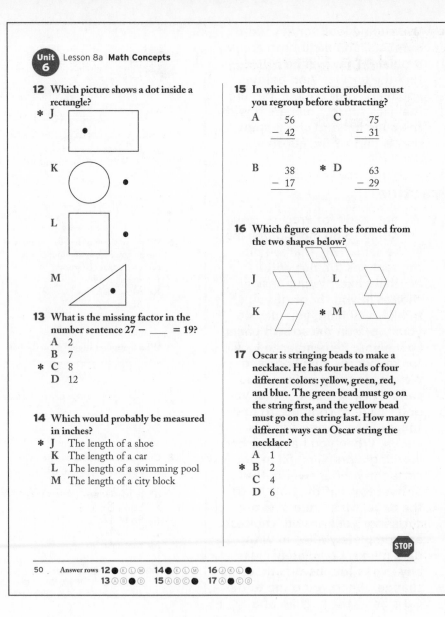

12 Which picture shows a dot inside a rectangle?

* **J**

K

L

M

13 What is the missing factor in the number sentence 27 − ___ = 19?
   A 2
   B 7
* C 8
   D 12

14 Which would probably be measured in inches?
* **J** The length of a shoe
   K The length of a car
   L The length of a swimming pool
   M The length of a city block

15 In which subtraction problem must you regroup before subtracting?

   A   56   C   75
      − 42   − 31

   B   38   * D   63
      − 17   − 29

16 Which figure cannot be formed from the two shapes below?

   J   L

   K   * M

17 Oscar is stringing beads to make a necklace. He has four beads of four different colors: yellow, green, red, and blue. The green bead must go on the string first, and the yellow bead must go on the string last. How many different ways can Oscar string the necklace?
   A 1
* B 2
   C 4
   D 6

STOP

50   Answer rows   12 ● Ⓚ Ⓛ Ⓜ   14 ● Ⓚ Ⓛ Ⓜ   16 Ⓙ Ⓚ Ⓛ ●
                   13 Ⓐ Ⓑ ● Ⓓ   15 Ⓐ Ⓑ Ⓒ ●   17 Ⓐ ● Ⓒ Ⓓ

Lesson 8b
Unit 6
Math Concepts

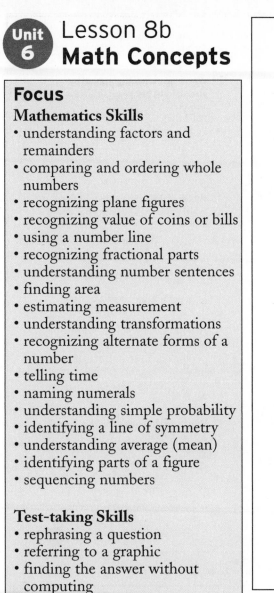

Focus
Mathematics Skills
- understanding factors and remainders
- comparing and ordering whole numbers
- recognizing plane figures
- recognizing value of coins or bills
- using a number line
- recognizing fractional parts
- understanding number sentences
- finding area
- estimating measurement
- understanding transformations
- recognizing alternate forms of a number
- telling time
- naming numerals
- understanding simple probability
- identifying a line of symmetry
- understanding average (mean)
- identifying parts of a figure
- sequencing numbers

Test-taking Skills
- rephrasing a question
- referring to a graphic
- finding the answer without computing
- working methodically

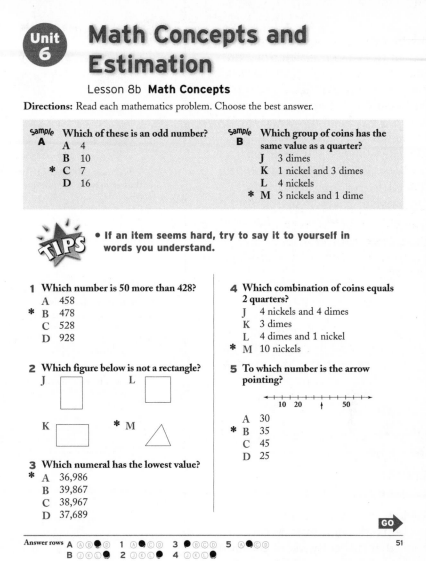

Samples A and B

Distribute scratch paper to the students.

Say Turn to Lesson 8b on page 51. In this lesson you will work on more mathematics problems. Read the directions at the top of the page to yourself.

Allow time for the students to read the directions.

Say Find Sample A. Read the question to yourselves. *(pause)* Which answer choice is correct? *(answer C)* Yes, answer C is correct because 7 is an odd number. Mark answer C for Sample A in the answer rows. Make sure the circle is completely filled in with a dark mark.

Check to see that the students have filled in the correct answer circle.

Say Now we'll do Sample B. Read the question to yourself. *(pause)* Which answer is correct? *(answer M)* Fill in answer M for Sample B in the answer rows at the bottom of the page. Be sure you fill in the circle with a dark mark.

Check to see that the students have filled in the correct answer circle.

★**TIPS**

Say Now let's look at the tip.

Have a volunteer read the tip aloud to the group.

Say Sometimes an item might seem a little difficult to understand. One thing you can do is say the question to yourself in words you understand better. This will help you find the right answer.

Practice

Say We are ready for Practice. You are going to do more problems in the same way that we did the Samples. Do not write anything except your answer choices in your book. If you think it will help, you may do your work on scratch paper. When you have finished working a problem, fill in the circle for your answer in the answer rows at the bottom of the page. Make sure that the circles for your answer choices are completely filled in with dark marks. Completely erase any marks for answers that you change. When you come to the GO sign at the bottom of the page, turn the page and continue working. Work until you come to the STOP sign at the bottom of page 52. Do you have any questions? Start working now.

Allow time for the students to fill in their answers.

Say You may stop working now. You have finished Lesson 8b.

Review the answers with the students. If any problems caused particular difficulty, work through each of the answer choices. It may be helpful to have volunteers solve each problem at the chalkboard and discuss the strategy they used.

Have the students indicate completion of the lesson by entering their score for this activity on the progress chart at the beginning of the book.

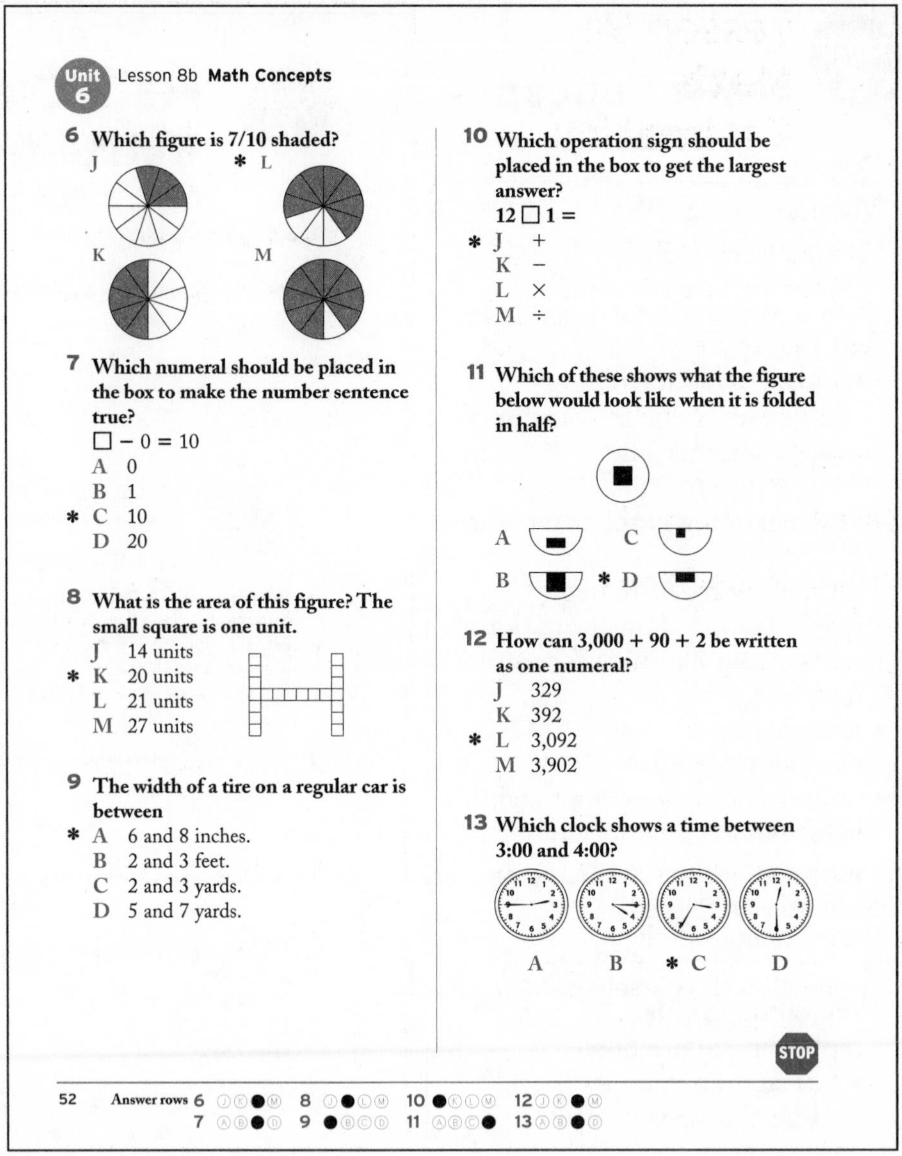

---

6 Which figure is 7/10 shaded?

J   * L

K   M

7 Which numeral should be placed in the box to make the number sentence true?

$\square - 0 = 10$

A   0
B   1
* C   10
D   20

8 What is the area of this figure? The small square is one unit.

J   14 units
* K   20 units
L   21 units
M   27 units

9 The width of a tire on a regular car is between

* A   6 and 8 inches.
B   2 and 3 feet.
C   2 and 3 yards.
D   5 and 7 yards.

10 Which operation sign should be placed in the box to get the largest answer?

$12 \square 1 =$

* J   +
K   −
L   ×
M   ÷

11 Which of these shows what the figure below would look like when it is folded in half?

A   C

B   * D

12 How can $3,000 + 90 + 2$ be written as one numeral?

J   329
K   392
* L   3,092
M   3,902

13 Which clock shows a time between 3:00 and 4:00?

A   B   * C   D

STOP

52   Answer rows   6 ⒥⒦●Ⓜ   8 ⒥●ⓁⓂ   10 ●⒦ⓁⓂ   12 ⒥⒦●Ⓜ
              7 Ⓐ⒝●Ⓓ   9 ●ⒷⒸⒹ   11 ⒶⒷⒸ●   13 ⒶⒷ●Ⓓ

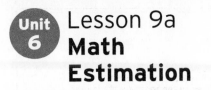
Unit 6

Focus

Mathematics Skill
• estimating and rounding

Test-taking Skills
• working methodically
• finding the answer without computing

Samples A and B

Distribute scratch paper to the students.

Say Turn to Lesson 9a on page 53. In this lesson you will solve mathematics problems involving estimation. Read the directions at the top of the page to yourself.

Allow time for the students to read the directions.

Say Find Sample A. Read the question to yourselves. *(pause)* Think about how to solve the problem. Which answer choice is correct? *(answer D)* Yes, answer D is correct. If you round the numbers in the problem and solve it, the answer is *60*. Mark answer D for Sample A in the answer rows. Make sure the circle is completely filled in with a dark mark.

Check to see that the students have filled in the correct answer circle.

Say Now we'll do Sample B. Read the question to yourself. Remember to round before you solve the problem. *(pause)* Which answer is correct? *(answer K)* Fill in answer K for Sample B in the answer rows at the bottom of the page. Be sure you fill in the circle with a dark mark.

Check to see that the students have filled in the correct answer circle. If necessary, elaborate on the solutions to the sample items and review the rules for rounding numbers.

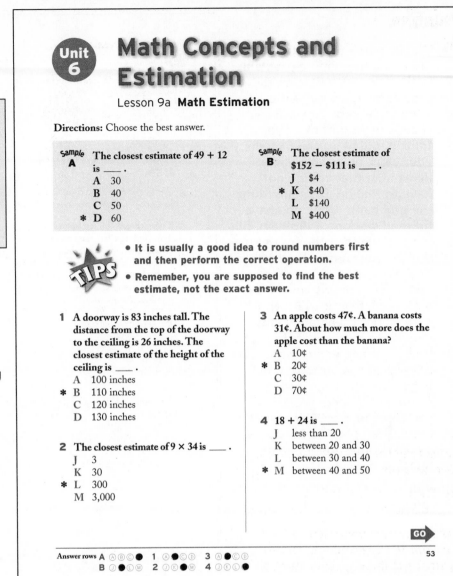

Unit 6

Math Concepts and Estimation

Lesson 9a Math Estimation

Directions: Choose the best answer.

Sample A The closest estimate of 49 + 12 is ___ .
A 30
B 40
C 50
* D 60

Sample B The closest estimate of $152 − $111 is ___ .
J $4
* K $40
L $140
M $400

TIPS
• It is usually a good idea to round numbers first and then perform the correct operation.
• Remember, you are supposed to find the best estimate, not the exact answer.

1 A doorway is 83 inches tall. The distance from the top of the doorway to the ceiling is 26 inches. The closest estimate of the height of the ceiling is ___ .
A 100 inches
* B 110 inches
C 120 inches
D 130 inches

2 The closest estimate of 9 × 34 is ___ .
J 3
K 30
* L 300
M 3,000

3 An apple costs 47¢. A banana costs 31¢. About how much more does the apple cost than the banana?
A 10¢
* B 20¢
C 30¢
D 70¢

4 18 + 24 is ___ .
J less than 20
K between 20 and 30
L between 30 and 40
* M between 40 and 50

GO

Answer rows A Ⓐ Ⓑ Ⓒ ● 1 Ⓐ ● Ⓒ Ⓓ 3 Ⓐ ● Ⓒ Ⓓ
B Ⓙ ● Ⓛ Ⓜ 2 Ⓙ Ⓚ ● Ⓜ 4 Ⓙ Ⓚ Ⓛ ●

53

★TIPS

Say Now let's look at the tips.

Have a volunteer read the tips aloud to the group.

Say Estimation problems are different from other math problems because you do not have to find an exact answer. The first thing you should do is round the numbers in the problem. After that, you should solve the problem and choose the answer that is the best estimate of the exact answer.

Practice

Say We are ready for Practice. You are going to do more problems in the same way that we did the Samples. Do not write anything except your answer choices in your book. If you think it will help, you may do your work on scratch paper. Remember that you do not have to find an exact answer to the problems. When you have finished working a problem, fill in the circle for your answer in the answer rows at the bottom of the page. Make sure that the circles for your answer choices are completely filled in with dark marks. Completely erase any marks for answers that you change. When you come to the GO sign at the bottom of the page, turn the page and continue working. Work until you come to the STOP sign at the bottom of page 54. Do you have any questions? Start working now.

Allow time for the students to fill in their answers.

Say You may stop working now. You have finished Lesson 9a.

Review the answers with the students. If any problems caused particular difficulty, work through each of the answer choices. It may be helpful to have volunteers solve each problem at the chalkboard and discuss the rounding and estimation skills they used.

Have the students indicate completion of the lesson by entering their score for this activity on the progress chart at the beginning of the book.

Unit 6 — Lesson 9a **Math Estimation**

5 The closest estimate of the total cost of the kites is ___ .

5 kites
$2.95 each

- A $3
- B $8
- C $10
- * D $15

6 Three classes line up to go to recess. The kindergarten class has 28 students, the first grade has 12 students, and the second grade has 22 students. Which best shows how to get the closest estimate of the total number of students?

- * J 30 + 10 + 20
- K 30 + 20 + 20
- L 20 + 10 + 20
- M 30 + 10 + 30

7 The closest estimate of 719 − 186 is ___ .

- A 5
- B 50
- * C 500
- D 5,000

8 An elm tree in the park is 76 feet tall. A maple tree in the same park is 39 feet tall. The closest estimate of how much taller the elm tree is than the maple tree is ___ .

- J 60 feet
- K 50 feet
- * L 40 feet
- M 30 feet

9 The closest estimate of $6.58 − $2.61 is ___ .

- A $3
- * B $4
- C $5
- D $6

54   Answer rows   5 Ⓐ Ⓑ Ⓒ ● 6 ● Ⓚ Ⓛ Ⓜ 7 Ⓐ Ⓑ ● Ⓓ 8 Ⓙ Ⓚ ● Ⓜ 9 Ⓐ ● Ⓒ Ⓓ

Math Estimation

Focus

Mathematics Skill
• estimating and rounding

Test-taking Skills
• finding the answer without computing
• working methodically

Samples A and B

Distribute scratch paper to the students.

Say Turn to Lesson 9b on page 55. In this lesson you will solve more problems involving estimation. Read the directions at the top of the page to yourself.

Allow time for the students to read the directions.

Say Find Sample A. Read the question to yourselves. *(pause)* Think about how to solve the problem. Which answer choice is correct? *(answer A)* Yes, answer A is correct. If you round the numbers in the problem and then add, the answer is *30*. Mark answer A for Sample A in the answer rows. Make sure the circle is completely filled in with a dark mark.

Check to see that the students have filled in the correct answer circle.

Say Now we'll do Sample B. Read the question to yourself. Remember to round before you solve the problem. *(pause)* Which answer is correct? *(answer L)* Fill in answer L for Sample B in the answer rows at the bottom of the page. Be sure you fill in the circle with a dark mark.

Check to see that the students have filled in the correct answer circle. If necessary, elaborate on the solutions to the sample items.

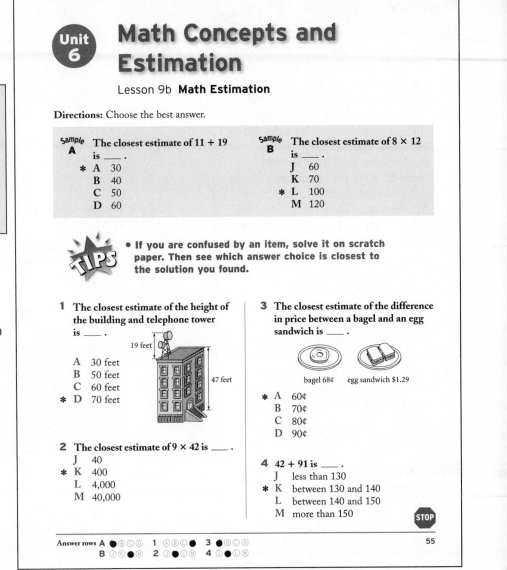

Unit 6 Math Concepts and Estimation

Lesson 9b **Math Estimation**

Directions: Choose the best answer.

Sample A The closest estimate of 11 + 19 is ___ .
* A 30
  B 40
  C 50
  D 60

Sample B The closest estimate of 8 × 12 is ___ .
  J 60
  K 70
* L 100
  M 120

TIPS
• If you are confused by an item, solve it on scratch paper. Then see which answer choice is closest to the solution you found.

1 The closest estimate of the height of the building and telephone tower is ___ .
   19 feet
   47 feet
   A 30 feet
   B 50 feet
   C 60 feet
 * D 70 feet

2 The closest estimate of 9 × 42 is ___ .
   J 40
 * K 400
   L 4,000
   M 40,000

3 The closest estimate of the difference in price between a bagel and an egg sandwich is ___ .
   bagel 68¢   egg sandwich $1.29
 * A 60¢
   B 70¢
   C 80¢
   D 90¢

4 42 + 91 is ___ .
   J less than 130
 * K between 130 and 140
   L between 140 and 150
   M more than 150
   STOP

Answer rows A ●ⒷⒸⒹ 1 ⒶⒷⒸ● 3 ●ⒷⒸⒹ
             B ⒿⓀ●Ⓜ 2 Ⓙ●ⓁⓂ 4 Ⓙ●ⓁⓂ   55

TIPS

Say Now let's look at the tip.

Have a volunteer read the tip aloud to the group.

Say Sometimes a problem may seem confusing. When this happens, solve the problem on scratch paper. Round the numbers in the problem, solve the problem, and then match your solution with the answer choices.

Review rounding rules with the students if necessary.

Practice

Say We are ready for Practice. You are going to do more problems in the same way that we did the Samples. Do not write anything except your answer choices in your book. If you think it will help, you may do your work on scratch paper. Remember that you do not have to find an exact answer to the problems. When you have finished working on a problem, fill in the circle for your answer in the answer rows at the bottom of the page. Make sure that the circles for your answer choices are completely filled in with dark marks. Completely erase any marks for answers that you change. Work until you come to the STOP sign at the bottom of the page. Do you have any questions? Start working now.

Allow time for the students to fill in their answers.

Say You may stop working now. You have finished Lesson 9b.

Review the answers with the students. If any problems caused particular difficulty, work through each of the answer choices. It may be helpful to have volunteers solve each problem at the chalkboard, emphasizing front-end rounding.

Have the students indicate completion of the lesson by entering their score for this activity on the progress chart at the beginning of the book.

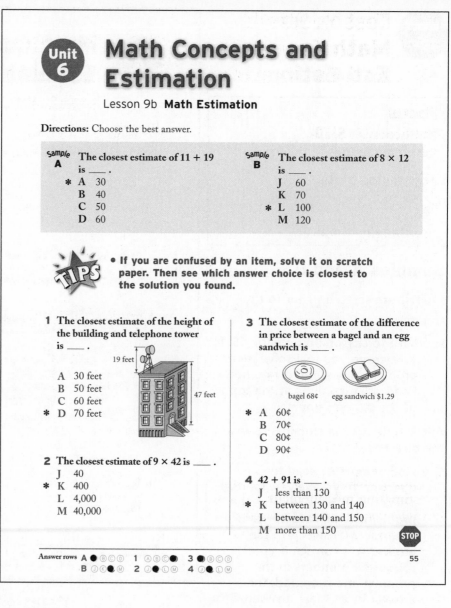

Focus

Mathematics Skills

- comparing metric and standard units
- comparing whole numbers
- understanding number sentences
- understanding characteristics of related numbers
- identifying parts of a figure
- identifying the best measurement unit
- understanding permutations and combinations
- identifying problem-solving strategies
- understanding place value
- recognizing value of coins or bills
- using a number line
- recognizing fractional parts
- understanding special properties of zero
- finding area
- estimating measurement
- understanding transformations
- recognizing alternate forms of a number
- telling time
- estimating and rounding

Test-taking Skills

- managing time effectively
- identifying and using key words, numbers, and pictures
- referring to a graphic
- finding the answer without computing
- working methodically
- evaluating answer choices
- rephrasing a question

This lesson simulates an actual test-taking experience. Therefore, it is recommended that the directions be read verbatim and that the suggested procedures and time allowances be followed.

Test Yourself: Math Concepts and Estimation

Directions: Read each mathematics problem. Choose the best answer.

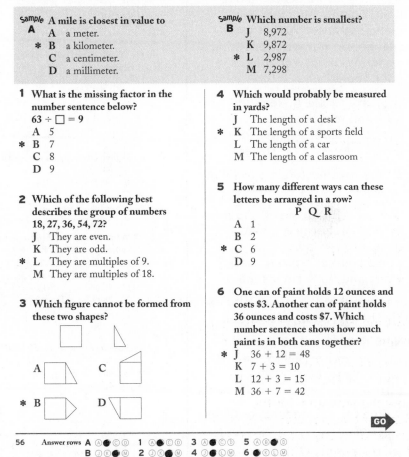

Sample A A mile is closest in value to
- A   a meter.
- *B   a kilometer.
- C   a centimeter.
- D   a millimeter.

Sample B Which number is smallest?
- J   8,972
- K   9,872
- *L   2,987
- M   7,298

1 What is the missing factor in the number sentence below?
$63 \div \square = 9$
- A   5
- *B   7
- C   8
- D   9

2 Which of the following best describes the group of numbers 18, 27, 36, 54, 72?
- J   They are even.
- K   They are odd.
- *L   They are multiples of 9.
- M   They are multiples of 18.

3 Which figure cannot be formed from these two shapes?

4 Which would probably be measured in yards?
- J   The length of a desk
- *K   The length of a sports field
- L   The length of a car
- M   The length of a classroom

5 How many different ways can these letters be arranged in a row?
P Q R
- A   1
- B   2
- *C   6
- D   9

6 One can of paint holds 12 ounces and costs $3. Another can of paint holds 36 ounces and costs $7. Which number sentence shows how much paint is in both cans together?
- *J   36 + 12 = 48
- K   7 + 3 = 10
- L   12 + 3 = 15
- M   36 + 7 = 42

GO

56   Answer rows A Ⓐ●ⓒⓓ 1 Ⓐ●ⓒⓓ 3 Ⓐ●ⓒⓓ 5 Ⓐⓑ●ⓓ
                    B Ⓙⓚ●Ⓜ 2 Ⓙⓚ●Ⓜ 4 Ⓙ●ⓛⓜ 6 ●ⓚⓛⓜ

Directions

Administration Time: approximately 30 minutes

Distribute scratch paper to the students.

Say Turn to the Test Yourself lesson on page 56.

Point out to the students that this Test Yourself lesson is timed like a real test, but that they will score it themselves to see how well they are doing. Encourage them to read each question carefully, to think about what they are supposed to do, and to work carefully on scratch paper when necessary. They should skip difficult problems, return to them later, and take the best guess when they are unsure of the answer.

Say This lesson will check how well you can solve mathematics problems. Remember to make sure that the circles for your answer choices are completely filled in. Press your pencil firmly so that your marks come out dark. Completely erase any marks for answers that you change. Do not write anything except your answer choices in your books.

Look at Sample A. Read the question and the answer choices. Mark the circle for the answer you think is correct.

Allow time for the students to fill in their answers.

Say The circle for answer B should be filled in because a mile is closest to *a kilometer*. If you chose another answer, erase yours and fill in circle B now.

Check to see that the students have filled in the correct answer circle.

Say Now read Sample B and the answer choices. Fill in the circle for the answer you think is correct.

Allow time for the students to fill in their answers.

Say The circle for answer L should be filled in. If you chose another answer, erase yours and fill in circle L now.

Check to see that the students have filled in the correct answer circle.

Say Now you will do more mathematics problems. You may use the scratch paper I gave you. When you come to a GO sign at the bottom of a page, turn the page and continue working. Work until you come to the STOP sign at the bottom of page 60. Make sure that the circles for your answers are completely filled in with dark marks. Be sure to fill in the circle in the answer row for the problem you are working on. Completely erase any marks for answers that you change. You will have 25 minutes to solve the problems. You may begin.

Allow 25 minutes.

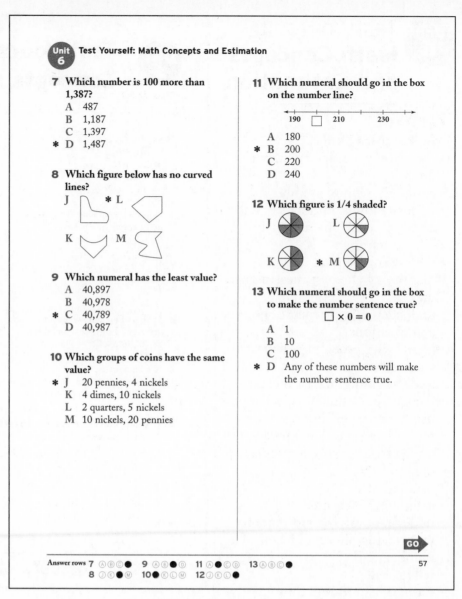

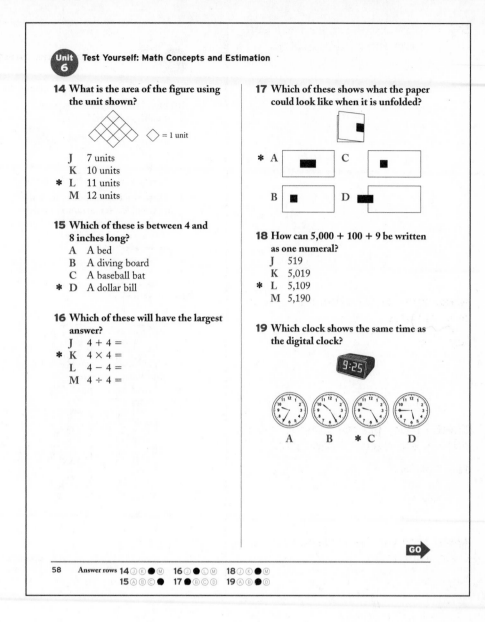

14 What is the area of the figure using the unit shown?

◇ = 1 unit

  J 7 units
  K 10 units
* L 11 units
  M 12 units

15 Which of these is between 4 and 8 inches long?
  A A bed
  B A diving board
  C A baseball bat
* D A dollar bill

16 Which of these will have the largest answer?
  J $4 + 4 =$
* K $4 \times 4 =$
  L $4 - 4 =$
  M $4 \div 4 =$

17 Which of these shows what the paper could look like when it is unfolded?

* A   C
  B   D

18 How can $5,000 + 100 + 9$ be written as one numeral?
  J 519
  K 5,019
* L 5,109
  M 5,190

19 Which clock shows the same time as the digital clock?

9:25

  A   B * C   D

GO

Directions: For questions 20–27, choose the best answer.

20 The closest estimate of the total number of flowers is ___ .

J   50
K   60
* L   70
M   80

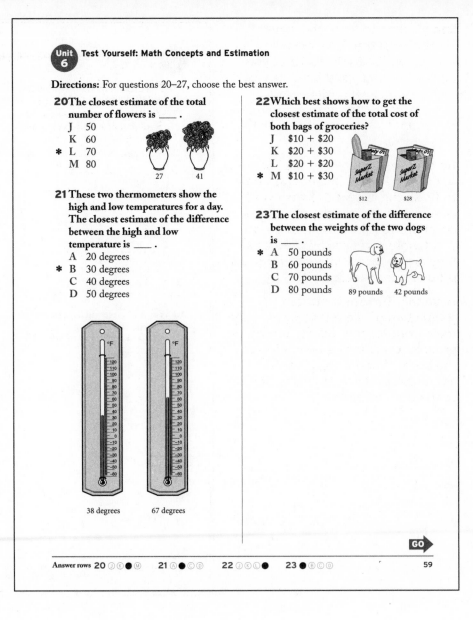

27   41

21 These two thermometers show the high and low temperatures for a day. The closest estimate of the difference between the high and low temperature is ___ .

A   20 degrees
* B   30 degrees
C   40 degrees
D   50 degrees

38 degrees   67 degrees

22 Which best shows how to get the closest estimate of the total cost of both bags of groceries?

J $10 + $20
K $20 + $30
L $20 + $20
* M $10 + $30

SuperZ Market   SuperZ Market
$12 $28

23 The closest estimate of the difference between the weights of the two dogs is ___ .

* A   50 pounds
B   60 pounds
C   70 pounds
D   80 pounds

89 pounds   42 pounds

GO

Answer rows **20** Ⓙ Ⓚ ● Ⓜ   **21** Ⓐ ● Ⓒ Ⓓ   **22** Ⓙ Ⓚ Ⓛ ●   **23** ● Ⓑ Ⓒ Ⓓ

59

Say It's time to stop. You have finished the Test Yourself lesson. Check to see that you have completely filled in your answer circles. Make sure that any marks for answers that you changed have been completely erased.

Go over the lesson with the students. Ask whether they had enough time to finish the lesson. Did they work carefully on scratch paper? Which questions required them to guess? What were some of the problems they experienced? Work through any problems that caused difficulty.

Have the students indicate completion of the lesson by entering their score for this activity on the progress chart at the beginning of the book. If necessary, provide additional practice problems similar to the ones in this unit.

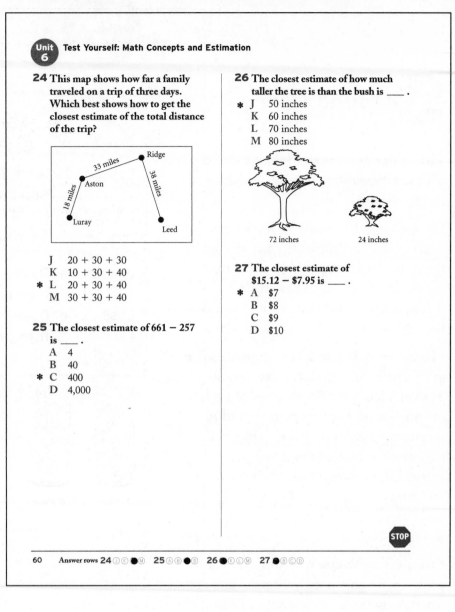

24 This map shows how far a family traveled on a trip of three days. Which best shows how to get the closest estimate of the total distance of the trip?

- 33 miles (Aston to Ridge)
- 18 miles (Luray to Aston)
- 38 miles (Ridge to Leed)

Ridge · Aston · Luray · Leed

- J   20 + 30 + 30
- K   10 + 30 + 40
- * L   20 + 30 + 40
- M   30 + 30 + 40

25 The closest estimate of 661 − 257 is ___ .
- A   4
- B   40
- * C   400
- D   4,000

26 The closest estimate of how much taller the tree is than the bush is ___ .
- * J   50 inches
- K   60 inches
- L   70 inches
- M   80 inches

72 inches   24 inches

27 The closest estimate of $15.12 − $7.95 is ___ .
- * A $7
- B $8
- C $9
- D $10

STOP

60   Answer rows **24** ⓙ Ⓚ ● Ⓜ   **25** Ⓐ Ⓑ ● Ⓓ   **26** ● Ⓚ Ⓛ Ⓜ   **27** ● Ⓑ Ⓒ Ⓓ

Unit 7

Background

This unit contains five lessons that deal with math problem solving and data interpretation skills.

• **In Lessons 10a and 10b,** students solve word problems. Students analyze questions and indicate that the correct answer is not given. They work methodically, convert items to a workable format, and avoid attractive distractors.

• **In Lessons 11a and 11b,** students solve problems involving data interpretation. Students learn the importance of finding the answer without computing and of skimming a chart or graph. They evaluate answer choices, transfer numbers accurately, perform the correct operation, and compute carefully. They use charts and graphs and convert items to a workable format.

• **In the Test Yourself lesson,** the math problem solving, data interpretation, and test-taking skills introduced in Lessons 10a through 11b are reinforced and presented in a format that gives students the experience of taking an achievement test. Techniques for managing time effectively when taking a standardized test are reinforced.

Instructional Objectives

Lesson 10a	**Math Problem Solving**	Given a word problem, students identify which of four answer choices is correct.
Lesson 10b	**Math Problem Solving**	
Lesson 11a	**Data Interpretation**	Given a problem involving a chart, diagram, or graph, students identify which of four answer choices is correct.
Lesson 11b	**Data Interpretation**	
	Test Yourself	Given questions similar to those in Lessons 10a through 11b, students utilize problem solving, data interpretation, and test-taking strategies on achievement test formats.

Lesson 10a
Math Problem Solving

Focus

Mathematics Skill
• solving word problems

Test-taking Skills
• analyzing a question
• indicating that the correct answer is not given
• working methodically
• converting items to a workable format

Samples A and B

Distribute scratch paper to the students.

Say Turn to Lesson 10a on page 61. In this lesson you will solve word problems. Read the directions at the top of the page to yourself.

Allow time for the students to read the directions.

Say Find Sample A. Read the question to yourselves. *(pause)* Which operation should you use to solve the problem? *(subtraction)* Which answer choice is correct? You may use scratch paper to find the answer. *(answer B)* Yes, answer B is correct because there were 5 bagels left. Mark answer B for Sample A in the answer rows. Make sure the circle is completely filled in with a dark mark.

Check to see that the students have filled in the correct answer circle.

Say Now we'll do Sample B. Read the question to yourself. Choose the answer you think is correct. If the correct solution is not one of the choices, choose answer M, Not given. *(pause)* Which answer is correct? *(answer M)* The solution to the problem is 25 fish, but this is not one of the choices. Fill in answer M for Sample B in the answer rows at the bottom of the page. Be sure you fill in the circle with a dark mark.

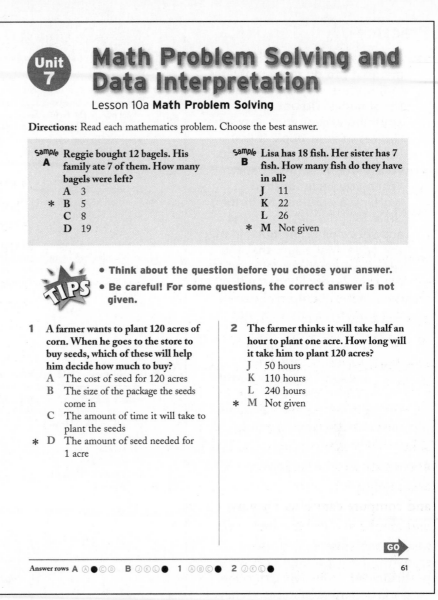

Unit 7

Math Problem Solving and Data Interpretation

Lesson 10a **Math Problem Solving**

Directions: Read each mathematics problem. Choose the best answer.

Sample A Reggie bought 12 bagels. His family ate 7 of them. How many bagels were left?
A 3
*B 5
C 8
D 19

Sample B Lisa has 18 fish. Her sister has 7 fish. How many fish do they have in all?
J 11
K 22
L 26
*M Not given

TIPS
• Think about the question before you choose your answer.
• Be careful! For some questions, the correct answer is not given.

1 A farmer wants to plant 120 acres of corn. When he goes to the store to buy seeds, which of these will help him decide how much to buy?
A The cost of seed for 120 acres
B The size of the package the seeds come in
C The amount of time it will take to plant the seeds
*D The amount of seed needed for 1 acre

2 The farmer thinks it will take half an hour to plant one acre. How long will it take him to plant 120 acres?
J 50 hours
K 110 hours
L 240 hours
*M Not given

GO

Answer rows A Ⓐ●ⒸⒹ B ⒥ⓀⓁ● 1 Ⓐ ⒷⒸ● 2 ⒥ⓀⓁ● 61

Check to see that the students have filled in the correct answer circle.

★TIPS

Say Now let's look at the tips.

Have a volunteer read the tips aloud to the group.

Say When you solve word problems, be sure to read them carefully and think about what the question is asking. Use scratch paper, if necessary, and if the answer you find is not one of the choices, mark the last answer, Not given.

Solve the two sample items on the chalkboard, if appropriate, demonstrating how to set the problems up correctly on scratch paper.

Practice

Say We are ready for Practice. You are going to do more problems in the same way that we did the samples. Do not write anything except your answer choices in your book. If you think it will help, you may do your work on scratch paper. When you have finished working a problem, fill in the circle for your answer in the answer rows at the bottom of the page. Make sure that the circles for your answer choices are completely filled in with dark marks. Completely erase any marks for answers that you change. When you come to the GO sign at the bottom of the page, turn the page and continue working. Work until you come to the STOP sign at the bottom of page 62. Do you have any questions? Start working now.

Allow time for the students to fill in their answers.

Say You may stop working now. You have finished Lesson 10a.

Review the answers with the students. If any problems caused particular difficulty, work through each of the answer choices. It may be helpful to have volunteers solve each problem at the chalkboard and discuss the strategy they used.

Have the students indicate completion of the lesson by entering their score for this activity on the progress chart at the beginning of the book.

---

3 Larissa sells some of the corn the farmer grows. She bought 10 bushels of corn from the farmer for $2.00 a bushel. She hopes to sell it for $4.00 a bushel. To find out how much she will make for each bushel she sells, Larissa should
A   add $2.00 to 10.
B   subtract $4.00 from 10.
* C   subtract $2.00 from $4.00.
D   add $4.00 to 10.

4 Larissa also sells apples. She sold 17 on Monday and 14 on Tuesday. On Wednesday, she sold 5 more than she did on Tuesday. How many apples did she sell on Wednesday?
J   11
* K   19
L   22
M   23

5 School starts at 8:15. It takes Louise 25 minutes to walk to school. Joe can walk to school in 15 minutes. To find out how much longer it takes Louise to walk to school than Joe, you should
A   subtract 15 from 8:15.
B   add 15 and 25.
C   subtract 25 from 8:15.
* D   Not given

6 Louise is 10 years old and is 52 inches tall. Her sister Nadia is 9 years old and is 48 inches tall. To find out how much taller Louise is, you should
J   add 10 and 9.
K   add 48 and 52.
* L   subtract 48 from 52.
M   subtract 9 from 52.

7 Joe's mother, Mrs. Jacobs, worked 8 hours on Monday, 7 hours on Tuesday, and 5 hours on Wednesday. How many hours did she work in all ?
A   14
B   19
C   21
* D   Not given

8 Joe read 12 pages of his book on Monday and 7 on Tuesday. Louise read 8 pages of her book on Monday and 9 on Thursday. How many total pages did they read on both days?
* J   36
K   37
L   39
M   Not given

STOP

62   Answer rows 3 Ⓐ Ⓑ ● Ⓓ   5 Ⓐ Ⓑ Ⓒ ●   7 Ⓐ Ⓑ Ⓒ ●
4 Ⓙ ● Ⓛ Ⓜ   6 Ⓙ Ⓚ ● Ⓜ   8 ● Ⓚ Ⓛ Ⓜ

Unit 7

Lesson 10b
Math Problem Solving

Focus

Mathematics Skill
• solving word problems

Test-taking Skills
• working methodically
• avoiding attractive distractors
• indicating that the correct answer is not given

Samples A and B

Distribute scratch paper to the students.

Say Turn to Lesson 10b on page 63. In this lesson you will solve more word problems. Read the directions at the top of the page to yourself.

Allow time for the students to read the directions.

Say Find Sample A. Read the question to yourselves and find the answer. *(pause)* Which answer choice is correct? *(answer D)* Yes, answer D is correct because the solution to the problem, 5, is not one of the answer choices. Mark answer D for Sample A in the answer rows. Make sure the circle is completely filled in with a dark mark.

Check to see that the students have filled in the correct answer circle.

Say Now do Sample B. Read the problem to yourself. Think about the process you should use before you solve the problem. *(pause)* Which answer is correct? *(answer L)* Fill in answer L for Sample B in the answer rows at the bottom of the page. Be sure you fill in the circle with a dark mark.

Check to see that the students have filled in the correct answer circle. If necessary, elaborate on the solutions to the sample items.

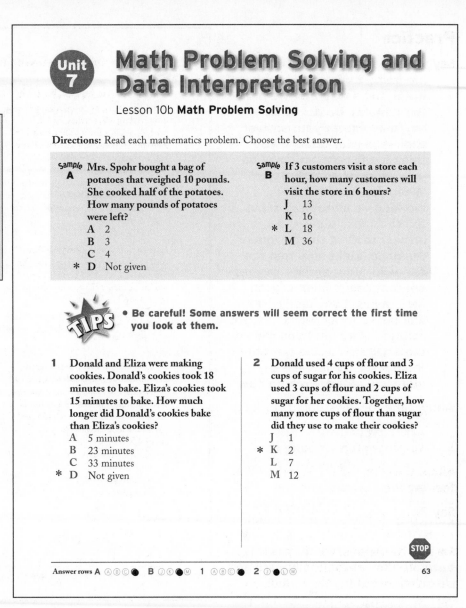

Unit 7

Math Problem Solving and Data Interpretation

Lesson 10b **Math Problem Solving**

Directions: Read each mathematics problem. Choose the best answer.

Sample A Mrs. Spohr bought a bag of potatoes that weighed 10 pounds. She cooked half of the potatoes. How many pounds of potatoes were left?
A 2
B 3
C 4
* D Not given

Sample B If 3 customers visit a store each hour, how many customers will visit the store in 6 hours?
J 13
K 16
* L 18
M 36

TIPS
• Be careful! Some answers will seem correct the first time you look at them.

1 Donald and Eliza were making cookies. Donald's cookies took 18 minutes to bake. Eliza's cookies took 15 minutes to bake. How much longer did Donald's cookies bake than Eliza's cookies?
A 5 minutes
B 23 minutes
C 33 minutes
* D Not given

2 Donald used 4 cups of flour and 3 cups of sugar for his cookies. Eliza used 3 cups of flour and 2 cups of sugar for her cookies. Together, how many more cups of flour than sugar did they use to make their cookies?
J 1
* K 2
L 7
M 12

STOP

Answer rows A ⒶⒷⒸ● B ⒿⓀ●Ⓜ 1 ⒶⒷⒸ● 2 Ⓙ●ⓁⓂ   63

⭐**TIPS**

Say Now let's look at the tip.

Have a volunteer read the tip aloud to the group.

Say For some mathematics problems, one or more of the answer choices might seem correct the first time you look at them. You should take your time, solve the problem, and then look at the answer choices. Don't be fooled by choices that use a number from the problem or the wrong operation.

Practice

Say We are ready for Practice. You are going to do more problems in the same way that we did the samples. Do not write anything except your answer choices in your book. If you think it will help, you may do your work on scratch paper. When you have finished working on a problem, fill in the circle for your answer in the answer rows at the bottom of the page. Make sure that the circles for your answer choices are completely filled in with dark marks. Completely erase any marks for answers that you change. Work until you come to the STOP sign at the bottom of the page. Do you have any questions? Start working now.

Allow time for the students to fill in their answers.

Say You may stop working now. You have finished Lesson 10b.

Review the answers with the students. If any problems caused particular difficulty, work through each of the answer choices. It may be helpful to have volunteers solve each problem at the chalkboard and discuss the strategy they used.

Have the students indicate completion of the lesson by entering their score for this activity on the progress chart at the beginning of the book.

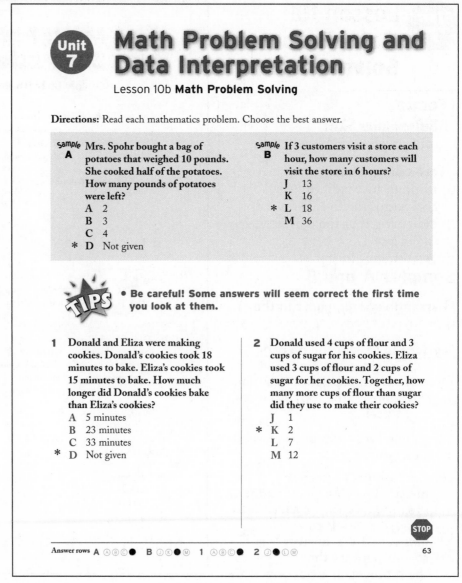

Unit 7 — Math Problem Solving and Data Interpretation

Lesson 10b **Math Problem Solving**

Directions: Read each mathematics problem. Choose the best answer.

Sample A Mrs. Spohr bought a bag of potatoes that weighed 10 pounds. She cooked half of the potatoes. How many pounds of potatoes were left?
A 2
B 3
C 4
* D Not given

Sample B If 3 customers visit a store each hour, how many customers will visit the store in 6 hours?
J 13
K 16
* L 18
M 36

TIPS
• Be careful! Some answers will seem correct the first time you look at them.

1 Donald and Eliza were making cookies. Donald's cookies took 18 minutes to bake. Eliza's cookies took 15 minutes to bake. How much longer did Donald's cookies bake than Eliza's cookies?
A 5 minutes
B 23 minutes
C 33 minutes
* D Not given

2 Donald used 4 cups of flour and 3 cups of sugar for his cookies. Eliza used 3 cups of flour and 2 cups of sugar for her cookies. Together, how many more cups of flour than sugar did they use to make their cookies?
J 1
* K 2
L 7
M 12

STOP

Answer rows A ⒶⒷⒸ● B ⒿⓀ●Ⓜ 1 ⒶⒷⒸ● 2 Ⓙ●ⓁⓂ   63

Focus

Mathematics Skill
• interpreting tables and graphs

Test-taking Skills
• finding the answer without computing
• skimming a chart or graph
• evaluating answer choices
• performing the correct operation
• computing carefully
• using charts and graphs
• transferring numbers accurately

Sample A

Distribute scratch paper to the students.

Say Turn to Lesson 11a on page 64. In this lesson you will solve problems involving a graph or chart. Read the directions at the top of the page to yourself.

Allow time for the students to read the directions.

Say Find Sample A. Look at the table and read the question to yourselves. Use the information in the table to find the answer. *(pause)* Which answer choice is correct? *(answer A)* Yes, answer A is correct. In 2004, 41 people attended the reunion. Mark answer A for Sample A in the answer rows. Make sure the circle is completely filled in with a dark mark.

Check to see that the students have filled in the correct answer circle.

★**TIPS**

Say Now let's look at the tip.

Have a volunteer read the tip aloud to the group.

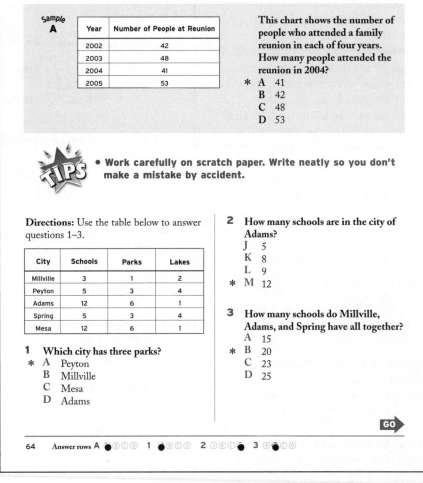

Unit 7

Math Problem Solving and Data Interpretation
Lesson 11a **Data Interpretation**

Year	Number of People at Reunion
2002	42
2003	48
2004	41
2005	53

This chart shows the number of people who attended a family reunion in each of four years. How many people attended the reunion in 2004?

* A   41
  B   42
  C   48
  D   53

TIPS

• Work carefully on scratch paper. Write neatly so you don't make a mistake by accident.

Directions: Use the table below to answer questions 1–3.

City	Schools	Parks	Lakes
Millville	3	1	2
Peyton	5	3	4
Adams	12	6	1
Spring	5	3	4
Mesa	12	6	1

1 Which city has three parks?
* A   Peyton
  B   Millville
  C   Mesa
  D   Adams

2 How many schools are in the city of Adams?
  J   5
  K   8
  L   9
* M   12

3 How many schools do Millville, Adams, and Spring have all together?
  A   15
* B   20
  C   23
  D   25

GO

64   Answer rows   A ⬤ⒷⒸⒹ   1 ⬤ⒷⒸⒹ   2 ⒥ⓀⓁ⬤   3 Ⓐ⬤ⒸⒹ

Say It's a good idea to skim a chart or graph, read a question, and then look back at the chart or graph to answer the question. Don't try to memorize the chart or graph. You should also be sure you know what the question is asking. If you begin working without thinking about the question, you will probably get the wrong answer.

Practice

Say We are ready for Practice. You are going to do more problems in the same way that we did the sample. Be sure to look back at the graph or chart when you solve the problems. Do not write anything except your answer choices in your book. If you think it will help, you may do your work on scratch paper. When you have finished working a problem, fill in the circle for your answer in the answer rows at the bottom of the page. Make sure that the circles for your answer choices are completely filled in with dark marks. Completely erase any marks for answers that you change. When you come to the GO sign at the bottom of the page, continue working. Work until you come to the STOP sign at the bottom of page 65. Do you have any questions? Start working now.

Allow time for the students to fill in their answers.

Say You may stop working now. You have finished Lesson 11a.

Review the answers with the students. If any problems caused particular difficulty, work through each of the answer choices. It may be helpful to have volunteers solve each problem at the chalkboard and discuss the strategy they used. You may also want to review the information in the graph and chart to be sure the students understand how to use them.

Have the students indicate completion of the lesson by entering their score for this activity on the progress chart at the beginning of the book.

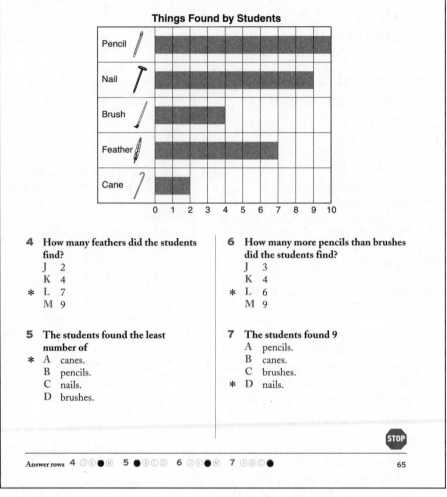

Unit 7 Lesson 11a **Data Interpretation**

Directions: The graph below shows the things some students found on a scavenger hunt. Use the graph to answer questions 4–7.

Things Found by Students

4 How many feathers did the students find?
J 2
K 4
* L 7
M 9

5 The students found the least number of
* A canes.
B pencils.
C nails.
D brushes.

6 How many more pencils than brushes did the students find?
J 3
K 4
* L 6
M 9

7 The students found 9
A pencils.
B canes.
C brushes.
* D nails.

STOP

Answer rows 4 ⓙⓚ●ⓜ 5 ●ⓑⓒⓓ 6 ⓙⓚ●ⓜ 7 ⓐⓑⓒ● 65

Focus

Mathematics Skill
- interpreting tables and graphs

Test-taking Skills
- working methodically
- converting items to a workable format
- finding the answer without computing
- using charts and graphs

Sample A

Say Turn to Lesson 11b on page 66. In this lesson you will solve more problems involving a chart. Read the directions to yourself.

Allow time for the students to read the directions.

Say Find Sample A. Look at the table; it is the same table we used in the last lesson. Read the question to yourselves. Use the information in the table to find the answer. *(pause)* Which answer choice is correct? *(answer D, 2005)* The most people attended the reunion in *2005*. Mark answer D for Sample A in the answer rows. Make sure the circle is completely filled in with a dark mark.

Check to see that the students have filled in the correct answer circle.

★TIPS

Say Now let's look at the tip.

Have a volunteer read the tip aloud to the group.

Say When you solve the problems in this lesson, you may have to solve some problems on scratch paper. When you do, work neatly so you don't confuse yourself. When you have finished solving a problem, you may even want to cross out your work so it doesn't confuse you on the next problem.

Unit 7
Math Problem Solving and Data Interpretation
Lesson 11b Data Interpretation

Sample A

Year	Number of People at Reunion
2002	42
2003	48
2004	41
2005	53

In which year did the most people attend the reunion?

A 2002
B 2003
C 2004
* D 2005

TIPS
- Work carefully on scratch paper. Write neatly so you don't make a mistake by accident.

Directions: Use the table below to do questions 1–3.

Student	Age (yrs)	Height (in.)	Weight (lbs)
Rudy	10	56	68
Lisa	9	52	62
Sharissa	11	56	77
Brendan	7	47	51
Colette	9	51	60

1 What two children are the same age?
A Rudy and Sharissa
B Brendan and Colette
C Sharissa and Lisa
* D Colette and Lisa

2 Which student weighs the most?
J Rudy
K Lisa
* L Sharissa
M Brendan

3 How much taller than Colette is Sharissa?
A 3 inches
* B 5 inches
C 7 inches
D 9 inches

STOP

66   Answer rows A Ⓐ Ⓑ Ⓒ ●   1 Ⓐ Ⓑ Ⓒ ●   2 Ⓙ Ⓚ ● Ⓜ   3 Ⓐ ● Ⓒ Ⓓ

Practice

Say We are ready for Practice. You are going to do more problems in the same way that we did the sample. Do not write anything except your answer choices in your book. If you think it will help, you may do your work on scratch paper, but be sure to work carefully. When you have finished working a problem, fill in the circle for your answer in the answer rows at the bottom of the page. Make sure that the circles for your answer choices are completely filled in with dark marks. Completely erase any marks for answers that you change. Work until you come to the STOP sign at the bottom of the page. Do you have any questions? Start working now.

Allow time for the students to fill in their answers.

Say You may stop working now. You have finished Lesson 11b.

Review the answers with the students. If any problems caused particular difficulty, work through each of the answer choices. It may be helpful to have volunteers solve each problem and discuss the strategy they used.

Have the students indicate completion of the lesson by entering their score for this activity on the progress chart at the beginning of the book.

Unit 7

Math Problem Solving and Data Interpretation

Lesson 11b **Data Interpretation**

Sample A

Year	Number of People at Reunion
2002	42
2003	48
2004	41
2005	53

In which year did the most people attend the reunion?
A 2002
B 2003
C 2004
* D 2005

TIPS
• Work carefully on scratch paper. Write neatly so you don't make a mistake by accident.

Directions: Use the table below to do questions 1–3.

Student	Age (yrs)	Height (in.)	Weight (lbs)
Rudy	10	56	68
Lisa	9	52	62
Sharissa	11	56	77
Brendan	7	47	51
Colette	9	51	60

1 What two children are the same age?
A Rudy and Sharissa
B Brendan and Colette
C Sharissa and Lisa
* D Colette and Lisa

2 Which student weighs the most?
J Rudy
K Lisa
* L Sharissa
M Brendan

3 How much taller than Colette is Sharissa?
A 3 inches
* B 5 inches
C 7 inches
D 9 inches

STOP

66   Answer rows A ⒶⒷⒸ● 1 ⒶⒷⒸ● 2 ⒿⓀ●Ⓜ 3 Ⓐ●ⒸⒹ

---

82   **Unit 7** Lesson 11b **Data Interpretation**

Test Yourself: Math Problem Solving and Data Interpretation

Focus

Mathematics Skills
- solving word problems
- interpreting tables and graphs

Test-taking Skills
- managing time effectively
- analyzing a question
- indicating that the correct answer is not given
- working methodically
- converting items to a workable format
- avoiding attractive distractors
- finding the answer without computing
- skimming a chart or graph
- evaluating answer choices
- performing the correct operation
- computing carefully
- transferring numbers accurately
- using charts and graphs

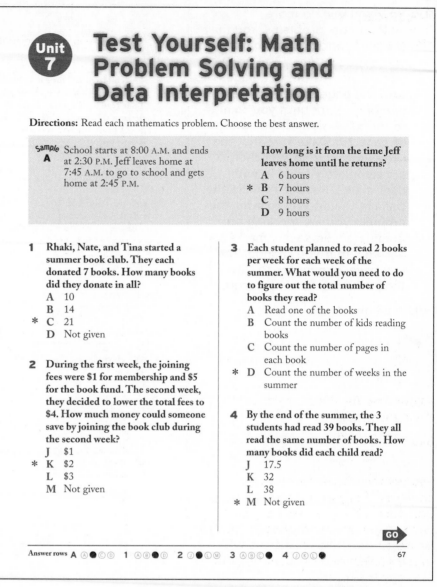

This lesson simulates an actual test-taking experience. Therefore, it is recommended that the directions be read verbatim and that the suggested procedures and time allowances be followed.

Directions

Administration Time: approximately 25 minutes

Distribute scratch paper to the students.

Say Turn to the Test Yourself lesson on page 67.

Point out to the students that this Test Yourself lesson is timed like a real test, but that they will score it themselves to see how well they are doing. Encourage them to read each question carefully, to think about what they are supposed to do, and to work carefully on scratch paper when necessary. They should skip difficult problems and return to them later and take the best guess when they are unsure of the answer.

Say This lesson will check how well you can solve mathematics problems like the ones we practiced before. Remember to make sure that the circles for your answer choices are completely filled in. Press your pencil firmly so that your marks come out dark. Completely erase any marks for answers that you change. Do not write anything except your answer choices in your books.

Look at Sample A. Read the story, the question, and the answer choices. Mark the circle for the answer you think is correct.

Allow time for the students to fill in their answers.

Say The circle for answer B should be filled in. If you chose another answer, erase yours and fill in circle B now.

Check to see that the students have filled in the correct answer circle.

Say Now you will do more mathematics problems. You may use the scratch paper I gave you. When you come to a GO sign at the bottom of a page, turn the page and continue working. Work until you come to the STOP sign at the bottom of page 70. Make sure that the circles for your answer choices are completely filled in with dark marks. Be sure to fill in the circle in the answer row for the problem you are working on. Completely erase any marks for answers that you change. You will have 20 minutes to solve the problems. You may begin.

Allow 20 minutes.

5 The children read for 2 hours each morning and 4 hours each evening. They read for 7 days. How can they figure out how many hours they read?
  A Add (2 + 4 + 7)
  B Multiply (2 × 4) and then add 7
* C Add (2 + 4) and then multiply by 7
  D Add (2 + 4) and then subtract the result from 7

Directions: This table shows the distance in yards that some students kicked a soccer ball. Use the information in the table below to do questions 6–9.

Student	Distance
Cody	5
Lizzie	12
Ted	6
Juliana	10
Sabil	11
Arny	9

6 Which student kicked the ball the farthest?
  J Cody
* K Lizzie
  L Ted
  M Juliana

7 How far did Ted kick the soccer ball?
  A 5 yards
* B 6 yards
  C 8 yards
  D 10 yards

8 How many times farther did Juliana kick the ball than Cody?
* J 2
  K 3
  L 4
  M 5

9 How far did Sabil and Arny kick the ball all together?
  A 2 yards
  B 19 yards
* C 20 yards
  D 29 yards

GO ➤

68   Answer rows **5** Ⓐ Ⓑ ⬤ Ⓓ **6** Ⓙ ⬤ Ⓛ Ⓜ **7** Ⓐ ⬤ Ⓒ Ⓓ **8** ⬤ Ⓚ Ⓛ Ⓜ **9** Ⓐ Ⓑ ⬤ Ⓓ

Directions: This chart shows the different colors found on cars in a grocery store parking lot. Use the chart below to answer questions 10–13.

Color of Cars Found in Grocery Store Parking Lot

Red	◎ ◎ ◎ ◎		
Black	◎ ◎ ◎ ◎ ◎ ◎ ◎
Green	◎ ◎ ◎
Yellow	◎
Silver	◎ ◎ ◎ ◎ ◎ ◎
Blue	◎ ◎ ◎ ◎ ◎

Each ◎ stands for one car

10 How many colors were found on at least 5 cars?
  J 1
  K 2
* L 3
  M 4

11 Which color was found on half as many cars as silver?
  A Yellow
* B Green
  C Blue
  D Black

12 If there were 2 more red cars, how many red cars would there be in all?
  J 4
  K 5
* L 6
  M 7

13 How many more black cars than silver cars were there?
* A 1
  B 6
  C 7
  D 13

GO

Answer rows **10** ⓙ ⓚ ● ⓜ **11** Ⓐ ● Ⓒ Ⓓ **12** ⓙ ⓚ ● ⓜ **13** ● Ⓑ Ⓒ Ⓓ   69

Say It's time to stop. You have finished the Test Yourself lesson. Check to see that you have completely filled in your answer circles. Make sure that any marks for answers that you changed have been completely erased.

Go over the lesson with the students. Ask whether they had enough time to finish the lesson. Did they work carefully on scratch paper? Which questions required them to guess? What were some of the problems they experienced? Work through any problems that caused difficulty.

Have the students indicate completion of the lesson by entering their score for this activity on the progress chart at the beginning of the book. If necessary, provide additional practice problems similar to the ones in this unit.

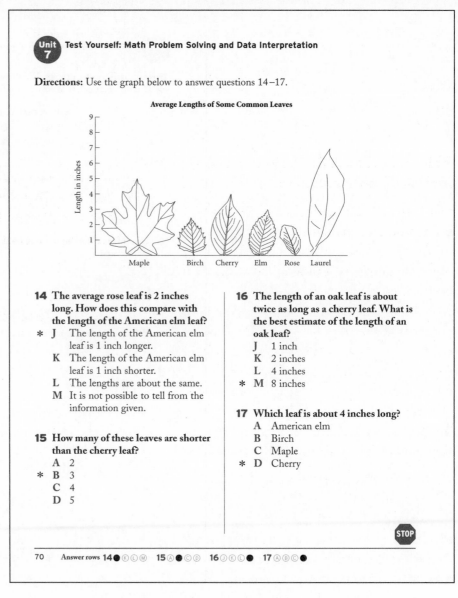

Unit 7 Test Yourself: Math Problem Solving and Data Interpretation

Directions: Use the graph below to answer questions 14–17.

14 The average rose leaf is 2 inches long. How does this compare with the length of the American elm leaf?
* J The length of the American elm leaf is 1 inch longer.
  K The length of the American elm leaf is 1 inch shorter.
  L The lengths are about the same.
  M It is not possible to tell from the information given.

15 How many of these leaves are shorter than the cherry leaf?
  A 2
* B 3
  C 4
  D 5

16 The length of an oak leaf is about twice as long as a cherry leaf. What is the best estimate of the length of an oak leaf?
  J 1 inch
  K 2 inches
  L 4 inches
* M 8 inches

17 Which leaf is about 4 inches long?
  A American elm
  B Birch
  C Maple
* D Cherry

STOP

70   Answer rows 14 ● Ⓚ Ⓛ Ⓜ   15 Ⓐ ● Ⓒ Ⓓ   16 Ⓙ Ⓚ Ⓛ ●   17 Ⓐ Ⓑ Ⓒ ●

Unit 8

Background

This unit contains five lessons that deal with math computation skills.

• **In Lessons 12a through 13b,** students solve problems involving addition, subtraction, multiplication, and division of whole numbers. Students practice performing the correct operation, computing carefully, and transferring numbers accurately. They indicate that the correct answer is not given, convert items to a workable format, and work methodically. They also learn about reworking a problem, checking items by the opposite operation, and taking the best guess when unsure of the answer.

• **In the Test Yourself lesson,** the math computation and test-taking skills introduced in Lessons 12a through 13b are reinforced and presented in a format that gives students the experience of taking an achievement test. Techniques for managing time effectively when taking a standardized test are reinforced.

Instructional **Objectives**

Lesson 12a	**Computation**	Given a problem involving computation, students identify which of three answer choices is correct or indicate that the correct answer is not given.
Lesson 12b	**Computation**	
Lesson 13a	**Computation**	
Lesson 13b	**Computation**	

Test Yourself	Given questions similar to those in Lessons 12a through 13b, students utilize computation skills and test-taking strategies on achievement test formats.

Unit 8 Lesson 12a Computation

Focus

Mathematics Skill
- adding, subtracting, multiplying, and dividing whole numbers

Test-taking Skills
- performing the correct operation
- computing carefully
- transferring numbers accurately
- indicating that the correct answer is not given
- converting items to a workable format
- reworking a problem

Samples A and B

Distribute scratch paper to the students.

Say Turn to Lesson 12a on page 71. In this lesson you will solve addition, subtraction, multiplication, and division problems. Read the directions at the top of the page to yourself while I read them out loud.

Read the directions out loud to the students.

Say Let's do Sample A. Read the problem and find the answer. If the answer you find is not one of the choices, choose the last answer, N. Which answer choice is correct? *(answer C)* Answer C is correct because the solution to the problem is 2,400. Mark answer circle C for Sample A in the answer rows at the bottom of the page. Make sure the circle is completely filled in with a dark mark.

Check to see that the students have filled in the correct answer circle.

Say Do Sample B yourself. Read the problem and choose the answer you think is correct. *(pause)* What is the correct answer? *(answer M)* Answer M is correct because 709 plus 132 is 841, and this is not one of the choices. Fill in circle M for Sample B in the answer rows. Make sure it is completely filled in with a dark mark.

Unit 8 Math Computation
Lesson 12a Computation

Directions: Solve each problem. Choose the answer you think is correct. If the correct answer is not given, fill in the space for the last answer, N.

| Sample A | $600 \times 4 =$ | A 24
 B 240
 * C 2,400
 D N | Sample B | $709 + 132 =$ | J 831
 K 842
 L 941
 * M N |

TIPS • Copy numbers carefully when you work on scratch paper.

1 $\begin{array}{r} 2,000 \\ \times\ 6 \end{array}$
A 1,200
B 2,600
C 120,000
* D N

5 $\begin{array}{r} 299 \\ -\ 8 \end{array}$
* A 291
B 297
C 307
D N

2 $13 + 4 + 211 =$
J 217
K 218
* L 228
M N

6 $\begin{array}{r} 294 \\ +\ 71 \end{array}$
J 223
K 255
L 355
* M N

3 $\begin{array}{r} 427 \\ +\ 815 \end{array}$
* A 1,242
B 2,252
C 1,342
D N

7 $3 \times 422 =$
A 425
* B 1,266
C 2,166
D N

4 $27 \div 3 =$
J 7
K 8
L 24
* M N

8 $\begin{array}{r} 926 \\ -\ 815 \end{array}$
J 101
* K 111
L 1,741
M N

STOP

Answer rows A Ⓐ Ⓑ ● Ⓓ   1 Ⓐ Ⓑ Ⓒ ●   3 ● Ⓑ Ⓒ Ⓓ   5 ● Ⓑ Ⓒ Ⓓ   7 Ⓐ ● Ⓒ Ⓓ
B Ⓙ Ⓚ Ⓛ ●   2 Ⓙ Ⓚ ● Ⓜ   4 Ⓙ Ⓚ Ⓛ ●   6 Ⓙ Ⓚ Ⓛ ●   8 Ⓙ ● Ⓛ Ⓜ

Check to see that the students have filled in the correct answer circle.

TIPS

Say Now let's look at the tip.

Have a volunteer read the tip aloud to the group.

Say Be sure you read the problem carefully, look at the numbers, and think about the operation you are supposed to perform. If you solve the problem and your solution is not one of the choices, work the problem again. If your answer is still not one of the choices, choose the last answer, N.

Practice

Say We are ready for Practice. You are going to do more problems in the same way that we did the samples. Do not write anything in your book except your answer choices. If you need to, use scratch paper to work the problems. Transfer numbers accurately to scratch paper and be sure to compute carefully. Pay careful attention to the operation sign for each problem. Work until you come to the STOP sign at the bottom of the page. Make sure that the circles for your answer choices are completely filled in with dark marks. Erase any marks for answers that you change. You may begin.

Allow time for the students to fill in their answers.

Say It's time to stop. You have finished Lesson 12a.

Review the answers with the students. If any problems caused particular difficulty, work through each of the answer choices. Be sure to demonstrate each computation process in detail.

Have the students indicate completion of the lesson by entering their score for this activity on the progress chart at the beginning of the book.

Unit 8

Math Computation

Lesson 12a **Computation**

Directions: Solve each problem. Choose the answer you think is correct. If the correct answer is not given, fill in the space for the last answer, N.

Sample A	$600 \times 4 =$		Sample B	$709 + 132 =$	
		A 24			J 831
		B 240			K 842
		*C 2,400			L 941
		D N			*M N

TIPS • Copy numbers carefully when you work on scratch paper.

1	$2,000$ $\times\ 6$	A 1,200 B 2,600 C 120,000 *D N	5	299 $-\ 8$	*A 291 B 297 C 307 D N
2	$13 + 4 + 211 =$	J 217 K 218 *L 228 M N	6	294 $+\ 71$	J 223 K 255 L 355 *M N
3	427 $+\ 815$	*A 1,242 B 2,252 C 1,342 D N	7	$3 \times 422 =$	A 425 *B 1,266 C 2,166 D N
4	$27 \div 3 =$	J 7 K 8 L 24 *M N	8	926 $-\ 815$	J 101 *K 111 L 1,741 M N

STOP

Answer rows A Ⓐ Ⓑ ● Ⓓ   1 Ⓐ Ⓑ ● ●   3 ● Ⓑ Ⓒ Ⓓ   5 ● Ⓑ Ⓒ Ⓓ   7 Ⓐ ● Ⓒ Ⓓ
B Ⓙ Ⓚ Ⓛ ●   2 Ⓙ Ⓚ ● Ⓜ   4 Ⓙ Ⓚ Ⓛ ●   6 Ⓙ Ⓚ Ⓛ ●   8 Ⓙ ● Ⓛ Ⓜ

71

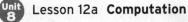

Unit 8 Lesson 12b
Computation

Focus

Mathematics Skill
- adding, subtracting, multiplying, and dividing

Test-taking Skills
- performing the correct operation
- computing carefully
- transferring numbers accurately
- indicating that the correct answer is not given
- converting items to a workable format
- taking the best guess when unsure of the answer

Samples A and B

Distribute scratch paper to the students.

Say Turn to Lesson 12b on page 72. In this lesson you will solve more addition, subtraction, multiplication, and division problems. Read the directions at the top of the page to yourself while I read them out loud.

Read the directions out loud to the students.

Say Let's do Sample A. Read the problem and find the answer. You may work on the scratch paper I gave you. *(pause)* Which answer choice is correct? *(answer B, 600)* Mark answer circle B for Sample A in the answer rows at the bottom of the page. Make sure the circle is completely filled in with a dark mark.

Check to see that the students have filled in the correct answer circle.

Say Do Sample B yourself. Read the problem and choose the answer you think is correct. *(pause)* What is the correct answer? *(answer K)* Fill in circle K for Sample B in the answer rows. Make sure it is completely filled in with a dark mark.

Math Computation
Lesson 12b **Computation**

Directions: Solve each problem. Choose the answer you think is correct. If the correct answer is not given, fill in the space for the last answer, N.

Sample A	$300 \times 2 =$		Sample B	$14 \div 2 =$	
		A 32 * B 600 C 6,000 D N			J 8 * K 7 L 6 M N

TIPS • Copy numbers carefully when you work on scratch paper.

1	$7 + 7 =$	A 17 B 12 * C 14 D N	4	$113 \times 2 =$	J 115 * K 226 L 336 M N
2	92 − 67	* J 25 K 35 L 29 M N	5	3,000 × 9	A 3,009 B 2,700 * C 27,000 D N
3	3 32 18 + 7	A 47 B 56 C 67 * D N	6	$18 \div 6 =$	* J 3 K 15 L 21 M N

STOP

---

72   Answer rows   A ⓐ●ⓒⓓ   1 ⓐⓑ●ⓓ   3 ⓐⓑⓒ●   5 ⓐⓑ●ⓓ
                   B ⓙ●ⓛⓜ   2 ●ⓚⓛⓜ   4 ⓙ●ⓛⓜ   6 ●ⓚⓛⓜ

Check to see that the students have filled in the correct answer circle. Review the solutions to the problems on the chalkboard, emphasizing working neatly and explaining each step of the solutions.

★**TIPS**

Say Now let's look at the tip.

Have a volunteer read the tip aloud to the group.

Say Be sure to work carefully on scratch paper. Transfer numbers accurately, perform the correct operation, and compute carefully. If you make a careless error, you might get the wrong answer even though you know how to solve the problem.

Practice

Say We are ready for Practice. You are going to do more problems in the same way that we did the samples. Do not write anything in your book except your answer choices. If you need to, use scratch paper to work the problems. Pay careful attention to the operation sign for each problem, and arrange the problem on scratch paper in a way that will help you solve it. If you are not sure which answer is correct, be sure to take your best guess. Work until you come to the STOP sign at the bottom of the page. Make sure that the circles for your answer choices are completely filled in with dark marks. Erase any marks for answers that you change. You may begin.

Allow time for the students to fill in their answers.

Say It's time to stop. You have finished Lesson 12b.

Review the answers with the students. If any problems caused particular difficulty, work through each of the answer choices. Demonstrate how to convert problems to a workable format.

Have the students indicate completion of the lesson by entering their score for this activity on the progress chart at the beginning of the book.

Math Computation
Lesson 12b **Computation**

Directions: Solve each problem. Choose the answer you think is correct. If the correct answer is not given, fill in the space for the last answer, N.

Sample A	$300 \times 2 =$			Sample B	$14 \div 2 =$		
		A	32			J	8
		* B	600			* K	7
		C	6,000			L	6
		D	N			M	N

TIPS • Copy numbers carefully when you work on scratch paper.

1 $7 + 7 =$
- A 17
- B 12
- * C 14
- D N

2 $92 - 67$
- * J 25
- K 35
- L 29
- M N

3 $3 \; 32 \; 18 \; + 7$
- A 47
- B 56
- C 67
- * D N

4 $113 \times 2 =$
- J 115
- * K 226
- L 336
- M N

5 $3,000 \times 9$
- A 3,009
- B 2,700
- * C 27,000
- D N

6 $18 \div 6 =$
- * J 3
- K 15
- L 21
- M N

STOP

72   Answer rows   A Ⓐ●ⒸⒹ   1 ⒶⒷ●Ⓓ   3 ⒶⒷⒸ●   5 ⒶⒷ●Ⓓ
                     B Ⓙ●ⓁⓂ   2 ●ⓀⓁⓂ   4 Ⓙ●ⓁⓂ   6 ●ⓀⓁⓂ

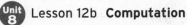

Lesson 13a
Computation

Focus

Mathematics Skill
• adding, subtracting, multiplying, and dividing whole numbers

Test-taking Skills
• performing the correct operation
• computing carefully
• transferring numbers accurately
• indicating that the correct answer is not given
• converting items to a workable format
• working methodically

Samples A and B

Distribute scratch paper to the students.

Say Turn to Lesson 13a on page 73. In this lesson you will solve addition, subtraction, multiplication, and division problems. Read the directions at the top of the page to yourself while I read them out loud.

Read the directions out loud to the students.

Say Let's do Sample A. Read the problem and find the answer. You may work on the scratch paper I gave you. If you do work on scratch paper, be sure to transfer numbers accurately and compute carefully. *(pause)* Which answer choice is correct? *(answer B, 651)* What operation did you use to get this answer? *(addition)* Mark answer circle B for Sample A in the answer rows at the bottom of the page. Make sure the circle is completely filled in with a dark mark.

Check to see that the students have filled in the correct answer circle.

Say Do Sample B yourself. Read the problem and choose the answer you think is correct. *(pause)* What is the correct answer? *(answer K)* Yes, answer K is correct because 63 divided by 7 is 9. Fill in circle K for Sample B in the answer rows. Make sure it is completely filled in with a dark mark.

Math Computation
Lesson 13a Computation

Directions: Solve each problem. Choose the answer you think is correct. If the correct answer is not given, fill in the space for the last answer, N.

Sample A	$619 + 32 =$		A 627 * B 651 C 661 D N	Sample B	$63 \div 7 =$		J 8 * K 9 L 70 M N

TIPS
• Look at the operation sign before you begin computing.
• Rewrite horizontal problems so you can solve them.

1	$\begin{array}{r} 8 \\ \times\ 4 \\ \hline \end{array}$	A 24 * B 32 C 35 D N	5	$\begin{array}{r} 14 \\ -\ 9 \\ \hline \end{array}$	A 4 * B 5 C 23 D N
2	$\begin{array}{r} 36 \\ \times\ 3 \\ \hline \end{array}$	J 404 K 405 * L 108 M N	6	$\begin{array}{r} 814 \\ +\ 14 \\ \hline \end{array}$	* J 828 K 838 L 855 M N
3	$\begin{array}{r} 318 \\ +\ 904 \\ \hline \end{array}$	A 1,212 B 1,221 * C 1,222 D N	7	$45 \div 9 =$	A 3 B 4 * C 5 D N
4	$81 \div 9 =$	J 7 K 8 * L 9 M N	8	$\begin{array}{r} 674 \\ -\ 213 \\ \hline \end{array}$	J 451 K 457 L 462 * M N

STOP

Answer rows A Ⓐ●ⓒⒹ 1 Ⓐ●ⓒⒹ 3 ⒶⒷ●Ⓓ 5 Ⓐ●ⓒⒹ 7 ⒶⒷ●Ⓓ   73
          B Ⓙ●ⓁⓂ 2 ⒿⓀ●Ⓜ 4 ⒿⓀ●Ⓜ 6 ●ⓀⓁⓂ 8 ⒿⓀⓁ●

Check to see that the students have filled in the correct answer circle.

TIPS

Say Now let's look at the tips.

Have a volunteer read the tips aloud to the group.

Say Be sure you think about the operation you are supposed to perform before you solve the problem. Rearrange problems on scratch paper so you can work them, and compute carefully so you don't make an accidental mistake.

Point out to the students that it would be easy to make a mistake in Sample B by adding instead of dividing.

Practice

Say We are ready for Practice. You are going to do more problems in the same way that we did the samples. Do not write anything in your book except your answer choices. If you need to, use scratch paper to work the problems. Transfer numbers accurately to scratch paper and be sure to compute carefully. Pay careful attention to the operation sign for each problem. If you are not sure which answer is correct, be sure to take your best guess. Work until you come to the STOP sign at the bottom of the page. Make sure that the circles for your answer choices are completely filled in with dark marks. Erase any marks for answers that you change. You may begin.

Allow time for the students to fill in their answers.

Say It's time to stop. You have finished Lesson 13a.

Review the answers with the students. If any problems caused particular difficulty, work through each of the answer choices.

Have the students indicate completion of the lesson by entering their score for this activity on the progress chart at the beginning of the book.

 Math Computation

Lesson 13a **Computation**

Directions: Solve each problem. Choose the answer you think is correct. If the correct answer is not given, fill in the space for the last answer, N.

Sample A	619 + 32 =		A 627	Sample B	63 ÷ 7 =		J 8
		*	B 651			*	K 9
			C 661				L 70
			D N				M N

TIPS
- Look at the operation sign before you begin computing.
- Rewrite horizontal problems so you can solve them.

1	8 × 4		A 24 * B 32 C 35 D N	5	14 − 9		A 4 * B 5 C 23 D N
2	36 × 3		J 404 K 405 * L 108 M N	6	814 + 14	*	J 828 K 838 L 855 M N
3	318 + 904		A 1,212 B 1,221 * C 1,222 D N	7	45 ÷ 9 =		A 3 B 4 * C 5 D N
4	81 ÷ 9 =		J 7 K 8 * L 9 M N	8	674 − 213		J 451 K 457 L 462 * M N

STOP

Answer rows
A Ⓐ●©Ⓓ 1 Ⓐ●©Ⓓ 3 ⒶⒷ●Ⓓ 5 ●Ⓑ©Ⓓ 7 ⒶⒷ●Ⓓ
B Ⓙ●ⓁⓂ 2 ⒿⓀ●Ⓜ 4 ⒿⓀ●Ⓜ 6 ●ⓀⓁⓂ 8 ⒿⓀⓁ●

73

Unit 8
Lesson 13b
Computation

Focus

Mathematics Skill
- adding, subtracting, multiplying, and dividing whole numbers

Test-taking Skills
- performing the correct operation
- computing carefully
- transferring numbers accurately
- indicating that the correct answer is not given
- converting items to a workable format
- reworking a problem
- checking items by the opposite operation

Samples A and B

Distribute scratch paper to the students.

Say Turn to Lesson 13b on page 74. In this lesson you will solve more addition, subtraction, multiplication, and division problems. Read the directions at the top of the page to yourself while I read them out loud.

Read the directions out loud to the students.

Say Let's do Sample A. Read the problem and find the answer. You may work on the scratch paper I gave you. If the correct answer is not given, choose the last anwer, N. *(pause)* Which answer choice is correct? *(answer C, 117)* Mark answer circle C for Sample A in the answer rows at the bottom of the page. Make sure the circle is completely filled in with a dark mark.

Check to see that the students have filled in the correct answer circle.

Say Do Sample B yourself. Read the problem and choose the answer you think is correct. *(pause)* What is the correct answer? *(answer K)* Yes, answer K is correct. Fill in circle K for Sample B in the answer rows. Make sure it is completely filled in with a dark mark.

Unit 8
Math Computation
Lesson 13b Computation

Directions: Solve each problem. Choose the answer you think is correct. If the correct answer is not given, fill in the space for the last answer, N.

Sample A 128 − 11 =
- A 17
- B 18
- *C 117
- D N

Sample B 13 + 20 + 35 =
- J 60
- *K 68
- L 79
- M N

• Remember, you can sometimes check an answer by using the opposite operation.

1. 411 − 7
- *A 404
- B 405
- C 418
- D N

2. 2 + 203 + 14 =
- *J 219
- K 220
- L 226
- M N

3. 349 − 5 =
- A 334
- B 345
- C 354
- *D N

4. 4 × 322 =
- J 128
- *K 1,288
- L 1,298
- M N

5. 25 − 12 =
- A 3
- B 12
- C 14
- *D N

6. 372 − 46
- *J 326
- K 334
- L 336
- M N

7. 221 + 34
- *A 255
- B 265
- C 555
- D N

8. 35 − 28 =
- J 3
- K 4
- *L 7
- M N

STOP

74 Answer rows A Ⓐ Ⓑ ● Ⓓ   1 ● Ⓑ Ⓒ Ⓓ   3 Ⓐ Ⓑ Ⓒ ●   5 Ⓐ Ⓑ Ⓒ ●   7 ● Ⓑ Ⓒ Ⓓ
B Ⓙ ● Ⓛ Ⓜ   2 ● Ⓚ Ⓛ Ⓜ   4 Ⓙ ● Ⓛ Ⓜ   6 ● Ⓚ Ⓛ Ⓜ   8 Ⓙ Ⓚ ● Ⓜ

Check to see that the students have filled in the correct answer circle.

★TIPS

Say Now let's look at the tip.

Have a volunteer read the tip aloud to the group.

Say Sometimes you can check a problem by performing the opposite operation. In Sample A, you can add 11 to 117 to get 128. This shows that 117 is the correct answer. You can use your scratch paper to check problems.

94   Lesson 13b **Computation**

Practice

Say We are ready for Practice. You are going to do more problems in the same way that we did the samples. Do not write anything in your book except your answer choices. If you need to, use scratch paper to work the problems. Pay careful attention to the operation sign for each problem, and if you are not sure an answer is correct, check it by performing the opposite operation. Work until you come to the STOP sign at the bottom of the page. Make sure that the circles for your answer choices are completely filled in with dark marks. Erase any marks for answers that you change. You may begin.

Allow time for the students to fill in their answers.

Say It's time to stop. You have finished Lesson 13b.

Review the answers with the students. If any problems caused particular difficulty, work through each of the answer choices. Demonstrate how to check answers by using the opposite operation.

Have the students indicate completion of the lesson by entering their score for this activity on the progress chart at the beginning of the book.

Unit 8 — Math Computation
Lesson 13b **Computation**

Directions: Solve each problem. Choose the answer you think is correct. If the correct answer is not given, fill in the space for the last answer, N.

Sample A	$128 - 11 =$		A 17
			B 18
		*	C 117
			D N

Sample B	$13 + 20 + 35 =$		J 60
		*	K 68
			L 79
			M N

TIPS
- Remember, you can sometimes check an answer by using the opposite operation.

1. $\begin{array}{r} 411 \\ -\ 7 \end{array}$
    * A 404
    B 405
    C 418
    D N

2. $2 + 203 + 14 =$
    * J 219
    K 220
    L 226
    M N

3. $349 - 5 =$
    A 334
    B 345
    C 354
    * D N

4. $4 \times 322 =$
    J 128
    * K 1,288
    L 1,298
    M N

5. $25 - 12 =$
    A 3
    B 12
    C 14
    * D N

6. $\begin{array}{r} 372 \\ -\ 46 \end{array}$
    * J 326
    K 334
    L 336
    M N

7. $\begin{array}{r} 221 \\ +\ 34 \end{array}$
    * A 255
    B 265
    C 555
    D N

8. $35 - 28 =$
    J 3
    K 4
    * L 7
    M N

STOP

74   Answer rows   A Ⓐ Ⓑ ● Ⓓ   1 ● Ⓑ Ⓒ Ⓓ   3 Ⓐ Ⓑ Ⓒ ●   5 Ⓐ Ⓑ Ⓒ ●   7 ● Ⓑ Ⓒ Ⓓ
                  B Ⓙ ● Ⓛ Ⓜ   2 ● Ⓚ Ⓛ Ⓜ   4 Ⓙ ● Ⓛ Ⓜ   6 ● Ⓚ Ⓛ Ⓜ   8 Ⓙ Ⓚ ● Ⓜ

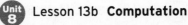

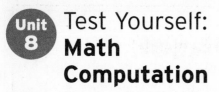

Focus

Mathematics Skill
• adding, subtracting, multiplying, and dividing whole numbers

Test-taking Skills
• managing time effectively
• performing the correct operation
• computing carefully
• transferring numbers accurately
• indicating that the correct answer is not given
• converting items to a workable format
• reworking a problem
• taking the best guess when unsure of the answer
• checking items by the opposite operation
• working methodically

This lesson simulates an actual test-taking experience. Therefore, it is recommended that the directions be read verbatim and that the suggested procedures and time allowances be followed.

Unit 8 Test Yourself: Math Computation

Directions: Solve each problem. Choose the answer you think is correct. If the correct answer is not given, fill in the space for the last answer, N.

Sample A	534 − 5 =	* A 529
		B 531
		C 539
		D N

Sample B	34 + 26 =	J 50
		K 51
		* L 60
		M N

1 6 × 5 =
  A 1
  B 11
* C 30
  D N

2 849 − 8
  J 831
* K 841
  L 857
  M N

3 45 + 202 =
  A 67
  B 207
* C 247
  D N

4 6 × 4
  J 10
* K 24
  L 42
  M N

5 454 + 412
  A 42
* B 866
  C 976
  D N

6 78 − 9 =
* J 69
  K 71
  L 87
  M N

7 89 − 40
  A 40
  B 45
* C 49
  D N

8 29 + 2 =
  J 27
* K 31
  L 49
  M N

STOP

75

Answer rows A ●ⒷⒸⒹ   1 ⒶⒷ●Ⓓ   3 ⒶⒷ●Ⓓ   5 Ⓐ●ⒸⒹ   7 ⒶⒷ●Ⓓ
            B ⒿⓀ●Ⓜ   2 Ⓙ●ⓁⓂ   4 ●ⓀⓁⓂ   6 ●ⓀⓁⓂ   8 Ⓙ●ⓁⓂ

Directions

Administration Time: approximately 15 minutes

Distribute scratch paper to the students.

Say Turn to the Test Yourself lesson on page 75.

Point out to the students that this Test Yourself lesson is timed like a real test, but that they will score it themselves to see how well they are doing. Encourage them to read each question carefully, to think about what they are supposed to do, and to work carefully on scratch paper when necessary. They should skip difficult problems and return to them later and take the best guess when they are unsure of the answer.

Say This lesson will check how well you can solve computation problems. Remember to make sure that the circles for your answer choices are completely filled in. Press your pencil firmly so that your marks come out dark. Completely erase any marks for answers that you change. Do not write anything except your answer choices in your books.

Look at Sample A. Read the question and the answer choices. Mark the circle for the answer you think is correct.

Allow time for the students to fill in their answers.

Say The circle for answer A should be filled in because 534 minus 5 is 529. If you chose another answer, erase yours and fill in circle A now.

Check to see that the students have filled in the correct answer circle.

Say Now do Sample B. Solve the problem and fill in the circle for the answer you think is correct.

Allow time for the students to fill in their answers.

Say The circle for answer L should be filled in because 34 plus 26 is 60. If you chose another answer, erase yours and fill in circle L now.

Check to see that the students have filled in the correct answer circle.

Say Now you will do more mathematics problems. You may use the scratch paper I gave you. Remember, for some items, the correct answer is not given. When this happens, choose the last answer. Work until you come to the STOP sign at the bottom of the page. Make sure that the circles for your answer choices are completely filled in with dark marks. Be sure to fill in the circle in the answer row for the problem you are working on. Completely erase any marks for answers that you change. You will have 10 minutes to solve the problems. You may begin.

Allow 10 minutes.

Say It's time to stop. You have finished the Test Yourself lesson. Check to see that you have completely filled in your answer circles. Make sure that any marks for answers that you changed have been completely erased.

Go over the lesson with the students. Ask if they had enough time to finish the lesson. Did they work carefully on scratch paper? Which questions required them to guess? What were some of the problems they experienced? Work through any problems that caused difficulty.

Have the students indicate completion of the lesson by entering their score for this activity on the progress chart at the beginning of the book. If necessary, provide additional practice problems similar to the ones in this unit.

Unit 8 — Test Yourself: Math Computation

Directions: Solve each problem. Choose the answer you think is correct. If the correct answer is not given, fill in the space for the last answer, N.

Sample A	$534 - 5 =$			Sample B	$34 + 26 =$		
		* A	529			J	50
		B	531			K	51
		C	539			* L	60
		D	N			M	N

1 $6 \times 5 =$
- A 1
- B 11
- * C 30
- D N

2 849
    $- 8$
- J 831
- * K 841
- L 857
- M N

3 $45 + 202 =$
- A 67
- B 207
- * C 247
- D N

4   6
   $\times 4$
- J 10
- * K 24
- L 42
- M N

5 454
   $+ 412$
- A 42
- * B 866
- C 976
- D N

6 $78 - 9 =$
- * J 69
- K 71
- L 87
- M N

7   89
   $- 40$
- A 40
- B 45
- * C 49
- D N

8 $29 + 2 =$
- J 27
- * K 31
- L 49
- M N

STOP

75

Answer rows A ●ⒷⒸⒹ 1 ⒶⒷ●Ⓓ 3 ⒶⒷ●Ⓓ 5 Ⓐ●ⒸⒹ 7 ⒶⒷ●Ⓓ
B ⒿⓀ●Ⓜ 2 Ⓙ●ⓁⓂ 4 Ⓙ●ⓁⓂ 6 ●ⓀⓁⓂ 8 Ⓙ●ⓁⓂ

Background

This unit contains seven lessons that deal with study skills.

• **In Lessons 14a and 14b,** students answer questions about a calendar, map, or diagram. They work methodically and skim or refer to a reference source. They also reread questions and identify and use key words, numbers, and pictures.

• **In Lesson 15a through 16b,** students use a dictionary, differentiate among reference sources, use a table of contents, and alphabetize words or names. In addition to reviewing the test-taking skills introduced in previous lessons, students learn the importance of comparing answer choices, analyzing questions, evaluating answer choices, and taking the best guess when unsure of the answer.

• **In the Test Yourself lesson,** the study skills and test-taking skills introduced in Lessons 14a through 16b are reinforced and presented in a format that gives students the experience of taking an achievement test. Techniques for managing time effectively when taking a standardized test are reinforced.

Instructional Objectives

Lesson 14a **Maps and Diagrams** Lesson 14b **Maps and Diagrams**	Given a question about a calendar, map or diagram, students identify which of four answer choices is correct.
Lesson 15a **Reference Materials** Lesson 15b **Reference Materials** Lesson 16a **Reference Materials** Lesson 16b **Reference Materials**	Given a question about a reference source, table of contents, dictionary or alphabetical order, students identify which of four answer choices is correct.
Test Yourself	Given questions similar to those in Lessons 14a through 16b, students utilize study skills and test-taking strategies on achievement test formats.

Lesson 14a
Maps and Diagrams

Unit 9

Focus

Reference Skills
- using a calendar
- understanding a map

Test-taking Skills
- working methodically
- referring to a reference source

Sample A

Say Turn to Lesson 14a on page 76. In this lesson you will practice using a map or calendar. Read the directions at the top of the page to yourself.

Allow time for the students to read the directions.

Say Look at the map for Sample A and read the question. What is the correct answer to the question? *(pause)* Answer C is correct because the Swim Beach is to the east of the Boat Ramp. Mark circle C for Sample A in the answer rows at the bottom of the page. Make sure the circle is completely filled in. Press your pencil firmly so that your mark comes out dark.

Check to see that the students have filled in the correct answer circle. Discuss with the students how to use the map to find the answer.

★TIPS

Say Now let's look at the tips.

Have a volunteer read the tips aloud.

Say It is important that you use the map or calendar to answer questions in this lesson. The answer will always be found in the reference source. Before you mark your answer, look carefully again at the map or calendar.

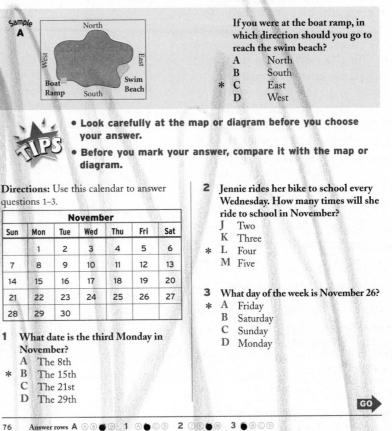

Maps, Diagrams, and Reference Materials

Unit 9

Lesson 14a **Maps and Diagrams**

Directions: Read each question. Choose the best answer.

Sample A

If you were at the boat ramp, in which direction should you go to reach the swim beach?
A North
B South
* C East
D West

TIPS
- Look carefully at the map or diagram before you choose your answer.
- Before you mark your answer, compare it with the map or diagram.

Directions: Use this calendar to answer questions 1–3.

November

Sun	Mon	Tue	Wed	Thu	Fri	Sat
	1	2	3	4	5	6
7	8	9	10	11	12	13
14	15	16	17	18	19	20
21	22	23	24	25	26	27
28	29	30				

1 What date is the third Monday in November?
A The 8th
* B The 15th
C The 21st
D The 29th

2 Jennie rides her bike to school every Wednesday. How many times will she ride to school in November?
J Two
K Three
* L Four
M Five

3 What day of the week is November 26?
* A Friday
B Saturday
C Sunday
D Monday

GO

76   Answer rows A Ⓐ Ⓑ ● Ⓓ   1 Ⓐ ● Ⓒ Ⓓ   2 Ⓙ Ⓚ ● Ⓜ   3 ● Ⓑ Ⓒ Ⓓ

Practice

Say Let's do the Practice items now. There are different kinds of items in this lesson, so you should read the directions for each section carefully. Think about what the questions are asking and be sure to refer to the calendar or map to answer the questions. When you come to the GO sign at the bottom of the page, continue working. Work until you come to the STOP sign at the bottom of page 77. Remember to make sure that your answer circles are completely filled in with dark marks. Completely erase any marks for answers that you change. Any questions? Start working now.

Allow time for the students to mark their answers.

Say It's time to stop. You have finished Lesson 14a.

Review the answers with the students. If any questions caused particular difficulty, work through each of the answer choices.

Have the students indicate completion of the lesson by entering their score for this activity on the progress chart at the beginning of the book.

Directions: Use this map to answer questions 4–7.

4 Which lake is farthest north?
  A Bear Creek Lake
  B Chatfield Reservoir
  C Cherry Creek Lake
* D Standley Lake Reservoir

5 Which major highway goes east and west?
  J I-25
* K I-70
  L I-76
  M I-225

6 Which of these is closest to the state capitol?
* A The U.S. Mint
  B City Park
  C Denver International Airport
  D Lowry Air Force Base

7 Which information can you find in the box at the bottom of the map?
  J How many feet in a mile
  K How many meters in a kilometer
* L How far in miles an inch on the map is equal to
  M How far it is from Denver to Grand Junction, Colorado

STOP

Answer rows 4 Ⓐ Ⓑ Ⓒ ● 5 Ⓙ ● Ⓛ Ⓜ 6 ● Ⓑ Ⓒ Ⓓ 7 Ⓙ Ⓚ ● Ⓜ

77

Unit 9 # Lesson 14b Maps and Diagrams

Focus

Reference Skills
• understanding a map
• understanding a diagram

Test-taking Skills
• skimming a reference source
• rereading a question
• referring to a reference source
• identifying and using key words, numbers, and pictures

Sample A

Say Turn to Lesson 14b on page 78. In this lesson you will practice reading a map. Read the directions at the top of the page to yourself.

Allow time for the students to read the directions.

Say Look at the map for Sample A and read the question. What is the correct answer to the question? *(pause)* Answer D is correct. The Boat Ramp is in the southwest corner of the map. Mark circle D for Sample A in the answer rows at the bottom of the page. Make sure the circle is completely filled in. Press your pencil firmly so that your mark comes out dark.

Check to see that the students have filled in the correct answer circle. Discuss with the students how to use the map to find the answer.

★TIPS

Say Now let's look at the tip.

Have a volunteer read the tip aloud.

Say It's a good idea to read a question twice before choosing your answer. Look for important words in the question and be sure you know what the question is asking.

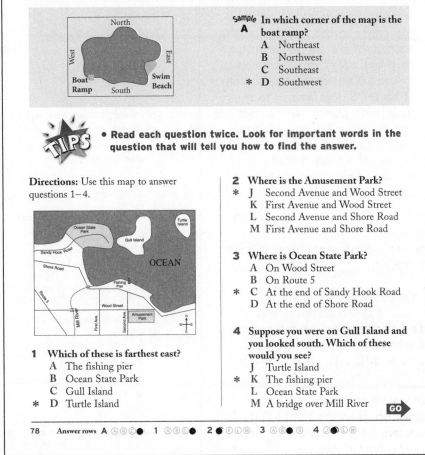

Unit 9 # Maps, Diagrams, and Reference Materials

Lesson 14b Maps and Diagrams

Directions: Read each question. Choose the best answer.

Sample A In which corner of the map is the boat ramp?
  A Northeast
  B Northwest
  C Southeast
* D Southwest

TIPS
• Read each question twice. Look for important words in the question that will tell you how to find the answer.

Directions: Use this map to answer questions 1–4.

1 Which of these is farthest east?
  A The fishing pier
  B Ocean State Park
  C Gull Island
* D Turtle Island

2 Where is the Amusement Park?
* J Second Avenue and Wood Street
  K First Avenue and Wood Street
  L Second Avenue and Shore Road
  M First Avenue and Shore Road

3 Where is Ocean State Park?
  A On Wood Street
  B On Route 5
* C At the end of Sandy Hook Road
  D At the end of Shore Road

4 Suppose you were on Gull Island and you looked south. Which of these would you see?
  J Turtle Island
* K The fishing pier
  L Ocean State Park
  M A bridge over Mill River

78 Answer rows A ⒶⒷⒸ● 1 ⒶⒷⒸ● 2 ●ⓀⓁⓂ 3 ⒶⒷ●Ⓓ 4 Ⓙ●ⓁⓂ

Practice

Say Let's do the Practice items now. Read each question twice before you choose an answer. Think about what the questions are asking and be sure to refer to the map or diagram to answer the questions. When you come to the GO sign at the bottom of the page, continue working. Work until you come to the STOP sign at the bottom of page 79. Remember to make sure that your answer circles are completely filled in with dark marks. Completely erase any marks for answers that you change. Any questions? Start working now.

Allow time for the students to mark their answers.

Say It's time to stop. You have finished Lesson 14b.

Review the answers with the students. If any questions caused particular difficulty, work through each of the answer choices.

Have the students indicate completion of the lesson by entering their score for this activity on the progress chart at the beginning of the book.

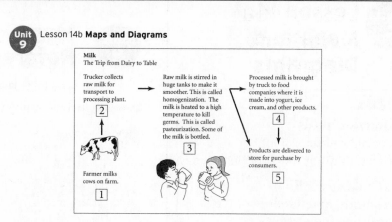

Unit 9 — Lesson 14b **Maps and Diagrams**

Milk
The Trip from Dairy to Table

Directions: This diagram shows what happens to milk as it goes from the cow to the store. Use the diagram to answer questions 5–10.

5 How does milk get to the processing plant?
  A By pipe
  B By plane
  C By train
* D By truck

6 Who are consumers?
  J People who work for farmers
  K People who make things
* L People who buy things
  M People who work in stores

7 Why does an arrow go from step 3 to step 5?
  A No food company wants it.
* B Some processed milk is sent to stores.
  C This milk is not processed.
  D It is a mistake.

8 Which of these happens at the processing plant?
  J Milk is sold to people.
* K Raw milk is pasteurized and homogenized.
  L Farmers make sure the milk tastes good.
  M Milk is put into trucks.

9 What goes to food companies?
* A Processed milk
  B Raw milk
  C Yogurt
  D Ice cream

10 Which of these probably takes place in step 4?
  J Farmers inspect the milk.
* K Milk is turned into cheese.
  L The drivers empty their trucks.
  M People buy the milk.

STOP

Answer rows 5 Ⓐ Ⓑ Ⓒ ●   7 Ⓐ ● Ⓒ Ⓓ   9 ● Ⓑ Ⓒ Ⓓ   79
        6 Ⓙ Ⓚ ● Ⓜ   8 Ⓙ ● Ⓛ Ⓜ   10 Ⓙ ● Ⓛ Ⓜ

Lesson 15a
Reference Materials

 Unit 9

Maps, Diagrams, and Reference Materials

Lesson 15a **Reference Materials**

Directions: Read each question. Choose the best answer.

Sample A

border (bor′ der)
The line that separates countries

bore (bor)
To make a hole in something

How should you spell the word that means the line that separates countries?

* A   border
B   bordir
C   boredir
D   boreder

TIPS

- Some lessons have different kinds of items from other lessons. Be sure you read the directions carefully.
- Think about what you are supposed to do before you choose your answer.

Directions: Decide what you should look up in a card catalog or enter into a computer to do a search for information.

1 To find books about the people who invented television, it would be best to look under
A   "invention" as a subject.
B   "people who invent" as a subject.
* C   "television" as a subject.
D   "people" as a subject.

2 To find out about marsupials, animals like kangaroos that have pouches, it would be best to look under the subject
* J   "marsupials."
K   "kangaroos."
L   "pouches."
M   "animals like kangaroos."

3 To find a collection of nature pictures by the famous photographer Ansel Adams, look under
A   "Ansel Adams" as an author.
B   "nature pictures" as a subject.
C   "famous photographers" as a subject.
* D   "Adams, Ansel" as an author.

4 To find out about the life of Wolfgang Amadeus Mozart, the famous composer, look under
J   "famous composer" as a subject.
* K   "Mozart, Wolfgang Amadeus" as a subject.
L   "life of composers" as a subject.
M   "Mozart, Wolfgang Amadeus" as an author.

STOP

80   Answer rows   A ●ⒷⒸⒹ   1 ⒶⒷ●Ⓓ   2 ●ⓀⓁⓂ   3 ⒶⒷⒸ●   4 Ⓙ●ⓁⓂ

Focus

Reference Skills
- using a dictionary
- differentiating among reference sources

Test-taking Skills
- working methodically
- comparing answer choices
- referring to a reference source

Sample A

Say Turn to Lesson 15a on page 80. In this lesson you will show how well you understand reference sources. Read the directions at the top of the page to yourself.

Allow time for the students to read the directions.

Say Look at the part of the dictionary for Sample A. Now read the question. Which answer is correct? *(pause)* Answer A is correct because this is the correct way to spell the word *border*. Mark circle A for Sample A in the answer rows at the bottom of the page. Make sure the circle is completely filled in. Press your pencil firmly so that your mark comes out dark.

Check to see that the students have filled in the correct answer circle.

★TIPS

Say Now let's look at the tips.

Have a volunteer read the tips aloud.

Say Read the directions carefully. A test often has different kinds of items, and you want to be sure you know what you are supposed to do. If you answer too quickly, you might make a mistake even though you know what the correct answer is.

Practice

Say Let's do the Practice items now. Read the directions for these items and think about what the questions are asking. Work until you come to the STOP sign at the bottom of the page. Remember to make sure that your answer circles are completely filled in with dark marks. Completely erase any marks for answers that you change. Any questions? Start working now.

Allow time for the students to mark their answers.

Say It's time to stop. You have finished Lesson 15a.

Review the answers with the students. If any questions caused particular difficulty, work through each of the answer choices.

Have the students indicate completion of the lesson by entering their score for this activity on the progress chart at the beginning of the book.

Unit 9

Maps, Diagrams, and Reference Materials

Lesson 15a Reference Materials

Directions: Read each question. Choose the best answer.

Sample A

border (bor' der)
The line that separates countries

bore (bor)
To make a hole in something

How should you spell the word that means the line that separates countries?

* **A** border
  B bordir
  C boredir
  D boreder

TIPS

- Some lessons have different kinds of items from other lessons. Be sure you read the directions carefully.
- Think about what you are supposed to do before you choose your answer.

Directions: Decide what you should look up in a card catalog or enter into a computer to do a search for information.

1 To find books about the people who invented television, it would be best to look under
  A "invention" as a subject.
  B "people who invent" as a subject.
* **C** "television" as a subject.
  D "people" as a subject.

2 To find out about marsupials, animals like kangaroos that have pouches, it would be best to look under the subject
* **J** "marsupials."
  K "kangaroos."
  L "pouches."
  M "animals like kangaroos."

3 To find a collection of nature pictures by the famous photographer Ansel Adams, look under
  A "Ansel Adams" as an author.
  B "nature pictures" as a subject.
  C "famous photographers" as a subject.
* **D** "Adams, Ansel" as an author.

4 To find out about the life of Wolfgang Amadeus Mozart, the famous composer, look under
  J "famous composer" as a subject.
* **K** "Mozart, Wolfgang Amadeus" as a subject.
  L "life of composers" as a subject.
  M "Mozart, Wolfgang Amadeus" as an author.

STOP

80   Answer rows A ●ⒷⒸⒹ 1 ⒶⒷ●Ⓓ 2 ●ⓀⓁⓂ 3 ⒶⒷⒸ● 4 Ⓙ●ⓁⓂ

Focus

Reference Skill
• differentiating among reference sources

Test-taking Skills
• working methodically
• analyzing questions
• referring to a reference source

Samples A and B

Say Turn to Lesson 15b on page 81. In this lesson you will show how well you understand how to use different reference sources. Read the directions at the top of the page to yourself.

Allow time for the students to read the directions.

Say Read the question for Sample A. Think about what the question is asking. Which answer is correct? *(pause)* Answer B is correct because the biography section contains books about people. Mark circle B for Sample A in the answer rows at the bottom of the page. Make sure the circle is completely filled in. Press your pencil firmly so that your mark comes out dark.

Check to see that the students have filled in the correct answer circle.

Say Now do Sample B. Which answer is correct? *(pause)* Answer L is correct because a book about volcanoes would be found in the science section. Mark circle L for Sample B in the answer rows at the bottom of the page. Make sure the circle is completely filled in. Press your pencil firmly so that your mark comes out dark.

Check to see that the students have filled in the correct answer circle.

Unit
9
Maps, Diagrams, and Reference Materials

Lesson 15b **Reference Materials**

Directions: Choose the best answer to each question.

Sample **A** Which of these would you find in a library's biography section?
    A   A book about plants and how they grow
 * B   A book about the life of Charles Dickens
    C   A book about using electric machines
    D   A book about the future of space travel

Sample **B** In which library section would you find a book on how volcanoes work?
    J   Fiction
    K   Travel
 * L   Science
    M   Biography

• This lesson has different kinds of items. Be sure you read the directions carefully.

Directions: Questions 1–4 are about using reference materials and books from a library. Choose the best answer to each question.

1 Which of these is usually found near the back of a book?
    A   The table of contents
 * B   The glossary
    C   The name of the author
    D   The title page

2 What book would tell you how a city began?
    J   A map book
 * K   A history book
    L   A science book
    M   A home-building book

3 Which of these would tell the most about the moon?
    A   An atlas
    B   A dictionary
 * C   An encyclopedia
    D   A history book

4 For which assignment should you use a dictionary?
    J   Find out what porcupines eat
    K   Find a tale about a porcupine
    L   Find several pictures of porcupines
 * M   Find out how to spell *porcupine*

STOP

Answer rows   A Ⓐ●ⒸⒹ   1 Ⓐ●ⒸⒹ   3 ⒶⒷ●Ⓓ   81
              B ⒿⓀ●Ⓜ   2 Ⓙ●ⓁⓂ   4 ⒿⓀⓁ●

⭐**TIPS**

Say Now let's look at the tip.

Have a volunteer read the tip aloud.

Say Read the directions on a test carefully. It's easy to make a mistake if you are not paying attention. Also, remember to read the question carefully. This will help you avoid careless mistakes.

Practice

Say Let's do the Practice items now. Think about what the questions are asking and look at the answer choices carefully. Work until you come to the STOP sign at the bottom of the page. Remember to make sure that your answer circles are completely filled in with dark marks. Completely erase any marks for answers that you change. Any questions? Start working now.

Allow time for the students to mark their answers.

Say It's time to stop. You have finished Lesson 15b.

Review the answers with the students. If any questions caused particular difficulty, work through each of the answer choices.

Have the students indicate completion of the lesson by entering their score for this activity on the progress chart at the beginning of the book.

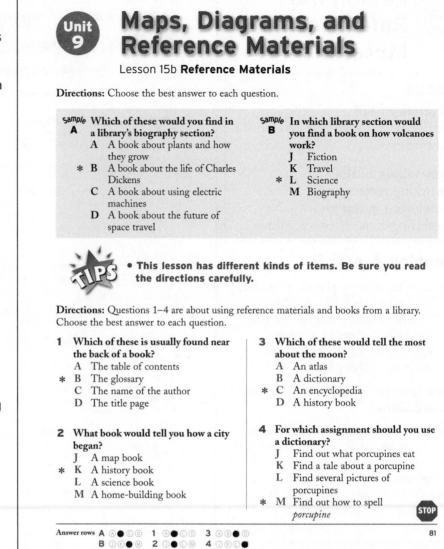

Unit 9 — Maps, Diagrams, and Reference Materials

Lesson 15b **Reference Materials**

Directions: Choose the best answer to each question.

Sample A Which of these would you find in a library's biography section?
  A A book about plants and how they grow
  *B A book about the life of Charles Dickens
  C A book about using electric machines
  D A book about the future of space travel

Sample B In which library section would you find a book on how volcanoes work?
  J Fiction
  K Travel
  *L Science
  M Biography

TIPS
• This lesson has different kinds of items. Be sure you read the directions carefully.

Directions: Questions 1–4 are about using reference materials and books from a library. Choose the best answer to each question.

1 Which of these is usually found near the back of a book?
  A The table of contents
  *B The glossary
  C The name of the author
  D The title page

2 What book would tell you how a city began?
  J A map book
  *K A history book
  L A science book
  M A home-building book

3 Which of these would tell the most about the moon?
  A An atlas
  B A dictionary
  *C An encyclopedia
  D A history book

4 For which assignment should you use a dictionary?
  J Find out what porcupines eat
  K Find a tale about a porcupine
  L Find several pictures of porcupines
  *M Find out how to spell *porcupine*

STOP

Answer rows A Ⓐ●ⒸⒹ   1 Ⓐ●ⒸⒹ   3 ⒶⒷ●Ⓓ   81
            B Ⓙ ⒦ ●Ⓜ   2 Ⓙ●ⓁⓂ   4 ⒿⓀⓁ●

Lesson 16a
Reference Materials

Focus

Reference Skills
• using a table of contents
• alphabetizing words or names

Test-taking Skills
• working methodically
• skimming a reference source
• referring to a reference source

Samples A and B

Say Turn to Lesson 16a on page 82. In this lesson you will show how well you understand a table of contents. Read the directions at the top of the page to yourself.

Allow time for the students to read the directions.

Say Look at the table of contents below the tips. Now read the question for Sample A. Which answer is correct? *(pause)* Answer B is correct because Chapter 6 is about tiny animals, and a giraffe is not tiny. Mark circle B for Sample A in the answer rows at the bottom of the page. Make sure the circle is completely filled in. Press your pencil firmly so that your mark comes out dark.

Check to see that the students have filled in the correct answer circle.

Say Look at the table of contents again and then read Sample B. Which answer is correct? *(pause)* Answer M is correct because the chapter about pets starts on page 73. Mark circle M for Sample B in the answer rows at the bottom of the page. Make sure the circle is completely filled in. Press your pencil firmly so that your mark comes out dark.

Check to see that the students have filled in the correct answer circle.

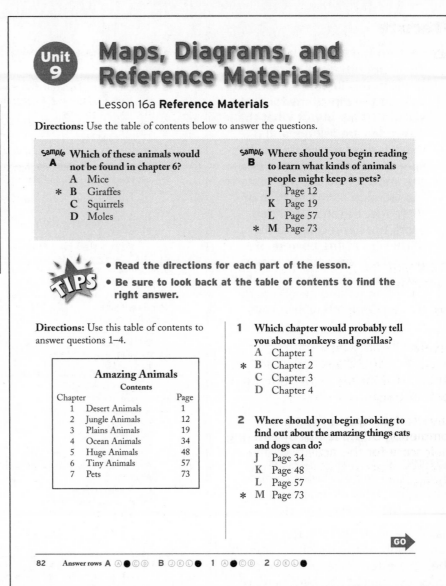

Unit 9

Maps, Diagrams, and Reference Materials

Lesson 16a **Reference Materials**

Directions: Use the table of contents below to answer the questions.

Sample A Which of these animals would not be found in chapter 6?
A   Mice
* B   Giraffes
C   Squirrels
D   Moles

Sample B Where should you begin reading to learn what kinds of animals people might keep as pets?
J   Page 12
K   Page 19
L   Page 57
* M   Page 73

TIPS
• Read the directions for each part of the lesson.
• Be sure to look back at the table of contents to find the right answer.

Directions: Use this table of contents to answer questions 1–4.

Amazing Animals
Contents

Chapter		Page
1	Desert Animals	1
2	Jungle Animals	12
3	Plains Animals	19
4	Ocean Animals	34
5	Huge Animals	48
6	Tiny Animals	57
7	Pets	73

1 Which chapter would probably tell you about monkeys and gorillas?
A   Chapter 1
* B   Chapter 2
C   Chapter 3
D   Chapter 4

2 Where should you begin looking to find out about the amazing things cats and dogs can do?
J   Page 34
K   Page 48
L   Page 57
* M   Page 73

GO

82   Answer rows   A ⒜ ● ⒞ ⒟   B ⒥ ⓚ ⓛ ●   1 ⒜ ● ⒞ ⒟   2 ⒥ ⓚ ⓛ ●

TIPS

Say Now let's look at the tips.

Have a volunteer read the tips aloud.

Say Read the directions for each set of items. If the item refers to a reference source, just skim the source and then look back at it to find the answers. Don't try to memorize the reference source.

Practice

Say Let's do the Practice items now. There are different kinds of items in this lesson, so be sure to read the directions for each section. Think about what the questions are asking, and if there is a reference source, be sure to refer back to it to find the answers. When you come to the GO sign at the bottom of the page, continue working. Work until you come to the STOP sign at the bottom of page 83. Remember to make sure that your answer circles are completely filled in with dark marks. Completely erase any marks for answers that you change. Any questions? Start working now.

Allow time for the students to mark their answers.

Say It's time to stop. You have finished Lesson 16a.

Review the answers with the students. If any questions caused particular difficulty, work through each of the answer choices.

Have the students indicate completion of the lesson by entering their score for this activity on the progress chart at the beginning of the book.

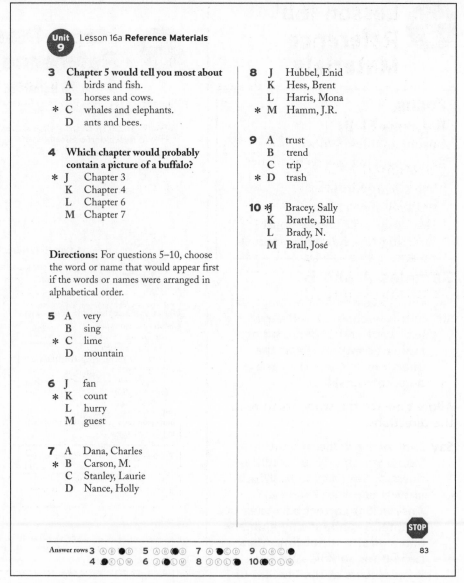

Unit 9 Lesson 16a **Reference Materials**

3 Chapter 5 would tell you most about
- A birds and fish.
- B horses and cows.
- *C whales and elephants.
- D ants and bees.

4 Which chapter would probably contain a picture of a buffalo?
- *J Chapter 3
- K Chapter 4
- L Chapter 6
- M Chapter 7

Directions: For questions 5–10, choose the word or name that would appear first if the words or names were arranged in alphabetical order.

5
- A very
- B sing
- *C lime
- D mountain

6
- J fan
- *K count
- L hurry
- M guest

7
- A Dana, Charles
- *B Carson, M.
- C Stanley, Laurie
- D Nance, Holly

8
- J Hubbel, Enid
- K Hess, Brent
- L Harris, Mona
- *M Hamm, J.R.

9
- A trust
- B trend
- C trip
- *D trash

10
- *J Bracey, Sally
- K Brattle, Bill
- L Brady, N.
- M Brall, José

STOP

Answer rows **3** Ⓐ Ⓑ ● ● **5** Ⓐ Ⓑ ● Ⓓ **7** Ⓐ ● Ⓒ Ⓓ **9** Ⓐ Ⓑ Ⓒ ● 83
4 ● Ⓚ Ⓛ Ⓜ **6** Ⓙ ● Ⓛ Ⓜ **8** Ⓙ Ⓚ Ⓛ ● **10** ● Ⓚ Ⓛ Ⓜ

Reference Materials

Focus

Reference Skill
• using a dictionary

Test-taking Skills
• working methodically
• evaluating answer choices
• referring to a reference source
• taking the best guess when unsure of the answer

Samples A and B

Say Turn to Lesson 16b on page 84. In this lesson you will practice using a dictionary. Read the directions at the top of the page to yourself.

Allow time for the students to read the directions.

Say Look at the dictionary entry below the tips and read the question for Sample A. Which answer is correct? *(pause)* Answer A is correct. Mark circle A for Sample A in the answer rows at the bottom of the page. Make sure the circle is completely filled in. Press your pencil firmly so that your mark comes out dark.

Check to see that the students have filled in the correct answer circle.

Say Now do Sample B. Look at the dictionary entry and decide which answer is correct. *(pause)* Answer K is correct. Mark circle K for Sample B in the answer rows at the bottom of the page. Make sure the circle is completely filled in. Press your pencil firmly so that your mark comes out dark.

Check to see that the students have filled in the correct answer circle. Discuss the sample items and explain how to find the correct answers by using the dictionary.

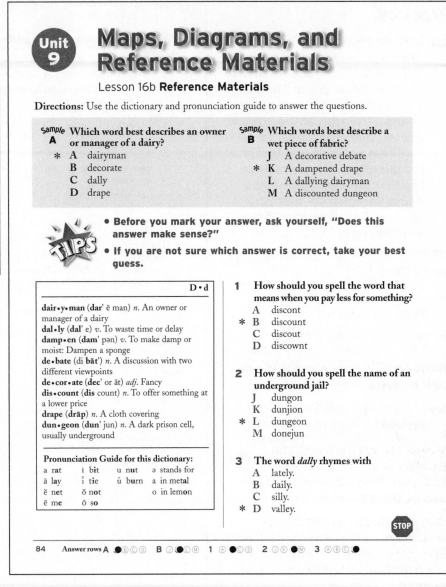

TIPS

Say Now let's look at the tips.

Have a volunteer read the tips aloud.

Say Before you mark an answer, be sure it makes sense. You should check it against the reference source to be sure it matches what is in the reference source. And remember, if you aren't sure which answer is correct, take your best guess.

Practice

Say Let's do the Practice items now. Read the question and answer choices carefully, and be sure to use the dictionary to find the answers. Work until you come to the STOP sign at the bottom of the page. Remember to make sure that your answer circles are completely filled in with dark marks. Completely erase any marks for answers that you change. Any questions? Start working now.

Allow time for the students to mark their answers.

Say It's time to stop. You have finished Lesson 16b.

Review the answers with the students. If any questions caused particular difficulty, work through each of the answer choices.

Have the students indicate completion of the lesson by entering their score for this activity on the progress chart at the beginning of the book.

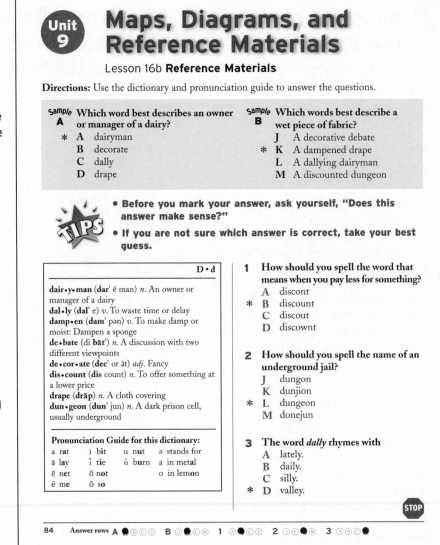

Unit 9 Maps, Diagrams, and Reference Materials

Lesson 16b **Reference Materials**

Directions: Use the dictionary and pronunciation guide to answer the questions.

Sample A Which word best describes an owner or manager of a dairy?
- * A dairyman
- B decorate
- C dally
- D drape

Sample B Which words best describe a wet piece of fabric?
- J A decorative debate
- * K A dampened drape
- L A dallying dairyman
- M A discounted dungeon

TIPS
- Before you mark your answer, ask yourself, "Does this answer make sense?"
- If you are not sure which answer is correct, take your best guess.

D • d

dair•y•man (dar' ē man) *n.* An owner or manager of a dairy
dal•ly (dal' e) *v.* To waste time or delay
damp•en (dam' pən) *v.* To make damp or moist: Dampen a sponge
de•bate (di bāt') *n.* A discussion with two different viewpoints
de•cor•ate (dec' or āt) *adj.* Fancy
dis•count (dis count) *n.* To offer something at a lower price
drape (drāp) *n.* A cloth covering
dun•geon (dun' jun) *n.* A dark prison cell, usually underground

Pronunciation Guide for this dictionary:
a rat	i bit	u nut	ə stands for
ā lay	ī tie	û burn	a in metal
ĕ net	ŏ not		o in lemon
ē me	ō so		

1 How should you spell the word that means when you pay less for something?
- A discont
- * B discount
- C discout
- D discownt

2 How should you spell the name of an underground jail?
- J dungon
- K dunjion
- * L dungeon
- M donejun

3 The word *dally* rhymes with
- A lately.
- B daily.
- C silly.
- * D valley.

STOP

84   Answer rows **A** ●ⒷⒸⒹ   **B** Ⓙ●ⓁⓂ   **1** Ⓐ●ⒸⒹ   **2** ⒿⓀ●Ⓜ   **3** ⒶⒷⒸ●

Test Yourself: Maps, Diagrams, and Reference Materials

Focus

Reference Skills
- using a table of contents
- using a calendar
- using a map
- using a dictionary
- alphabetizing words or names
- identifying key words
- differentiating among reference sources

Test-taking Skills
- managing time effectively
- following printed directions
- working methodically
- referring to a reference source
- skimming a reference source
- rereading a question
- identifying and using key words, numbers, and pictures
- comparing answer choices
- analyzing questions
- evaluating answer choices
- taking the best guess when unsure of the answer

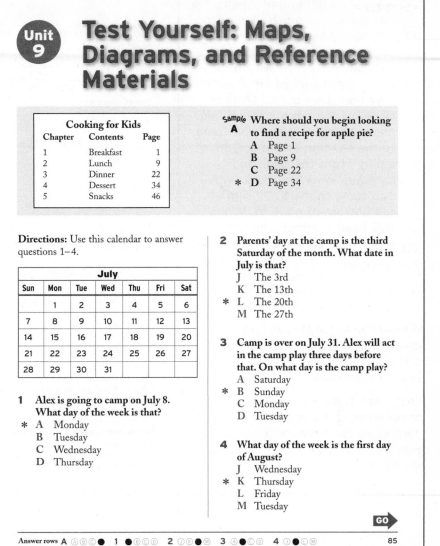

Unit 9 — Test Yourself: Maps, Diagrams, and Reference Materials

Cooking for Kids

Chapter	Contents	Page
1	Breakfast	1
2	Lunch	9
3	Dinner	22
4	Dessert	34
5	Snacks	46

Sample A Where should you begin looking to find a recipe for apple pie?
A   Page 1
B   Page 9
C   Page 22
* D   Page 34

Directions: Use this calendar to answer questions 1–4.

July

Sun	Mon	Tue	Wed	Thu	Fri	Sat
	1	2	3	4	5	6
7	8	9	10	11	12	13
14	15	16	17	18	19	20
21	22	23	24	25	26	27
28	29	30	31			

1   Alex is going to camp on July 8. What day of the week is that?
* A   Monday
B   Tuesday
C   Wednesday
D   Thursday

2   Parents' day at the camp is the third Saturday of the month. What date in July is that?
J   The 3rd
K   The 13th
* L   The 20th
M   The 27th

3   Camp is over on July 31. Alex will act in the camp play three days before that. On what day is the camp play?
A   Saturday
* B   Sunday
C   Monday
D   Tuesday

4   What day of the week is the first day of August?
J   Wednesday
* K   Thursday
L   Friday
M   Tuesday

GO

Answer rows A ⒶⒷⒸ●   1 ●ⒷⒸⒹ   2 ⒿⓀ●Ⓜ   3 Ⓐ●ⒸⒹ   4 Ⓙ●ⓁⓂ   85

This lesson simulates an actual test-taking experience. Therefore it is recommended that the directions be read verbatim and that the suggested procedures and time allowances be followed.

Directions
Administration Time: approximately 35 minutes

Say Turn to the Test Yourself lesson on page 85.

Point out to the students that this Test Yourself lesson is timed like a real test, but that they will score it themselves to see how well they are doing. Remind the students to work quickly and not to spend too much time on any one item. Encourage them to compare their answers with the reference material and to take the best guess when they are unsure of the answer.

Say This lesson will check how well you learned the reference skills you practiced in other lessons. Remember to make sure that the circles for your answer choices are completely filled in. Press your pencil firmly so that your marks come out dark. Completely erase any answers that you change. Do not write anything except your answer choices in your books.

Look at Sample A. Read the table of contents and the question. Mark the circle for the answer you think is correct.

Allow time for the students to mark their answers.

Say The circle for answer D should have been marked. If you chose another answer, erase yours and fill in circle D now.

Check to see that the students have marked the correct answer circle.

Say Now you will do more items. Do not spend too much time on any one question and pay attention to the directions for each section of the lesson. If you are not sure of an answer, take your best guess. Mark the circle for the answer you think might be right. When you come to the GO sign at the bottom of a page, turn the page and continue working. Work until you come to the STOP sign at the bottom of page 91. When you have finished, you can check over your answers to this lesson. Then wait for the rest of the group to finish. Do you have any questions? You will have 30 minutes. Begin working now.

Allow 30 minutes.

Unit 9 Test Yourself: Maps, Diagrams, and Reference Materials

Directions: This is a make-believe map of some countries. The key tells what the symbols on the map mean. Use the map to answer questions 5–10.

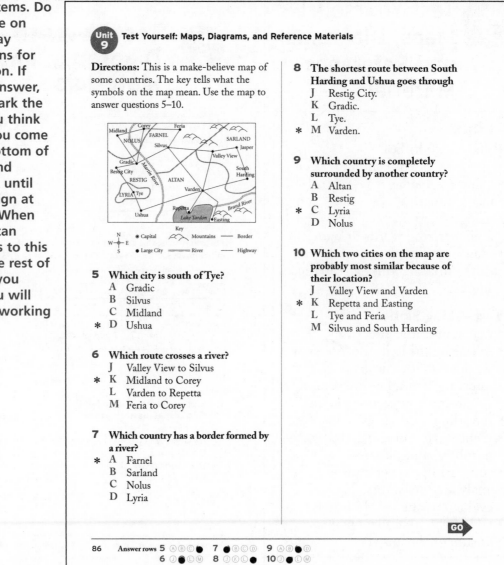

5 Which city is south of Tye?
A Gradic
B Silvus
C Midland
* D Ushua

6 Which route crosses a river?
J Valley View to Silvus
* K Midland to Corey
L Varden to Repetta
M Feria to Corey

7 Which country has a border formed by a river?
* A Farnel
B Sarland
C Nolus
D Lyria

8 The shortest route between South Harding and Ushua goes through
J Restig City.
K Gradic.
L Tye.
* M Varden.

9 Which country is completely surrounded by another country?
A Altan
B Restig
* C Lyria
D Nolus

10 Which two cities on the map are probably most similar because of their location?
J Valley View and Varden
* K Repetta and Easting
L Tye and Feria
M Silvus and South Harding

GO

Answer rows 5 Ⓐ Ⓑ Ⓒ ● 7 ● Ⓑ Ⓒ Ⓓ 9 Ⓐ Ⓑ ● Ⓓ
6 Ⓙ ● Ⓛ Ⓜ 8 Ⓙ Ⓚ Ⓛ ● 10 Ⓙ ● Ⓛ Ⓜ

Directions: This diagram shows the inside of a museum. Use the diagram to answer questions 11–16.

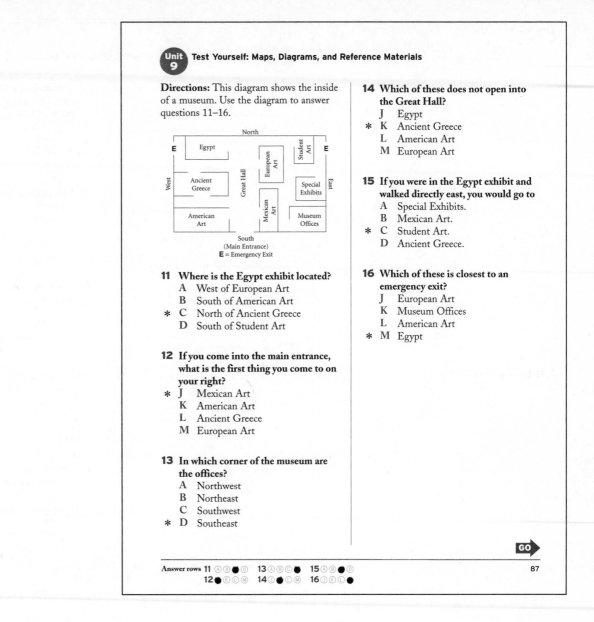

North

E | Egypt | Student Art | E
West | Ancient Greece | Great Hall | European Art | Special Exhibits | East
American Art | Mexican Art | Museum Offices

South
(Main Entrance)
E = Emergency Exit

11 Where is the Egypt exhibit located?
A West of European Art
B South of American Art
* C North of Ancient Greece
D South of Student Art

12 If you come into the main entrance, what is the first thing you come to on your right?
* J Mexican Art
K American Art
L Ancient Greece
M European Art

13 In which corner of the museum are the offices?
A Northwest
B Northeast
C Southwest
* D Southeast

14 Which of these does not open into the Great Hall?
J Egypt
* K Ancient Greece
L American Art
M European Art

15 If you were in the Egypt exhibit and walked directly east, you would go to
A Special Exhibits.
B Mexican Art.
* C Student Art.
D Ancient Greece.

16 Which of these is closest to an emergency exit?
J European Art
K Museum Offices
L American Art
* M Egypt

 GO

Answer rows   11 Ⓐ Ⓑ ● Ⓓ   13 Ⓐ Ⓑ Ⓒ ●   15 Ⓐ Ⓑ ● Ⓓ
12 ● Ⓚ Ⓛ Ⓜ   14 Ⓙ ● Ⓛ Ⓜ   16 Ⓙ Ⓚ Ⓛ ●

Directions: Use this dictionary to answer questions 17–22.

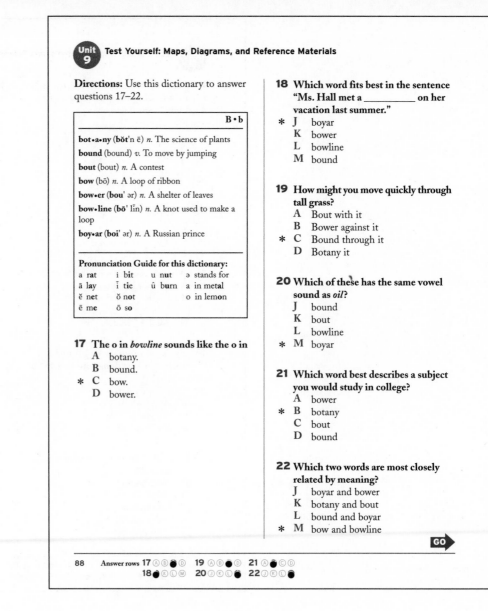

B • b

bot•a•ny (bŏt'n ē) *n.* The science of plants

bound (bound) *v.* To move by jumping

bout (bout) *n.* A contest

bow (bō) *n.* A loop of ribbon

bow•er (bou' ər) *n.* A shelter of leaves

bow•line (bō' lĭn) *n.* A knot used to make a loop

boy•ar (boi' ər) *n.* A Russian prince

Pronunciation Guide for this dictionary:

a rat	i bit	u nut	ə stands for
ā lay	ī tie	û burn	a in metal
ĕ net	ŏ not		o in lemon
ē me	ō so		

17 The o in *bowline* sounds like the o in
   A botany.
   B bound.
* C bow.
   D bower.

18 Which word fits best in the sentence "Ms. Hall met a _____ on her vacation last summer."
* J boyar
   K bower
   L bowline
   M bound

19 How might you move quickly through tall grass?
   A Bout with it
   B Bower against it
* C Bound through it
   D Botany it

20 Which of these has the same vowel sound as *oil*?
   J bound
   K bout
   L bowline
* M boyar

21 Which word best describes a subject you would study in college?
   A bower
* B botany
   C bout
   D bound

22 Which two words are most closely related by meaning?
   J boyar and bower
   K botany and bout
   L bound and boyar
* M bow and bowline

GO ▶

88   Answer rows 17 Ⓐ Ⓑ ● Ⓓ   19 Ⓐ Ⓑ ● Ⓓ   21 Ⓐ ● Ⓒ Ⓓ
                    18 ● Ⓚ Ⓛ Ⓜ   20 Ⓙ Ⓚ Ⓛ ●   22 Ⓙ Ⓚ Ⓛ ●

Directions: For questions 23–28, choose the word or name that would appear first if the words or names were arranged in alphabetical order.

23 A luck
B low
C let
* D less

24 J chase
* K chair
L chart
M chalk

25 A Varden, Tom
B Sanders, Lynn
* C Rice, Ann
D Toth, Brad

26 J breeze
* K bread
L brew
M brethren

27 A workshop
B worker
C workforce
* D workable

28 *J Mills, Carol
K Mills, Grant
L Mills, Stan
M Mills, Nellie

Directions: For questions 29–32, decide what you should look up in the card catalog or enter into a computer to find information.

29 To find a mystery book set in Africa written by Horace Michael Robertson, you should look under
A "mystery" as a subject.
B "Horace Michael Robertson" as a subject.
C "African mystery" as a subject.
* D "Robertson, Horace Michael" as an author.

30 Which of these subjects should you use to find books about Mars, Jupiter, and the other planets?
J "other planets"
* K "planets"
L "Mars"
M "Jupiter"

31 To find books about the natural wonders in Yellowstone National Park, it would be best to look under
* A "Yellowstone National Park" as a subject.
B "natural wonders" as a subject.
C "national park" as a subject.
D "wonders" as a subject.

32 To find a science fiction book about robots by Isaac Asimov, you should look under
J "Isaac" as an author.
K "robots" as a subject.
* L "Asimov, Isaac" as an author.
M "science fiction" as a subject.

GO

Answer rows 23 Ⓐ Ⓑ Ⓒ ● 25 Ⓐ Ⓑ ● Ⓓ 27 Ⓐ Ⓑ Ⓒ ● 29 Ⓐ Ⓑ Ⓒ ● 31 ● Ⓑ Ⓒ Ⓓ 89
24 Ⓙ ● Ⓛ Ⓜ 26 Ⓙ ● Ⓛ Ⓜ 28 ● Ⓚ Ⓛ Ⓜ 30 Ⓙ ● Ⓛ Ⓜ 32 Ⓙ Ⓚ ● Ⓜ

Directions: Use this table of contents to answer questions 33–38.

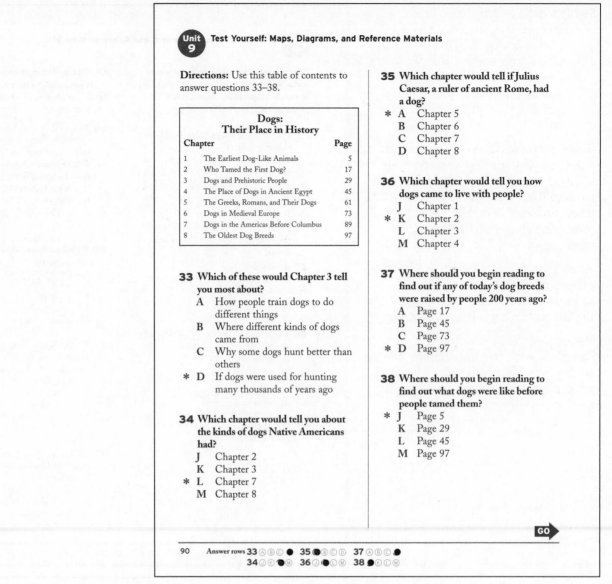

**Dogs:
Their Place in History**

Chapter		Page
1	The Earliest Dog-Like Animals	5
2	Who Tamed the First Dog?	17
3	Dogs and Prehistoric People	29
4	The Place of Dogs in Ancient Egypt	45
5	The Greeks, Romans, and Their Dogs	61
6	Dogs in Medieval Europe	73
7	Dogs in the Americas Before Columbus	89
8	The Oldest Dog Breeds	97

33 Which of these would Chapter 3 tell you most about?

  A How people train dogs to do different things

  B Where different kinds of dogs came from

  C Why some dogs hunt better than others

 * D If dogs were used for hunting many thousands of years ago

34 Which chapter would tell you about the kinds of dogs Native Americans had?

  J Chapter 2

  K Chapter 3

 * L Chapter 7

  M Chapter 8

35 Which chapter would tell if Julius Caesar, a ruler of ancient Rome, had a dog?

 * A Chapter 5

  B Chapter 6

  C Chapter 7

  D Chapter 8

36 Which chapter would tell you how dogs came to live with people?

  J Chapter 1

 * K Chapter 2

  L Chapter 3

  M Chapter 4

37 Where should you begin reading to find out if any of today's dog breeds were raised by people 200 years ago?

  A Page 17

  B Page 45

  C Page 73

 * D Page 97

38 Where should you begin reading to find out what dogs were like before people tamed them?

 * J Page 5

  K Page 29

  L Page 45

  M Page 97

GO ➡

90   **Answer rows** 33 Ⓐ Ⓑ Ⓒ ●   35 ● Ⓑ Ⓒ Ⓓ   37 Ⓐ Ⓑ Ⓒ ●
                           34 Ⓙ Ⓚ ● Ⓜ   36 Ⓙ ● Ⓛ Ⓜ   38 ● Ⓚ Ⓛ Ⓜ

Say It's time to stop. You have finished the Test Yourself lesson. Check to see that you have completely filled in your answer circles with dark marks. Make sure that any marks for answers that you changed have been completely erased.

Go over the lesson with the students. Ask them if they had enough time to finish the lesson. Did they remember to take their best guess when unsure of an answer? Did they refer to the reference sources to answer the questions?

Work through any questions that caused difficulty. If necessary, provide additional practice questions similar to the ones in this unit.

Have the students indicate completion of the lesson by entering their score for this activity on the progress chart at the beginning of the book.

Unit 9 Test Yourself: Maps, Diagrams, and Reference Materials

Directions: Questions 39–44 are about using reference materials and other books you would find in a library. Choose the best answer to each question.

39 Which of these would you find in an encyclopedia?
  A   A map of the airport in your town
  B   How to pronounce the word *pilot*
* C   A story about the history of flying
  D   Where you can buy plane tickets

40 Which section of the library would have a book about the painter Mary Cassatt?
  J   Fiction
  K   Sports
* L   Biography
  M   Science

41 What would you be most likely to find in an atlas?
  A   Word meanings
  B   Synonyms
* C   Maps
  D   Information about people

42 Where would you find the name of a person who wrote a book?
  J   The table of contents
* K   The title page
  L   The index
  M   The glossary

43 Which section of the library would have a book about gardening?
* A   Hobbies
  B   Fiction
  C   Science
  D   Biography

44 Which of these books would most likely be found in the section of the library labeled Health?
  J   A book about Dr. Spock
* K   A book about eating the right foods
  L   A book about people who travel to the future to find a special medicine
  M   A book about Mt. Everest

STOP

Answer rows **39** Ⓐ Ⓑ ● Ⓓ   **41** Ⓐ Ⓑ ● Ⓓ   **43** ● Ⓑ Ⓒ Ⓓ   91
              40 Ⓙ Ⓚ ● Ⓜ   **42** Ⓙ ● Ⓛ Ⓜ   **44** Ⓙ ● Ⓛ Ⓜ

Unit 10

This unit contains three lessons that deal with science skills.

• **In Lessons 17a and 17b,** students answer questions about science. They follow printed directions, refer to a graphic, and identify and use key words, numbers, and pictures. They skim questions, work methodically, reread questions, and prioritize questions.

• **In the Test Yourself lesson,** the science skills and test-taking skills introduced in Lessons 17a and 17b are reinforced and presented in a format that gives students the experience of taking an achievement test. Techniques for managing time effectively when taking a standardized test are reinforced.

Instructional **Objectives**

Lesson 17a **Science Skills** Lesson 17b **Science Skills**	Given a question about science, the student identifies which of four answer choices is correct.
Test Yourself	Given questions similar to those in Lessons 17a and 17b, the student utilizes science skills and test-taking strategies on achievement test formats.

Unit 10

Lesson 17a
Science Skills

Focus

Science Skills
- understanding weather, climate, and seasons
- understanding plant and animal behaviors and characteristics
- understanding fossilization
- recognizing forms, sources, and principles of energy
- understanding magnetism
- understanding diseases and their sources
- understanding scientific instruments, measurement, and processes
- recalling characteristics of Earth and bodies in space
- using illustrations, charts, and graphs
- recognizing importance of environmentally sound practices
- recognizing states and properties of matter
- classifying things based on characteristics
- recalling characteristics and functions of the human body
- understanding properties of light

Test-taking Skills
- following printed directions
- referring to a graphic
- identifying and using key words, numbers, and pictures
- skimming questions or answer choices

Samples A and B

Say Turn to Lesson 17a on page 92. In this lesson you will answer questions about science. Read the directions at the top of the page to yourself.

Allow time for the students to read the directions.

Say Look at Sample A at the top of the page and read the question. Which of these is an example of a weather event? *(pause)* The third

---

Unit 10

Science
Lesson 17a Science Skills

Directions: Read each question and the answer choices. Choose the best answer.

Sample A Which of these is an example of a weather event?
- A A volcano
- B An earthquake
- *C A hurricane
- D An avalanche

Sample B Which of these animals is a mammal?
- J A bird
- *K A whale
- L A spider
- M A snail

TIPS
- Read the question carefully. Look for important words that will help you find the answer.
- Read all the answer choices before choosing the one you think is right.

1 Which of these could be a fossil?
- A A tree blown down by the wind
- B A pile of stones from a river
- C A pine cone on the ground
- *D A leaf imprint in stone

2 Ben Franklin flew a kite with a key on it during a lightning storm. What kind of energy was he studying?
- *J Electrical energy
- K Heat energy
- L Light energy
- M Chemical energy

GO

92 Answer rows A Ⓐ Ⓑ ● Ⓓ   B Ⓙ ● Ⓛ Ⓜ   1 Ⓐ Ⓑ Ⓒ ●   2 ● Ⓚ Ⓛ Ⓜ

---

answer is correct because *a hurricane* is an example of a weather event. Mark answer C for Sample A in the answer rows at the bottom of the page. Make sure the circle is completely filled in. Press your pencil firmly so that your mark comes out dark.

Check to see that the students have filled in the correct answer circle.

Say Move over to Sample B. Read the question and answer choices. What is the correct answer to the question? *(pause)* The second answer is correct because *a whale* is a mammal. Mark answer K for Sample B in the answer rows at the bottom of the page.

Check to see that the students have filled in the correct answer circle. Review the answers to the sample items, if necessary.

Say Now let's look at the tips.

Have a volunteer read the tips aloud.

Say Be sure to read each question carefully. Look for important words as you did in other lessons. These words will help you find the right answer. You should be sure to read all the answer choices carefully, too. Only after reading all the answers should you choose the one you think is correct.

Practice

Say Let's do the Practice items now. Read each question and the answer choices carefully. Look for important words in the question that will help you find the answer. When you come to the GO sign at the bottom of the page, turn the page and continue working. Work until you come to the STOP sign at the bottom of page 97. Remember to make sure that your answer circles are completely filled in with dark marks. Completely erase any marks for answers that you change. Any questions? Start working now.

Allow time for the students to mark their answers.

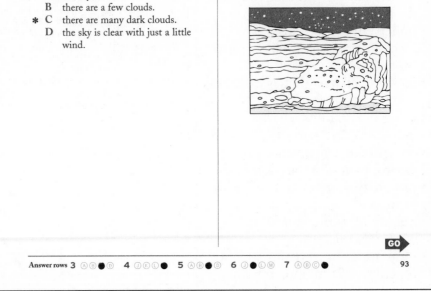

Unit 10 Lesson 17a **Science Skills**

3 A magnet could be used to
 A remove a juice stain from a shirt.
 B dig a hole in hard, rocky ground.
 * C pick up nails dropped on a driveway.
 D clean up water spilled on a floor.

4 You are most likely to spread germs when you
 J sit beside someone.
 K talk to someone.
 L walk near someone.
 * M sneeze near someone.

5 Lightning will most likely happen when
 A the sky is clear.
 B there are a few clouds.
 * C there are many dark clouds.
 D the sky is clear with just a little wind.

6 How do scientists figure out what color dinosaurs were?
 J Scientists have found living dinosaurs.
 * K Scientists guess by looking at today's animals.
 L Scientists study movies made by jungle explorers.
 M Scientists talk to people who have seen dinosaurs.

7 The moon is covered with holes called craters. These craters are
 A formed by wind.
 B covered with plants.
 C filled with water.
 * D caused by meteors.

GO

Answer rows 3 Ⓐ Ⓑ ● Ⓓ   4 Ⓙ Ⓚ Ⓛ ●   5 Ⓐ Ⓑ ● Ⓓ   6 Ⓙ ● Ⓛ Ⓜ   7 Ⓐ Ⓑ Ⓒ ●   93

Directions: Use the information below to answer questions 8–11.

Jan wondered if what was inside a can would affect how fast it rolled. She chose three cans that were the same size. She gently released them one at a time at the top of a short ramp. Then she did it a second time. The chart below shows her results.

Contents of Can	Type	Test 1	Test 2
Cooked pumpkin	solid	1:11 seconds	1:14 seconds
Vegetable soup	liquid & solid	1:07 seconds	1:06 seconds
Chicken broth	liquid	1:03 seconds	1:05 seconds

8 **Why did Jan let go of the cans gently?**
   J   So she had time to push the timer button
   K   So the cans would roll in the right direction
* L   So no cans would get an extra push
   M   So the cans would stop at the bottom of the ramp

9 **Which can rolled the fastest?**
   A   Cooked pumpkin, Test 2
* B   Chicken broth, Test 1
   C   Cooked pumpkin, Test 1
   D   Vegetable soup, Test 1

10 **How long did it take the can of chicken broth to roll down the ramp in Test 2?**
   J   1:14 seconds
   K   1:06 seconds
* L   1:05 seconds
   M   1:11 seconds

11 **Think about Jan's experiment. Which of these would probably roll the fastest?**
   A   A can of tuna
* B   A can of juice
   C   A can of peaches
   D   A can of apple sauce

12 Which bird has feet that are good for swimming?

* J Duck
* K Robin
* L Eagle
* M Owl

13 How long does it take for Earth to make one rotation on its axis?

* A 365 days
* B 12 hours
* C 18 hours
* D 24 hours

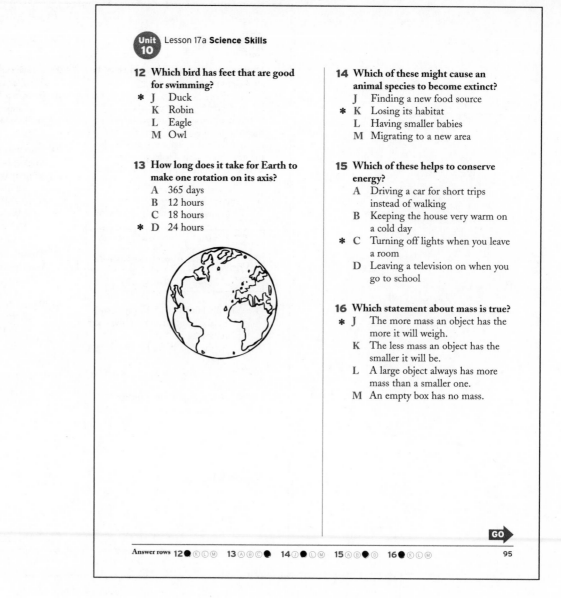

14 Which of these might cause an animal species to become extinct?

* J Finding a new food source
* K Losing its habitat
* L Having smaller babies
* M Migrating to a new area

15 Which of these helps to conserve energy?

* A Driving a car for short trips instead of walking
* B Keeping the house very warm on a cold day
* C Turning off lights when you leave a room
* D Leaving a television on when you go to school

16 Which statement about mass is true?

* J The more mass an object has the more it will weigh.
* K The less mass an object has the smaller it will be.
* L A large object always has more mass than a smaller one.
* M An empty box has no mass.

GO

Answer rows 12 ● Ⓚ Ⓛ Ⓜ   13 Ⓐ Ⓑ Ⓒ ●   14 Ⓙ ● Ⓛ Ⓜ   15 Ⓐ Ⓑ ● Ⓓ   16 ● Ⓚ Ⓛ Ⓜ   95

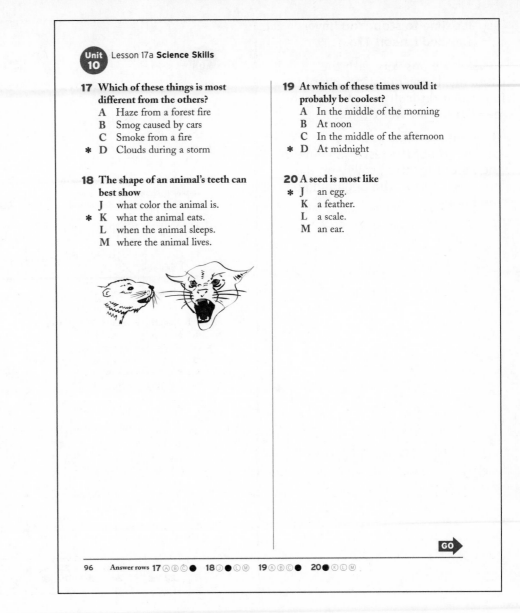
17 Which of these things is most different from the others?

  A Haze from a forest fire

  B Smog caused by cars

  C Smoke from a fire

∗ D Clouds during a storm

18 The shape of an animal's teeth can best show

  J what color the animal is.

∗ K what the animal eats.

  L when the animal sleeps.

  M where the animal lives.

19 At which of these times would it probably be coolest?

  A In the middle of the morning

  B At noon

  C In the middle of the afternoon

∗ D At midnight

20 A seed is most like

∗ J an egg.

  K a feather.

  L a scale.

  M an ear.

GO

96   Answer rows **17** Ⓐ Ⓑ Ⓒ ●   **18** Ⓙ ● Ⓛ Ⓜ   **19** Ⓐ Ⓑ Ⓒ ●   **20** ● Ⓚ Ⓛ Ⓜ

Say It's time to stop. You have finished Lesson 17a.

Review the answers with the students. If any questions caused particular difficulty, work through each of the answer choices.

Have the students indicate completion of the lesson by entering their score for this activity on the progress chart at the beginning of the book.

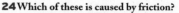

Unit 10 Lesson 17a **Science Skills**

21 The longest bone in your body is probably in your
  A chest.
  B foot.
  C hand.
* D leg.

22 Which of these is the best way to conserve water?
  J Drink only one glass of water a day.
* K Collect rainwater that runs off a roof.
  L Use just one ice cube to cool a drink.
  M Avoid swimming in a pond or lake.

23 Which of these will probably take up the most space?
* A A pound of feathers
  B A pound of iron
  C A pound of cement
  D A pound of wood

24 Which of these is caused by friction?
  J A ball bouncing after it is dropped
  K A ball floating when it is placed in water
* L A ball coming to a stop after it is rolled
  M A ball becoming warm from the sun

25 Lisa has a wooden box that is sealed completely. Which of these cannot be detected inside the box?
  A Sound
  B Air
  C Gravity
* D Light

26 Which of these are you least likely to see in nature?
  J A lion
* K A dinosaur
  L A giraffe
  M A whale

STOP

Answer rows **21** Ⓐ Ⓑ Ⓒ ● **23** ● Ⓑ Ⓒ Ⓓ **25** Ⓐ Ⓑ Ⓒ ●   97
            22 Ⓙ ● Ⓛ Ⓜ **24** Ⓙ Ⓚ ● Ⓜ **26** Ⓙ ● Ⓛ Ⓜ

Lesson 17b
Science Skills

Focus

Science Skills

- recalling characteristics and functions of the human body
- understanding scientific instruments, measurement, and processes
- understanding gravity, inertia, and friction
- recognizing characteristics of a habitat
- understanding life cycles and reproduction
- using illustrations, charts, and graphs
- understanding plant and animal behaviors and characteristics
- recognizing forms, sources, and principles of energy
- recognizing importance of environmentally sound practices
- recalling characteristics of Earth and bodies in space
- understanding weather, climate, and seasons
- understanding magnetism
- recognizing states and properties of matter

Test-taking Skills

- working methodically
- rereading a question
- skimming questions or answer choices
- prioritizing questions

Samples A and B

Say Turn to Lesson 17b on page 98. In this lesson you will answer questions about science. Read the directions at the top of the page to yourself.

Allow time for the students to read the directions.

Say Look at Sample A at the top of the page and read the question. Which of these organs is part of the circulatory system? *(pause)* The second answer is correct because the *heart* is

---

Unit 10 Science
Lesson 17b **Science Skills**

Directions: Read each question and the answer choices. Choose the best answer.

Sample A Which of these organs is part of the circulatory system?
  A Stomach
 *B Heart
  C Liver
  D Kidneys

Sample B The size of a dinosaur is usually determined by
  J comparing its teeth to those of today's animals.
  K determining how old it was.
  L finding out what it ate.
 *M measuring the size of its bones.

TIPS

- Read the question, choose the answer, then read the question again. Be sure you have chosen the right answer before marking it.
- Remember, skim the items and do the easiest ones first. Then come back and try the other items.

1 Which of the following statements is true about gravity?
  A Birds are not affected by gravity.
  B Gravity is the same as magnetism.
  C Only heavy things feel gravity.
 *D Gravity pulls objects toward Earth.

2 Which of these statements about soil is true?
  J Soil everywhere is exactly the same.
  K Soil is made in factories and is not found naturally.
 *L Soil determines how well plants will grow.
  M Soil is the same as sand.

GO

98   Answer rows   A Ⓐ●ⒸⒹ   B ⒿⓀⓁ●   1 ⒶⒷⒸ●   2 ⒿⓀ●Ⓜ

---

part of the circulatory system. Mark answer B for Sample A in the answer rows at the bottom of the page. Make sure the circle is completely filled in. Press your pencil firmly so that your mark comes out dark.

Check to see that the students have filled in the correct answer circle.

Say Move over to Sample B. Read the question and answer choices. What is the correct answer to the question? *(pause)* The last answer is correct. Mark answer M for Sample B in the answer rows at the bottom of the page.

Check to see that the students have filled in the correct answer circle. Review the answers to the sample items if necessary.

Say Now let's look at the tips.

Have a volunteer read the tips aloud.

Say It's a good idea to read a question, look at the answer choices, and then read the question again before choosing your answer. This is especially true if a question seems difficult or confusing. You should also skim the items and do the easiest ones first. After you answer the easy questions, come back and try the other items.

Practice

Say Let's do the Practice items now. Read a question, look at the answer choices, and then read the question again before choosing your answer. Skim the questions and try to answer the easiest items first.

When you come to the GO sign at the bottom of the page, turn the page and continue working. Work until you come to the STOP sign at the bottom of page 103. Remember to make sure that your answer circles are completely filled in with dark marks. Completely erase any marks for answers that you change. Any questions? Start working now.

Allow time for the students to mark their answers.

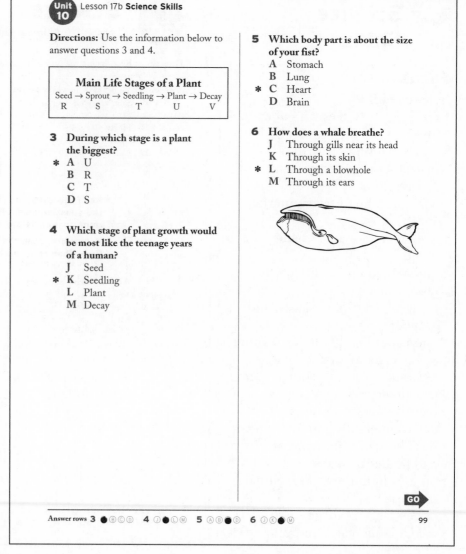

Unit 10 Lesson 17b **Science Skills**

Directions: Use the information below to answer questions 3 and 4.

Main Life Stages of a Plant
Seed → Sprout → Seedling → Plant → Decay
R   S   T   U   V

3 During which stage is a plant the biggest?
* A U
  B R
  C T
  D S

4 Which stage of plant growth would be most like the teenage years of a human?
  J Seed
* K Seedling
  L Plant
  M Decay

5 Which body part is about the size of your fist?
  A Stomach
  B Lung
* C Heart
  D Brain

6 How does a whale breathe?
  J Through gills near its head
  K Through its skin
* L Through a blowhole
  M Through its ears

GO

Answer rows **3** ●ⒷⒸⒹ **4** Ⓙ●ⓁⓂ **5** ⒶⒷ●Ⓓ **6** ⒿⓀ●Ⓜ   99

Directions: Use the information below to answer questions 7–10.

Anand planted bean seeds in each of two baby food jars. When the plants were five inches tall, he turned one jar on its side. He left the other jar standing upright. After a few weeks, the plant in the tipped jar had curved its stem toward the ceiling. Now both plants were growing upward in the same direction.

7 **What did Anand want to find out?**
  A Will bean plants grow in small jars?
  B What makes bean plants grow?
* C Do plants always grow upward?
  D Do different plants grow at different rates?

8 **Why did Anand tilt the jar?**
  J To keep it from getting much sunlight
* K To make the bean plant lie sideways
  L To be able to observe the plant better
  M To make it easier to measure the plant

9 **What do Anand's results tell him about bean plants?**
* A Bean plants grow upward.
  B Bean plants grow best indoors.
  C Bean plants grow best in glass jars.
  D Bean plants all grow at the same rate.

10 **Which of these is most like Anand's experiment?**
* J Trees growing straight up on the side of a mountain
  K Water rushing down a mountain in a stream
  L Birds flying over tall trees
  M Moss growing on the north side of a tree

100   **Answer rows**   **7** Ⓐ Ⓑ ● Ⓓ   **8** Ⓙ ● Ⓛ Ⓜ   **9** ● Ⓑ Ⓒ Ⓓ   **10** ● Ⓚ Ⓛ Ⓜ

11 Windmills have been used for centuries to do work for humans. Windmills get their energy from

  A gravity.
* B moving air.
  C shining sun.
  D lightning.

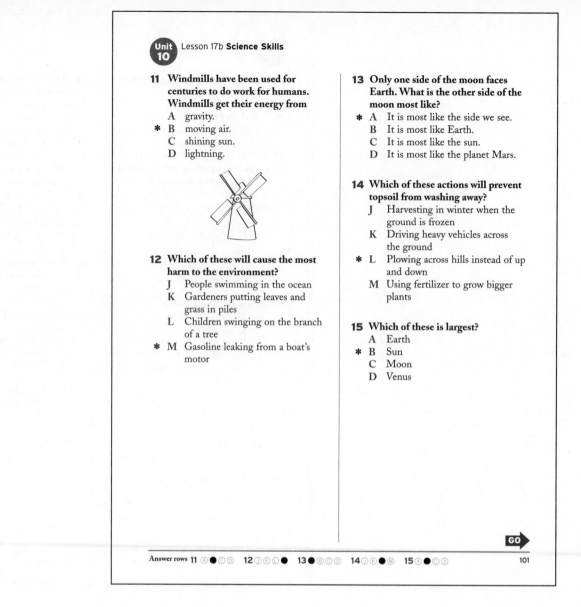

12 Which of these will cause the most harm to the environment?

  J People swimming in the ocean
  K Gardeners putting leaves and grass in piles
  L Children swinging on the branch of a tree
* M Gasoline leaking from a boat's motor

13 Only one side of the moon faces Earth. What is the other side of the moon most like?

* A It is most like the side we see.
  B It is most like Earth.
  C It is most like the sun.
  D It is most like the planet Mars.

14 Which of these actions will prevent topsoil from washing away?

  J Harvesting in winter when the ground is frozen
  K Driving heavy vehicles across the ground
* L Plowing across hills instead of up and down
  M Using fertilizer to grow bigger plants

15 Which of these is largest?

  A Earth
* B Sun
  C Moon
  D Venus

GO

16 How is electricity delivered to most homes?

   J   In batteries

*   K   Through wires

   L   In big trucks

   M   By antennas

17 What is inside of fruit?

   A   Tiny versions of the plant that grew it

   B   Tiny leaves that will grow bigger

*   C   Seeds of the plant that grew it

   D   Seeds of many different plants

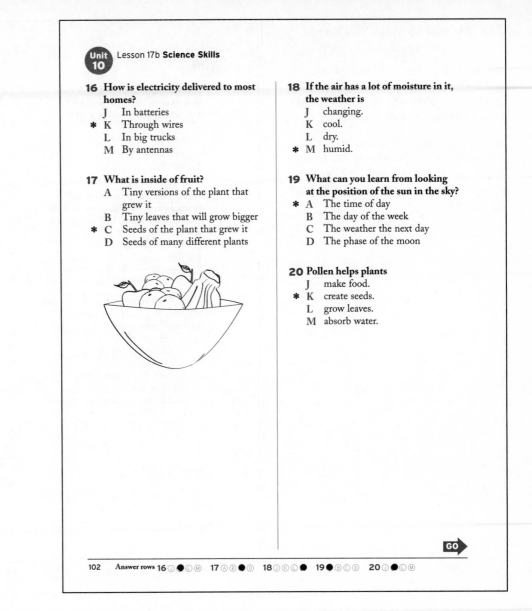

18 If the air has a lot of moisture in it, the weather is

   J   changing.

   K   cool.

   L   dry.

*   M   humid.

19 What can you learn from looking at the position of the sun in the sky?

*   A   The time of day

   B   The day of the week

   C   The weather the next day

   D   The phase of the moon

20 Pollen helps plants

   J   make food.

*   K   create seeds.

   L   grow leaves.

   M   absorb water.

Say It's time to stop. You have finished Lesson 17b.

Review the answers with the students. If any questions caused particular difficulty, work through each of the answer choices.

Have the students indicate completion of the lesson by entering their score for this activity on the progress chart at the beginning of the book.

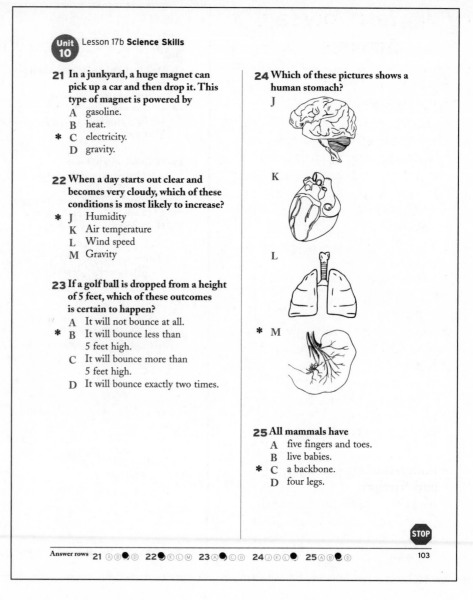

21 In a junkyard, a huge magnet can pick up a car and then drop it. This type of magnet is powered by
A gasoline.
B heat.
* C electricity.
D gravity.

22 When a day starts out clear and becomes very cloudy, which of these conditions is most likely to increase?
* J Humidity
K Air temperature
L Wind speed
M Gravity

23 If a golf ball is dropped from a height of 5 feet, which of these outcomes is certain to happen?
A It will not bounce at all.
* B It will bounce less than 5 feet high.
C It will bounce more than 5 feet high.
D It will bounce exactly two times.

24 Which of these pictures shows a human stomach?
J

K

L

* M

25 All mammals have
A five fingers and toes.
B live babies.
* C a backbone.
D four legs.

STOP

Answer rows 21 Ⓐ Ⓑ ● Ⓓ 22 ● Ⓚ Ⓛ Ⓜ 23 Ⓐ ● Ⓒ Ⓓ 24 Ⓙ Ⓚ Ⓛ ● 25 Ⓐ Ⓑ ● Ⓓ

Unit 10 Test Yourself: Science

Focus

Science Skills

- understanding plant and animal behaviors and characteristics
- understanding scientific instruments, measurement, and processes
- understanding properties of light
- understanding magnetism
- understanding diseases and their sources
- understanding the water cycle
- recalling characteristics of Earth and bodies in space
- recognizing importance of environmentally sound practices
- recognizing states and properties of matter
- understanding weather, climate, and seasons
- recognizing characteristics of a habitat
- understanding gravity, inertia, and friction
- recalling characteristics and functions of the human body
- recognizing forms, sources, and principles of energy
- understanding life cycles and reproduction
- recognizing moon phases

Test-taking Skills

- managing time effectively
- following printed directions
- referring to a graphic
- identifying and using key words, numbers, and pictures
- skimming questions or answer choices
- working methodically
- rereading a question
- prioritizing questions

This lesson simulates an actual test-taking experience. Therefore it is recommended that the directions be read verbatim and that the suggested procedures and time allowances be followed.

Unit 10 Test Yourself: Science

Directions: Read each question and the answer choices. Choose the best answer.

Sample A Which of these animal groups is extinct?
- A Birds
- *B Dinosaurs
- C Lizards
- D Turtles

Sample B The chemical that makes plants green also
- J becomes fruit.
- K turns into honey.
- L causes plants to grow colorful flowers.
- *M uses the sun's energy to make food.

1 Trace fossils can be dinosaur footprints and tail marks. They can tell scientists all of the following things except
- A if the dinosaur's tail dragged on the ground.
- B whether the dinosaur walked on two or four legs.
- C how the dinosaur's foot was shaped.
- *D whether the dinosaur was male or female.

2 When light passes through objects at an angle, it bends. Light is bent in this way by
- *J a magnifying glass.
- K a mirror.
- L a dark room.
- M a solid wall.

3 If two magnets repel each other, it means
- A their opposite poles are together.
- B they are made of different materials.
- *C their same poles are together.
- D they are no longer magnetized.

4 What causes a cold?
- J Dust
- *K Germs
- L Going outside without a coat
- M Getting your feet wet and catching a chill

GO

104   Answer rows   A Ⓐ●ⒸⒹ   1 ⒶⒷⒸ●   3 Ⓐ●ⒸⒹ
                      B ⒿⓀⓁ●   2 ●ⓀⓁⓂ   4 Ⓙ●ⓁⓂ

Directions

Administration Time: approximately 50 minutes

Say Turn to the Test Yourself lesson on page 104.

Point out to the students that this Test Yourself lesson is timed like a real test, but that they will score it themselves to see how well they are doing. Remind the students to work quickly and not to spend too much time on any one item.

Say This lesson will check how well you learned the science skills you practiced in other lessons. Remember to make sure that the circles for your answer choices are completely filled in. Press your pencil firmly so that your marks come out dark. Completely erase any answers that you change. Do not write anything except your answer choices in your books.

Look at Sample A. Read the question and answer choices. Mark the circle for the answer you think is correct.

Allow time for the students to mark their answers.

Say The circle for answer B should have been marked. If you chose another answer, erase yours and fill in circle B now.

Check to see that the students have marked the correct answer circle.

Say Move over to Sample B. Read the question and answer choices. Mark the circle for the answer you think is correct.

Allow time for the students to mark their answers.

Say The circle for answer M should have been marked. If you chose another answer, erase yours and fill in circle M now.

Check to see that the students have marked the correct answer circle.

Say Now you will do more items. Do not spend too much time on any one question and pay attention to the directions. If you are not sure of an answer, take your best guess. Mark the circle for the answer you think might be right. When you come to the GO sign at the bottom of a page, turn the page and continue working. Work until you come to the STOP sign at the bottom of page 113. When you have finished, you can check over your answers to this lesson. Then wait for the rest of the group to finish. Do you have any questions? You will have 45 minutes. Begin working now.

Allow 45 minutes.

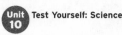 **Test Yourself: Science**

Directions: Use the information below to answer questions 5 and 6.

Fossils show that a small horse-like mammal with four toes lived long ago. Today's horses have one toe, or hoof. The chart below shows how horses' feet have changed.

Time Period	Number of Toes on Horses' Front Feet
50 million years ago	4 toes
30 million years ago	3 toes
20 million years ago	2 toes and 1 large hoof
Present day	1 hoof

5 How many years did it take for a horse with three toes to develop two toes and a hoof?
- A   30 million years
- B   20 million years
- C   50 million years
- * D   10 million years

6 Changes such as the number of toes on a horse
- J   are the result of bad weather.
- * K   help the animal survive.
- L   happen in just a few years.
- M   make it harder for the animal to live.

7 Which of these is <u>not</u> part of the water cycle?
- A   Rain and snow fall to the ground.
- B   Water collects in lakes, rivers, and oceans.
- C   Water evaporates from the ocean to form clouds.
- * D   Water is formed underground in dry river beds.

8 The planet closest to the sun is
- J   Mars.
- K   Venus.
- L   Earth.
- * M   Mercury.

[GO]

Answer rows   5 Ⓐ Ⓑ Ⓒ ●   6 Ⓙ ● Ⓛ Ⓜ   7 Ⓐ Ⓑ Ⓒ ●   8 Ⓙ Ⓚ Ⓛ ●   105

Directions: Use the information below to answer questions 9–12.

Semir taped two yardsticks to his desk far enough apart to make a track for his marbles to roll on. Then he set a red marble in the center of the track and flicked a blue marble so it hit the red one. The blue marble stopped, but the red marble rolled down the track. Next Semir put a red marble and a blue marble in the center of the track and rolled a yellow marble into them. The yellow marble hit the red marble and stopped, but the blue marble on the end rolled. He tried again with more marbles. His results are in the chart below.

Try	Marbles Flicked	Center Marbles	Marbles that Rolled After Colliding
W	Blue	Red	Red
X	Yellow	Red & Blue	Blue
Y	Green & Yellow	Red & Blue	Red & Blue
Z	Green & Purple	Yellow, Red, & Blue	Red & Blue

9 Which try shows what happens when one marble is flicked into two marbles?
A W
* B X
C Y
D Z

10 Semir thinks that however many marbles you flick, that's how many marbles will roll from the other end when they are hit. In how many of his tries did that happen?
J 1
K 2
L 3
* M 4

11 What will happen if Semir puts three marbles in the center in this order— red, blue, yellow—and flicks one green marble into the red one?
A The red marble will roll.
B The blue and yellow marbles will roll.
C The green marble will push all the marbles down the track.
* D The yellow marble will roll.

12 If Semir wants to make only two marbles move down the track, what should he do?
J Flick three marbles and put four in the center.
* K Flick two marbles and put three in the center.
L Flick two marbles and put one in the center.
M Flick three marbles and put three in the center.

GO

13 Which of the following is __not__ true about reptiles?

   A Reptiles are vertebrates with scaly skin.

 * B Most reptiles live in water.

   C Reptiles are cold-blooded.

   D Most reptiles lay eggs.

14 An animal species is considered endangered when

   J all of the animals in the species have died.

   K most of the animals in the species become a danger to humans.

 * L only a few animals in a species are living.

   M some of the animals in the species are a danger to one another.

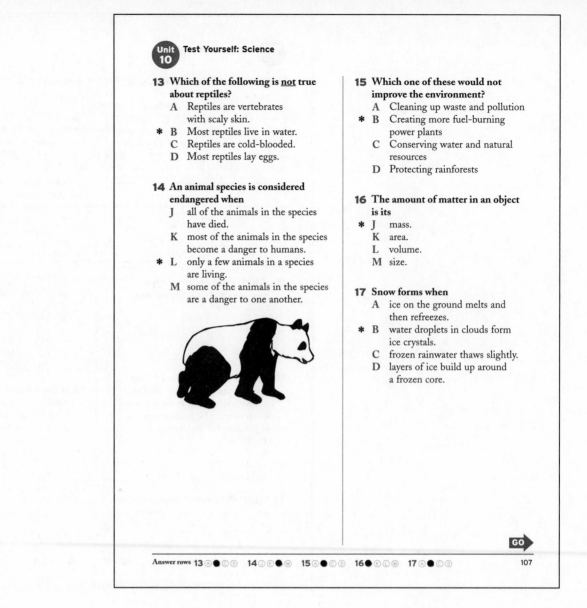

15 Which one of these would not improve the environment?

   A Cleaning up waste and pollution

 * B Creating more fuel-burning power plants

   C Conserving water and natural resources

   D Protecting rainforests

16 The amount of matter in an object is its

 * J mass.

   K area.

   L volume.

   M size.

17 Snow forms when

   A ice on the ground melts and then refreezes.

 * B water droplets in clouds form ice crystals.

   C frozen rainwater thaws slightly.

   D layers of ice build up around a frozen core.

GO

Answer rows 13 Ⓐ ● Ⓒ Ⓓ 14 Ⓙ Ⓚ ● Ⓜ 15 Ⓐ ● Ⓒ Ⓓ 16 ● Ⓚ Ⓛ Ⓜ 17 Ⓐ ● Ⓒ Ⓓ   107

18 One revolution of Earth around the sun determines
J   the cycle of day and night.
K   the position of the Equator.
* L   the length of one year.
M   how much Earth tilts on its axis.

19 At what temperature is it most likely to snow?
* A   Below 30°F
B   Between 35 and 40°F
C   Between 40 and 50°F
D   Above 55°F

20 What part of a plant absorbs water and minerals from the soil?
* J   The roots
K   The stem
L   The leaves
M   The petals

Directions: Use the food chain below to answer questions 21–22.

Food Chain
Owls → Weasels → Ducks → Grasshoppers → Seeds

21 All of these are true about this food chain <u>except</u>
A   weasels prey on ducks.
B   grasshoppers eat seeds.
C   grasshoppers are eaten by ducks.
* D   ducks prey on weasels.

22 If ducks were removed from the habitat, which of these would happen?
* J   Weasels would lose a food source.
K   Grasshoppers would disappear over time.
L   More predators would eat grasshoppers.
M   Owls would eat more weasels.

GO

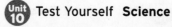

23 The moon's gravity is weaker than Earth's. If a can weighing one pound on Earth is placed on the moon,
  A the can will weigh nothing.
  B the can will weigh more.
* C the can will weigh less.
  D the can's weight will stay the same.

24 Which of the following is <u>not</u> true about rocks?
* J Rocks cannot be changed by heat and pressure.
  K Some rocks contain metals or gems.
  L Weathered rock turns to soil.
  M Rocks can be changed by wind and rain.

25 Food is partly digested in the
  A heart.
  B lungs.
* C stomach.
  D brain.

26 Mammals can do all of the following <u>except</u>
  J lay eggs.
  K give birth to live babies.
  L grow their young in pouches.
* M have hundreds of babies at once.

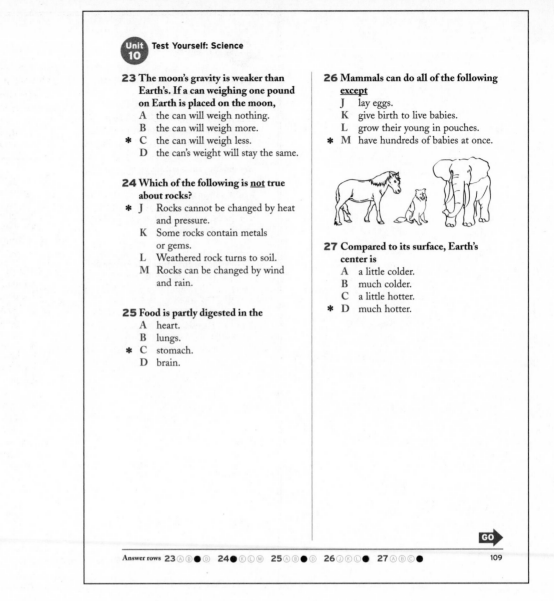

27 Compared to its surface, Earth's center is
  A a little colder.
  B much colder.
  C a little hotter.
* D much hotter.

GO

Directions: Use the information below to answer questions 28–31.

Caitlin had two spider plants. She put one in her mother's bedroom next to a radio that played classical music all day. She put the other on a table in the attic where it was quiet. Both plants had the same amount of light and water. After two weeks, the plant in her mother's room had five new "babies" (small plants hanging from the large plant). The plant in the attic had one "baby."

28 **What was Caitlin trying to find out?**

* J Does music affect plant growth?
  K What kind of music is best for plants?
  L Do plants grow better at higher altitudes?
  M Will plants grow better in different parts of the house?

29 **What did Caitlin find out through this experiment?**

A Attics are not the best place to grow plants.
B It is better to grow plants in a room where people stay.
* C A plant exposed to music has more babies.
D Spider plants often have babies.

30 **If Caitlin does this experiment again, which of these steps shouldn't she do?**

J Be sure both plants get the same amount of sunlight.
K Measure the amount of water she gives each plant.
L Use the same amount of soil for each plant.
* M Add fertilizer to the plant in the attic.

31 **For best results in this experiment, Caitlin should do all of the following except**

A give each plant the same amount of water.
B make sure both plants are the same size at the start.
* C switch the plants to different places every few days.
D measure and chart their growth often.

GO

32 What force causes a compass to work?
  J   Heat
  K   Sunlight
* L   Magnetism
  M   Gravity

33 One of the major differences between Earth and the moon is
  A   the moon does not get energy from the sun.
  B   the moon does not have any gravity.
  C   the moon's surface is very smooth.
* D   the moon has no atmosphere.

34 Which of these is a form of fertilizer?
* J   Decaying plant matter
  K   Beach sand
  L   Smooth river rocks
  M   Used oil from automobiles

35 Which statement best describes the size of the sun?
  A   It is about the same size as the moon.
* B   Its diameter is 100 times larger than Earth's.
  C   It is about the same size as Earth.
  D   Its diameter is two times larger than Earth's.

36 What does a car battery supply to a car?
  J   Heat
  K   Gasoline
* L   Electricity
  M   Motion

GO

Answer rows **32** ⓙ ⓚ ● ⓜ   **33** Ⓐ Ⓑ Ⓒ ●   **34** ● ⓚ ⓛ ⓜ   **35** Ⓐ ● Ⓒ Ⓓ   **36** ⓙ ⓚ ● ⓜ   111

37 The seeds of plants are carried from place to place by all of these <u>except</u>
  A the wind.
  B birds.
  C land animals.
 * D self-movement.

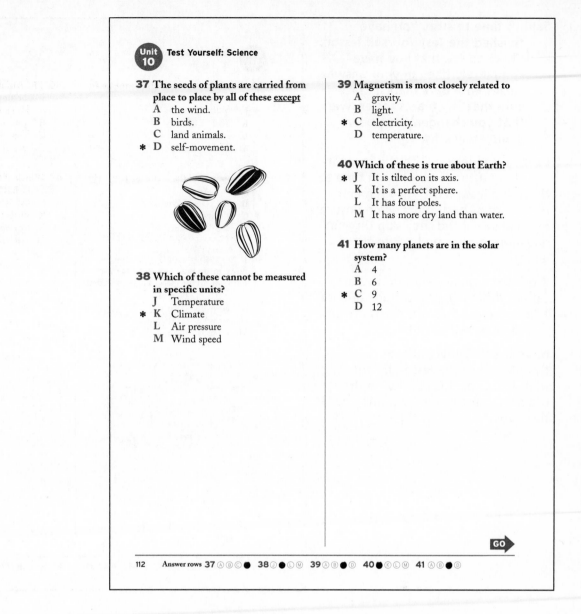

38 Which of these cannot be measured in specific units?
  J Temperature
 * K Climate
  L Air pressure
  M Wind speed

39 Magnetism is most closely related to
  A gravity.
  B light.
 * C electricity.
  D temperature.

40 Which of these is true about Earth?
 * J It is tilted on its axis.
  K It is a perfect sphere.
  L It has four poles.
  M It has more dry land than water.

41 How many planets are in the solar system?
  A 4
  B 6
 * C 9
  D 12

GO ➡

Say It's time to stop. You have finished the Test Yourself lesson. Check to see that you have completely filled in your answer circles with dark marks. Make sure that any marks for answers that you changed have been completely erased.

Go over the lesson with the students. Ask them if they had enough time to finish the lesson. Did they remember to take their best guess when unsure of an answer? Did they skip difficult questions and come back to them later?

Work through any questions that caused difficulty. If necessary, provide additional practice questions similar to the ones in this unit.

Have the students indicate completion of the lesson by entering their score for this activity on the progress chart at the beginning of the book.

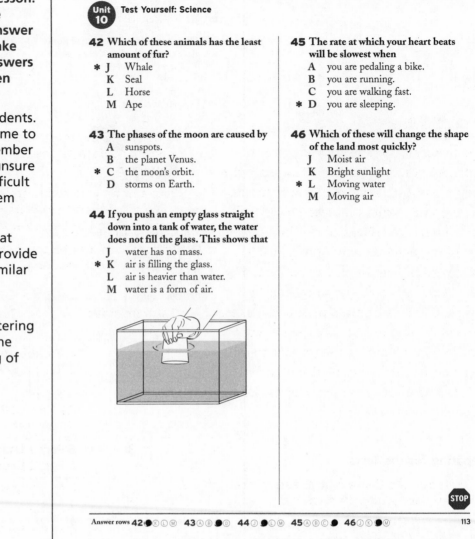

Unit 10 Test Yourself: Science

42 Which of these animals has the least amount of fur?
* **J** Whale
  K Seal
  L Horse
  M Ape

43 The phases of the moon are caused by
  A sunspots.
  B the planet Venus.
* **C** the moon's orbit.
  D storms on Earth.

44 If you push an empty glass straight down into a tank of water, the water does not fill the glass. This shows that
  J water has no mass.
* **K** air is filling the glass.
  L air is heavier than water.
  M water is a form of air.

45 The rate at which your heart beats will be slowest when
  A you are pedaling a bike.
  B you are running.
  C you are walking fast.
* **D** you are sleeping.

46 Which of these will change the shape of the land most quickly?
  J Moist air
  K Bright sunlight
* **L** Moving water
  M Moving air

STOP

Answer rows 42 ● K L M 43 A B ● D 44 J ● L M 45 A B C ● 46 J ● L M   113

Test Practice

To the Teacher:

The Test Practice unit provides the students with an opportunity to apply the reading, spelling, language, mathematics, science, study skills, and test-taking skills practiced in the lessons of this book. It is also a final practice activity to be used prior to administering the *Iowa Tests of Basic Skills®*. By following the step-by-step instructions on the subsequent pages, you will be able to simulate the structured atmosphere in which achievement tests are given. Take time to become familiar with the administrative procedures before the students take the tests.

Preparing for the Tests

1. **Remove the Name and Answer Sheet from each student's book.**

2. **Put a "Testing—Do Not Disturb" sign on the classroom door to eliminate unnecessary interruptions.**

3. **Make sure the students are seated at comfortable distances from each other and that their desks are clear.**

4. **Provide each student sharpened pencils with erasers. Have an extra supply of pencils available. For the mathematics items, provide each student with scratch paper.**

5. **Distribute the students' books and answer sheets.**

6. **Instruct the students in filling out the identifying data on their Name and Answer Sheets. Instructions are given on the next page of this Teacher's Edition.**

7. **Encourage the students with a "pep talk."**

Scheduling the Tests

Allow 10–15 minutes for the students to complete the identifying data on the Name and Answer Sheet before beginning Test 1.

Each test may be administered in a separate session, or you may follow the schedule below that indicates the recommended testing sessions.

Two sessions may be scheduled for the same day if a sufficient break in time is provided between sessions.

Recommended Session	Test	Administration Time (minutes)
1	1 Vocabulary	15
	2 Reading Comprehension	30
2	3 Spelling	15
	4 Capitalization	15
	5 Punctuation	15
3	6 Part 1 Usage	20
	6 Part 2 Expression	15
4	7 Part 1 Math Concepts	25
	7 Part 2 Math Estimation	15
5	8 Part 1 Math Problem Solving	15
	8 Part 2 Data Interpretation	15
	9 Math Computation	15
6	10 Maps and Diagrams	25
	11 Reference Materials	30
7	12 Science	45

Administering the Tests

1. Follow the time limit provided for each test by using a clock or a watch with a second hand to ensure accuracy.

2. Read the "Say" copy verbatim to the students and follow all the instructions given.

3. Make sure the students understand the directions for each test before proceeding.

4. Move about the classroom during testing to see that the directions are being followed. Make sure the students are working on the correct page and are marking their answers properly.

5. Without distracting the students, provide test-taking tips at your discretion. If you notice a student is unable to answer a question, encourage him or her to skip the question and go on to the next one. If students finish the test before time is called, suggest they go back to any skipped questions within that part of the test. However, do not provide help with the content of any question.

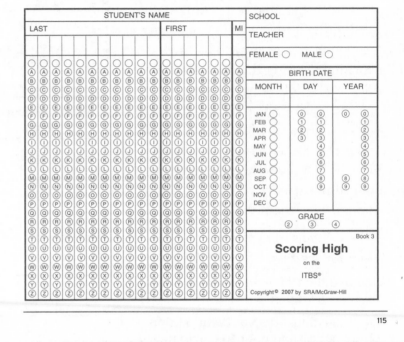

Name and Answer Sheet

To the Student:

Now that you have completed the lessons in this book, you are on your way to scoring high!

These tests will give you a chance to put the tips you have learned to work.

A few last reminders…

•   Be sure you understand all the directions before you begin each test. You may ask the teacher questions about the directions if you do not understand them.

•   Work as quickly as you can during each test.

•   When you change an answer, be sure to erase your first mark completely.

•   You can guess at an answer or skip difficult items and go back to them later.

•   Use the tips you have learned whenever you can.

•   It is okay to be a little nervous.

Preparing the Name and Answer Sheet

Proper marking of the grids on a machine-scorable answer sheet is necessary for the correct listing of students' test results. Use the directions below to give the students practice in completing the identifying data on an answer sheet.

Say You have to fill in some information on your Name and Answer Sheet before you begin the Test Practice section. I am going to tell you how to do this.

Make sure your Name and Answer Sheet is facing up and the heading STUDENT'S NAME is above the boxes with circles. In the boxes under the word LAST, print your last name. Start at the left and put one letter in each box. Print as many letters of your last name as will

fit before the heavy rule. In the boxes under the word FIRST, print your first name. Put one letter in each box and print only as many letters of your first name as will fit before the heavy rule. If you have a middle name, print your middle initial in the box under MI.

Allow time for the students to print their names.

Say Look at the columns of letters under the boxes. In each column, fill in the space for the letter you printed in the box. Fill in only one space in each column. Fill in the empty space at the top of a column if there is no letter in the box.

Allow time for the students to fill in the spaces. Give help to individual students as needed.

Say Print the name of your school after the word SCHOOL.

Print your teacher's last name after the word TEACHER.

Fill in the space after the word FEMALE if you are a girl. Fill in the space after the word MALE if you are a boy.

Look at the heading BIRTH DATE. In the box under the word MONTH, print the first three letters of the month in which you were born. In the column of months under the box, fill in the space for the month you printed in the box.

In the box under the word DAY, print the one or two numerals of your birth date. In the columns of numerals under the box, fill in the spaces for the numerals you printed in the box. If your birth date has just one numeral, fill in the space with a zero in it in the column on the left.

In the box under the word YEAR, print the last two numerals of your year of birth. In the columns of numerals under the box, fill in the spaces for the numerals you printed in the box.

Look at the heading GRADE. Fill in the space for the numeral that stands for your grade.

Check to see that the students have filled in all the identifying data correctly. Then have them identify the part of the Answer Sheet for each part of the Test Practice section.

TEST 1 VOCABULARY

TEST 2 READING COMPREHENSION

TEST 3 SPELLING

TEST 4 CAPITALIZATION

TEST 5 PUNCTUATION

TEST 6 USAGE AND EXPRESSION
Part 1 Usage

Part 2 Expression

116

TEST 7   MATH CONCEPTS AND ESTIMATION
Part 1   Math Concepts

A Ⓐ Ⓑ Ⓒ Ⓓ   3 Ⓐ Ⓑ Ⓒ Ⓓ   7 Ⓐ Ⓑ Ⓒ Ⓓ   11 Ⓐ Ⓑ Ⓒ Ⓓ   15 Ⓐ Ⓑ Ⓒ Ⓓ   19 Ⓐ Ⓑ Ⓒ Ⓓ
B Ⓙ Ⓚ Ⓛ Ⓜ   4 Ⓙ Ⓚ Ⓛ Ⓜ   8 Ⓙ Ⓚ Ⓛ Ⓜ   12 Ⓙ Ⓚ Ⓛ Ⓜ   16 Ⓙ Ⓚ Ⓛ Ⓜ
1 Ⓐ Ⓑ Ⓒ Ⓓ   5 Ⓐ Ⓑ Ⓒ Ⓓ   9 Ⓐ Ⓑ Ⓒ Ⓓ   13 Ⓐ Ⓑ Ⓒ Ⓓ   17 Ⓐ Ⓑ Ⓒ Ⓓ
2 Ⓙ Ⓚ Ⓛ Ⓜ   6 Ⓙ Ⓚ Ⓛ Ⓜ   10 Ⓙ Ⓚ Ⓛ Ⓜ   14 Ⓙ Ⓚ Ⓛ Ⓜ   18 Ⓙ Ⓚ Ⓛ Ⓜ

Part 2   Math Estimation

A Ⓐ Ⓑ Ⓒ Ⓓ   20 Ⓙ Ⓚ Ⓛ Ⓜ   21 Ⓐ Ⓑ Ⓒ Ⓓ   22 Ⓐ Ⓑ Ⓒ Ⓓ   23 Ⓐ Ⓑ Ⓒ Ⓓ
B Ⓙ Ⓚ Ⓛ Ⓜ

TEST 8   MATH PROBLEM SOLVING AND DATA INTERPRETATION
Part 1   Math Problem Solving

A Ⓐ Ⓑ Ⓒ Ⓓ   1 Ⓐ Ⓑ Ⓒ Ⓓ   2 Ⓙ Ⓚ Ⓛ Ⓜ   3 Ⓐ Ⓑ Ⓒ Ⓓ   4 Ⓙ Ⓚ Ⓛ Ⓜ
B Ⓙ Ⓚ Ⓛ Ⓜ

Part 2   Data Interpretation

A Ⓐ Ⓑ Ⓒ Ⓓ   B Ⓙ Ⓚ Ⓛ Ⓜ   5 Ⓐ Ⓑ Ⓒ Ⓓ   6 Ⓙ Ⓚ Ⓛ Ⓜ   7 Ⓐ Ⓑ Ⓒ Ⓓ

TEST 9   MATH COMPUTATION

A Ⓐ Ⓑ Ⓒ Ⓓ   1 Ⓐ Ⓑ Ⓒ Ⓓ   3 Ⓐ Ⓑ Ⓒ Ⓓ   5 Ⓐ Ⓑ Ⓒ Ⓓ   7 Ⓐ Ⓑ Ⓒ Ⓓ
B Ⓙ Ⓚ Ⓛ Ⓜ   2 Ⓙ Ⓚ Ⓛ Ⓜ   4 Ⓙ Ⓚ Ⓛ Ⓜ   6 Ⓙ Ⓚ Ⓛ Ⓜ   8 Ⓙ Ⓚ Ⓛ Ⓜ

TEST 10   MAPS AND DIAGRAMS

A Ⓐ Ⓑ Ⓒ Ⓓ   3 Ⓐ Ⓑ Ⓒ Ⓓ   6 Ⓙ Ⓚ Ⓛ Ⓜ   9 Ⓐ Ⓑ Ⓒ Ⓓ   12 Ⓙ Ⓚ Ⓛ Ⓜ
1 Ⓐ Ⓑ Ⓒ Ⓓ   4 Ⓙ Ⓚ Ⓛ Ⓜ   7 Ⓐ Ⓑ Ⓒ Ⓓ   10 Ⓙ Ⓚ Ⓛ Ⓜ
2 Ⓙ Ⓚ Ⓛ Ⓜ   5 Ⓐ Ⓑ Ⓒ Ⓓ   8 Ⓙ Ⓚ Ⓛ Ⓜ   11 Ⓐ Ⓑ Ⓒ Ⓓ

TEST 11   REFERENCE MATERIALS

A Ⓐ Ⓑ Ⓒ Ⓓ   3 Ⓐ Ⓑ Ⓒ Ⓓ   7 Ⓐ Ⓑ Ⓒ Ⓓ   11 Ⓐ Ⓑ Ⓒ Ⓓ   15 Ⓐ Ⓑ Ⓒ Ⓓ   19 Ⓐ Ⓑ Ⓒ Ⓓ
B Ⓙ Ⓚ Ⓛ Ⓜ   4 Ⓙ Ⓚ Ⓛ Ⓜ   8 Ⓙ Ⓚ Ⓛ Ⓜ   12 Ⓙ Ⓚ Ⓛ Ⓜ   16 Ⓙ Ⓚ Ⓛ Ⓜ   20 Ⓙ Ⓚ Ⓛ Ⓜ
1 Ⓐ Ⓑ Ⓒ Ⓓ   5 Ⓐ Ⓑ Ⓒ Ⓓ   9 Ⓐ Ⓑ Ⓒ Ⓓ   13 Ⓐ Ⓑ Ⓒ Ⓓ   17 Ⓐ Ⓑ Ⓒ Ⓓ   21 Ⓐ Ⓑ Ⓒ Ⓓ
2 Ⓙ Ⓚ Ⓛ Ⓜ   6 Ⓙ Ⓚ Ⓛ Ⓜ   10 Ⓙ Ⓚ Ⓛ Ⓜ   14 Ⓙ Ⓚ Ⓛ Ⓜ   18 Ⓙ Ⓚ Ⓛ Ⓜ

| A | Ⓐ Ⓑ ● Ⓓ |
| B | Ⓙ Ⓚ ● Ⓜ |

1	Ⓐ Ⓑ ● Ⓓ
2	● Ⓚ Ⓛ Ⓜ
3	Ⓐ ● Ⓒ Ⓓ
4	● Ⓚ Ⓛ Ⓜ
5	Ⓐ Ⓑ ●
6	Ⓙ Ⓚ ● Ⓜ

7	● Ⓑ Ⓒ Ⓓ
8	Ⓙ Ⓚ Ⓛ ●
9	Ⓐ Ⓑ ● Ⓓ
10	Ⓙ Ⓚ Ⓛ ●
11	Ⓐ Ⓑ ● Ⓓ
12	Ⓙ ● Ⓛ Ⓜ
13	● Ⓑ Ⓒ Ⓓ
14	Ⓙ ● Ⓚ Ⓜ

15	Ⓐ ● Ⓒ Ⓓ
16	Ⓙ ● Ⓛ Ⓜ
17	Ⓐ Ⓑ ● Ⓓ
18	Ⓙ Ⓚ Ⓛ ●
19	Ⓐ Ⓑ ● Ⓓ
20	Ⓙ Ⓚ Ⓛ ●
21	Ⓐ Ⓑ ● Ⓓ
22	Ⓙ ● Ⓛ Ⓜ

23	Ⓐ ● Ⓒ Ⓓ
24	Ⓙ Ⓚ ● Ⓜ
25	Ⓐ ● Ⓒ Ⓓ
26	Ⓙ Ⓚ ● Ⓜ
27	● Ⓑ Ⓒ Ⓓ
28	Ⓙ Ⓚ Ⓛ ●
29	Ⓐ Ⓑ ● Ⓓ
30	Ⓙ ● Ⓛ Ⓜ

31	Ⓐ Ⓑ ● Ⓓ
32	● Ⓚ Ⓛ Ⓜ
33	Ⓐ ● Ⓒ Ⓓ
34	● Ⓚ Ⓛ Ⓜ
35	Ⓐ ● Ⓒ Ⓓ
36	Ⓙ Ⓚ Ⓛ ●
37	● Ⓑ Ⓒ Ⓓ
38	Ⓙ Ⓚ ● Ⓜ

39	Ⓐ Ⓑ ● Ⓓ
40	Ⓙ ● Ⓛ Ⓜ
41	Ⓐ Ⓑ ● Ⓓ
42	Ⓙ Ⓚ ● Ⓜ
43	● Ⓑ Ⓒ Ⓓ
44	Ⓙ Ⓚ Ⓛ ●
45	Ⓐ Ⓑ ● Ⓓ
46	● Ⓚ Ⓛ Ⓜ

Administration Time: 15 minutes

Say Turn to the Test Practice section of your book on page 119. This is Test 1, Vocabulary.

Check to see that the students have found page 119.

Say Look at your answer sheet. Find the part called Test 1, Vocabulary. All your answers for this test should be marked on your answer sheet, not in your book.

Check to see that the students have found the correct part of the answer sheet.

Say This test will check how well you know vocabulary words. Remember to make sure that the circles for your answer choices are completely filled in. Press your pencil firmly so that your marks come out dark. Completely erase any marks for answers that you change.

Look at Sample A. Read the phrase and fill in the circle for the answer that means the same as the underlined word. Mark your answer in the row for Sample A on the answer sheet.

Allow time for the students to read the item and mark their answers.

Say You should have filled in answer circle C because a brake is a part of a car. If you did not fill in answer C, erase your answer and fill in answer C now.

Check to see that the students have filled in the correct answer circle.

Say Do Sample B now. Read the phrase and fill in the circle for the answer that means the same as the underlined word. Mark your answer in the row for Sample B on the answer sheet.

Allow time for the students to read the item and mark their answers.

Unit 11
Test Practice
Test 1 **Vocabulary**

Directions: Read the phrase and the answer choices. Choose the answer that means the same as the underlined word.

Sample A	Press the brake
	A button
	B seat of a chair
*	C part of a car
	D polish

Sample B	To stir the food
	J keep cool
	K eat slowly
	L cook outside
*	M mix with a spoon

1 To **blink** your eyes
    A close tightly
    B clean
    C hurt
* D open and close quickly

2 Heavy **lumber**
* J wood
    K metal
    L plastic
    M cloth

3 To **pack** the box
    A put tape on
    B carry
* C put things in
    D move

4 A **pleasant** day
    J cold
* K nice
    L busy
    M sticky

5 Speak to the **clerk**
    A person who teaches in a school
* B person who works in a store
    C person who fights fires
    D person who tells stories

6 Get a **reward**
* J something earned
    K lucky guess
    L long book
    M letter from a friend

7 The snake was **harmless**.
    A not colorful
    B not noisy
* C not dangerous
    D not hidden

8 To **guide** some people
    J call
* K lead
    L know
    M like

STOP

Say You should have filled in answer circle M because *stir* means to mix with a spoon. If you did not fill in answer M, erase your answer and fill in answer M now.

Say Now you will answer more questions. Read each item. Fill in the space for your answers on the answer sheet. Be sure the number of the answer row matches the item you are doing. Work by yourself. Work until you come to the STOP sign at the bottom of the page. When you have finished, you can check over your answers to this test. Then wait for the rest of the group to finish. Do you have any questions?

Answer any questions that the students have.

Say Start working now. You have 10 minutes.

Allow 10 minutes.

Say It's time to stop. You have completed Test 1. Check to see that you have completely filled in your answer circles with dark marks. Make sure that any marks for answers that you changed have been completely erased. Now you may close your books.

Review the items with the students. Have them indicate completion of the lesson by entering their score for this activity on the progress chart at the beginning of the book. Then collect the students' books and answer sheets if this is the end of the testing session.

Unit 11 Test Practice
Test 1 **Vocabulary**

Directions: Read the phrase and the answer choices. Choose the answer that means the same as the underlined word.

Sample A Press the <u>brake</u>
- A button
- B seat of a chair
- * C part of a car
- D polish

Sample B To <u>stir</u> the food
- J keep cool
- K eat slowly
- L cook outside
- * M mix with a spoon

1 To <u>blink</u> your eyes
- A close tightly
- B clean
- C hurt
- * D open and close quickly

2 Heavy <u>lumber</u>
- * J wood
- K metal
- L plastic
- M cloth

3 To <u>pack</u> the box
- A put tape on
- B carry
- * C put things in
- D move

4 A <u>pleasant</u> day
- J cold
- * K nice
- L busy
- M sticky

5 Speak to the <u>clerk</u>
- A person who teaches in a school
- * B person who works in a store
- C person who fights fires
- D person who tells stories

6 Get a <u>reward</u>
- * J something earned
- K lucky guess
- L long book
- M letter from a friend

7 The snake was <u>harmless</u>.
- A not colorful
- B not noisy
- * C not dangerous
- D not hidden

8 To <u>guide</u> some people
- J call
- * K lead
- L know
- M like

STOP

119

Administration Time: 30 minutes

Say Turn to the Test Practice section of your book on page 121. This is Test 2, Reading Comprehension.

Check to see that the students have found page 121.

Say Look at your answer sheet. Find the part called Test 2, Reading Comprehension. All your answers for this test should be marked on your answer sheet, not in your book.

Check to see that the students have found the correct part of the answer sheet.

Say This test will check your reading comprehension. Remember to make sure that the circles for your answer choices are completely filled in. Press your pencil firmly so that your marks come out dark. Completely erase any marks for answers that you change.

Look at the passage for Sample A. Read the passage to yourself. Then read the question beside the passage. On your answer sheet, find the answer circles for Sample A. Mark the circle for the answer you think is right.

Allow time for the students to read the item and mark their answers.

Say You should have filled in answer circle C. You can figure out from the passage that George saw elk. If you did not fill in answer C, erase your answer and fill in answer C now.

Check to see that the students have filled in the correct answer circle.

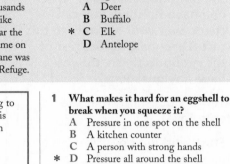

Unit 11 Test Practice

Test 2 **Reading Comprehension**

Directions: Read the passage and the answer choices. Choose the best answer.

Sample A
When the plane got close to the ground, George couldn't believe what he saw. There were thousands of huge animals that looked like deer grazing on the plains near the airport. Just then, the pilot came on the intercom. She said the plane was flying over the National Elk Refuge.

What kind of animals did George see?
A Deer
B Buffalo
* C Elk
D Antelope

One of the great parts of helping to bake is cracking an egg. The shell is thin and easy to break on a kitchen counter, but have you ever tried squeezing an egg in one hand?

Take an egg and hold it over the kitchen sink. Wrap your fingers around it. Then squeeze the egg as hard as you can. You'll find that no matter how hard you squeeze, the egg will not break. It seems strange at first, since eggs are so easy to crack on the counter.

The reason that the egg does not break has to do with pressure. When the pressure is spread out all around the egg, it is hard to break. When there is a lot of pressure in only one spot, however, the eggshell will break.

Next time you are helping to bake, you can show this trick to your family!

1 **What makes it hard for an eggshell to break when you squeeze it?**
A Pressure in one spot on the shell
B A kitchen counter
C A person with strong hands
* D Pressure all around the shell

2 **How do you hold the egg so that it doesn't break?**
* J Wrap your fingers around it.
K Press on it with the palms of both hands.
L Hold it with your middle finger and thumb.
M Use your fingertips to squeeze it.

3 **What would happen if you pressed hard against an eggshell on a counter with only your thumb?**
A The shell would not break.
B The egg would fly from your thumb.
* C The shell would crack.
D The egg would change shape.

Say Now you will answer more questions. Read the passages and the questions that follow them. Fill in the space for your answers on the answer sheet. Be sure the number of the answer row matches the item you are doing. Work by yourself. When you come to the GO sign at the bottom of a page, turn to the next page and continue working. Work until you come to the STOP sign at the bottom of page 124. When you have finished, you can check over your answers to this test. Then wait for the rest of the group to finish. Do you have any questions?

Answer any questions that the students have.

Say Start working now. You have 25 minutes.

Allow 25 minutes.

"Mom, may I take swimming lessons this summer?" Tiara asked.

Mom thought for a moment. "I tell you what, Tiara, if you read five books by the time the first lesson begins, you may take swimming lessons."

Tiara moaned. How would she ever be able to read five books? She enjoyed books, but sometimes it was hard for her to finish them. Because she really wanted to take swimming lessons, she agreed.

Tiara went to the library and chose two books to start. As she sat down in the library to begin reading, she was swept away by the story. It was about a girl who moved with her family to the frontier. By the time she left the library, she had read half the book!

By the second week of summer break, she had finished three books. She couldn't put them down. After she finished her chores, she went outside to the tree house and read until lunchtime.

"Swimming lessons begin next week," Tiara's mother said a month later. "How many books have you read?"

She smiled proudly and showed her the list of books. "Mom, I've read ten books already, and I'm almost finished with my eleventh. Your deal was the best deal I've ever made! I'm taking swimming lessons and have found a new hobby."

Tiara gave her mother a hug and went back to the tree house. She really enjoyed her new hobby.

GO

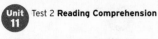

4 Why did Tiara moan when her mother made a deal with her?

  J She didn't know how to read.

  K She wanted to spend her summer at the pool.

 * L She had a hard time finishing books she started.

  M She didn't want to take swimming lessons.

5 What does it mean to say that Tiara was "swept away by the story"?

  A The story was about an ocean.

 * B Tiara enjoyed the book so much she lost track of time.

  C Tiara read her book at the swimming pool.

  D The girl in the story had a chore of sweeping the floor.

6 Why did Tiara read so many books?

 * J She learned to enjoy reading.

  K She wanted to take swimming lessons.

  L Her mother chose ten books.

  M Her mother promised her a gift.

7 What will Tiara probably do at the tree house?

  A Meet a friend

  B Build a fort

  C Think about other hobbies

 * D Read her book

8 Why did Tiara feel proud?

  J She did better in school than anyone expected.

  K Her mother gave her a hug.

 * L She had read more books than she thought possible.

  M She had learned to swim.

9 The first book Tiara read was about

  A a girl who surprised herself by learning to read.

 * B a girl who moved with her family to the frontier.

  C an interesting summer.

  D a mother and her daughter.

GO

123

Say It's time to stop. You have completed Test 2. Check to see that you have completely filled in your answer circles with dark marks. Make sure that any marks for answers that you changed have been completely erased. Now you may close your books.

Review the items with the students. Have them indicate completion of the lesson by entering their score for this activity on the progress chart at the beginning of the book. Then collect the students' books and answer sheets if this is the end of the testing session.

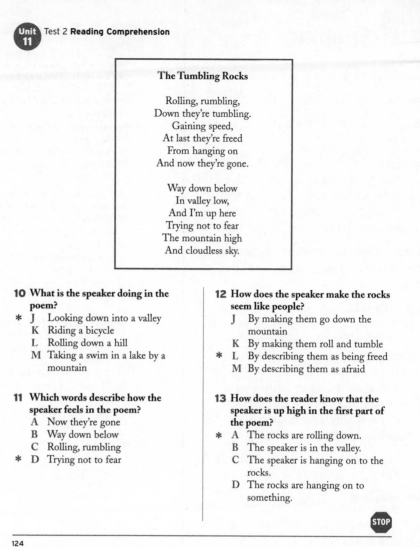

The Tumbling Rocks

Rolling, rumbling,
Down they're tumbling.
Gaining speed,
At last they're freed
From hanging on
And now they're gone.

Way down below
In valley low,
And I'm up here
Trying not to fear
The mountain high
And cloudless sky.

10 What is the speaker doing in the poem?

* **J** Looking down into a valley
  K Riding a bicycle
  L Rolling down a hill
  M Taking a swim in a lake by a mountain

11 Which words describe how the speaker feels in the poem?

  A Now they're gone
  B Way down below
  C Rolling, rumbling
* **D** Trying not to fear

12 How does the speaker make the rocks seem like people?

  J By making them go down the mountain
  K By making them roll and tumble
* **L** By describing them as being freed
  M By describing them as afraid

13 How does the reader know that the speaker is up high in the first part of the poem?

* **A** The rocks are rolling down.
  B The speaker is in the valley.
  C The speaker is hanging on to the rocks.
  D The rocks are hanging on to something.

STOP

Administration Time: 15 minutes

Say Turn to Test 3 on page 125.

Check to see that the students have found page 125.

Say Look at your answer sheet. Find the part called Test 3, Spelling. All your answers for this test should be marked on your answer sheet, not in your book.

Check to see that the students have found the correct part of the answer sheet.

Say This test will check how well you can find misspelled words. Remember to make sure that the circles for your answer choices are completely filled in. Press your pencil firmly so that your marks come out dark. Completely erase any marks for answers that you change.

Look at the words for Sample A. Find the word that has a spelling mistake. If none of the words has a mistake, choose the last answer, No mistakes. Mark the circle for your answer.

Allow time for the students to mark their answers.

Say Answer circle B, *m-i-n-i-t*, should have been marked because it is a misspelling of *m-i-n-u-t-e*. If you chose another answer, erase yours and fill in answer circle B now.

Check to see that the students have filled in the correct answer circle.

Say Look at Sample B. Find the word that has a spelling mistake. If none of the words has a mistake, choose the last answer, No mistakes. Mark the circle for your answer.

Allow time for the students to mark their answers.

Say Answer circle N should have been marked because all the words are spelled correctly. If you chose another answer, erase yours and fill in answer circle N now.

Check to see that the students have filled in the correct answer circle.

 Test Practice

Unit 11
Test 3 **Spelling**

Directions: Fill in the space for any word that has a spelling mistake. If there is no mistake, fill in the last answer space.

Sample A		Sample B	
A	order	J	across
*B	minit	K	thin
C	heavy	L	flies
D	dust	M	narrow
E	(No mistakes)	* N	(No mistakes)

1	A	either
	B	whisper
	C	hungry
*	D	shor
	E	(No mistakes)

2	J	front
*	K	graf
	L	decided
	M	weather
	N	(No mistakes)

3*	A	scheet
	B	cold
	C	dull
	D	stool
	E	(No mistakes)

4	J	unsure
	K	steam
*	L	beping
	M	nickel
	N	(No mistakes)

5	A	ocean
	B	kindness
	C	guess
	D	monkey
*	E	(No mistakes)

6*	J	partie
	K	cheek
	L	whether
	M	suppose
	N	(No mistakes)

7	A	thirsty
	B	comfort
	C	spider
*	D	leter
	E	(No mistakes)

8	J	seemed
*	K	koach
	L	pencil
	M	terrible
	N	(No mistakes)

STOP

125

Say Now you will do more spelling items. Look for a word that has a spelling mistake. If none of the words has a mistake, choose the last answer. Work by yourself. Work until you come to the STOP sign at the bottom of the page. When you have finished, you can check over your answers to this test. Then wait for the rest of the group to finish. Any questions?

Answer any questions that the students have.

Say Start working now. You will have 10 minutes.

Allow 10 minutes.

Say It's time to stop. You have completed Test 3. Check to see that you have completely filled in your answer circles with dark marks. Make sure that any marks for answers that you changed have been completely erased. Now you may close your books.

Review the items with the students. Have them indicate completion of the lesson by entering their score for this activity on the progress chart at the beginning of the book. Then collect the students' books and answer sheets if this is the end of the testing session.

Unit 11
Test Practice
Test 3 **Spelling**

Directions: Fill in the space for any word that has a spelling mistake. If there is no mistake, fill in the last answer space.

Sample A			Sample B		
	A	order		J	across
*	B	minit		K	thin
	C	heavy		L	flies
	D	dust		M	narrow
	E	(No mistakes)	*	N	(No mistakes)

1	A	either	5	A	ocean
	B	whisper		B	kindness
	C	hungry		C	guess
* D		shor		D	monkey
	E	(No mistakes)	* E		(No mistakes)

2	J	front	6 * J		partie
* K		graf		K	cheek
	L	decided		L	whether
	M	weather		M	suppose
	N	(No mistakes)		N	(No mistakes)

3 * A		scheet	7	A	thirsty
	B	cold		B	comfort
	C	dull		C	spider
	D	stool	* D		leter
	E	(No mistakes)		E	(No mistakes)

4	J	unsure	8	J	seemed
	K	steam	* K		koach
* L		beping		L	pencil
	M	nickel		M	terrible
	N	(No mistakes)		N	(No mistakes)

STOP

125

Test 4
Capitalization

Administration Time: 15 minutes

Say Turn to Test 4 on page 127.

Check to see that the students have found page 127.

Say Look at your answer sheet. Find the part called Test 4, Capitalization. All your answers for this test should be marked on your answer sheet, not in your book.

Check to see that the students have found the correct part of the answer sheet.

Say This test will check how well you can find capitalization mistakes. Remember to make sure that the circles for your answer choices are completely filled in. Press your pencil firmly so that your marks come out dark. Completely erase any marks for answers that you change.

Look at Sample A. Read the answer choices. Find the answer that has a capitalization mistake. If there is no mistake, choose the last answer. Mark the circle for your answer on the answer sheet.

Allow time for the students to mark their answers.

Say Answer circle D should have been marked because none of the answer choices has a mistake. If you chose another answer, erase yours and fill in answer circle D now.

Check to see that the students have filled in the correct answer circle.

Say Look at Sample B. Find the answer that has a capitalization mistake. If there is no mistake, choose the last answer. Mark the circle for your answer.

Allow time for the students to mark their answers.

Say Answer circle K should have been marked because the *m* in *Mr.* should have been capitalized. If you chose another answer, erase yours and fill in answer circle K now.

Test Practice
Test 4 Capitalization

Directions: Fill in the space for the answer that has a mistake in capitalization. Fill in the last answer space if there is no mistake.

Sample A
  A A small rabbit
  B has been eating the
  C plants in our garden.
 * D (No mistakes)

Sample B
 * K My teacher's name is mr. Fazio. He was a football
  L player when he went to college.
  M (No mistakes)

1 A "Sara, what are your plans
    B for your vacation time in
 * C december? I'm going skiing."
    D (No mistakes)

2 * J We went to the beach saturday.
    K Mina's mom and dad helped us
    L build a gigantic sandcastle.
    M (No mistakes)

3 A When my neighbor Tom
 * B had a broken leg, i helped
    C him with his yard work.
    D (No mistakes)

4 * J In the summer, mr. Fiori, the
    K music teacher, goes on a
    L trip. He enjoys his time off.
    M (No mistakes)

5 A America honors its soldiers
 * B on memorial day. It became
    C a holiday by law in 1971.
    D (No mistakes)

6 J Frank and his dad help at
    K the farm on Sunday afternoons.
    L Then they go for a bike ride.
 * M (No mistakes)

7 * A In july we pick sour cherries
    B with Aunt Beth. Then we make
    C jars of homemade jam.
    D (No mistakes)

8 J In our nation's capital,
 * K washington, D.C., there is a
    L statue of Abraham Lincoln.
    M (No mistakes)

STOP

127

Check to see that the students have filled in the correct answer circle.

Say Now you will do more items. Look for an answer that has a capitalization mistake. If none of the answers has a mistake, choose the last answer. Work by yourself until you come to the STOP sign at the bottom of the page. When you have finished, you can check over your answers to this test. Then wait for the rest of the group to finish. Any questions?

Answer any questions that the students have.

Say Start working now. You will have 10 minutes.

Allow 10 minutes.

Say It's time to stop. You have completed Test 4. Check to see that you have completely filled in your answer circles with dark marks. Make sure that any marks for answers that you changed have been completely erased. Now you may close your books.

Review the items with the students. Have them indicate completion of the lesson by entering their score for this activity on the progress chart at the beginning of the book. Then collect the students' books and answer sheets if this is the end of the testing session.

Unit 11

Test Practice
Test 4 **Capitalization**

Directions: Fill in the space for the answer that has a mistake in capitalization. Fill in the last answer space if there is no mistake.

Sample A
A A small rabbit
B has been eating the
C plants in our garden.
* D (No mistakes)

Sample B
J My teacher's name is
* K mr. Fazio. He was a football
L player when he went to
   college.
M (No mistakes)

1
A "Sara, what are your plans
B for your vacation time in
* C december? I'm going skiing."
D (No mistakes)

2
* J We went to the beach saturday.
K Mina's mom and dad helped us
L build a gigantic sandcastle.
M (No mistakes)

3
A When my neighbor Tom
* B had a broken leg, i helped
C him with his yard work.
D (No mistakes)

4
* J In the summer, mr. Fiori, the
K music teacher, goes on a
L trip. He enjoys his time off.
M (No mistakes)

5
A America honors its soldiers
* B on memorial day. It became
C a holiday by law in 1971.
D (No mistakes)

6
J Frank and his dad help at
K the farm on Sunday afternoons.
L Then they go for a bike ride.
* M (No mistakes)

7
* A In july we pick sour cherries
B with Aunt Beth. Then we make
C jars of homemade jam.
D (No mistakes)

8
J In our nation's capital,
* K washington, D.C., there is a
L statue of Abraham Lincoln.
M (No mistakes)

STOP

127

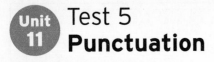

Test 5
Punctuation

Administration Time: 15 minutes

Say Turn to Test 5 on page 128.

Check to see that the students have found page 128.

Say Look at your answer sheet. Find the part called Test 5, Punctuation. All your answers for this test should be marked on your answer sheet, not in your book.

Check to see that the students have found the correct part of the answer sheet.

Say This test will check how well you can find punctuation mistakes. Remember to make sure that the circles for your answer choices are completely filled in. Press your pencil firmly so that your marks come out dark. Completely erase any marks for answers that you change.

Look at Sample A. Read the answer choices. Find the answer that has a punctuation mistake. If there is no mistake, choose the last answer. Mark the circle for your answer on the answer sheet.

Allow time for the students to mark their answers.

Say Answer circle C should have been marked because there should be a period after *dishes*. If you chose another answer, erase yours and fill in answer circle C now.

Check to see that the students have filled in the correct answer circle.

Say Look at Sample B. Find the answer that has a punctuation mistake. If there is no mistake, choose the last answer. Mark the circle for your answer.

Allow time for the students to mark their answers.

Say Answer circle J should have been marked. A colon should be included in the time 9:15. If you chose another answer, erase yours and fill in answer circle J now.

Test Practice
Test 5 **Punctuation**

Directions: Fill in the space for the answer that has a mistake in punctuation. Fill in the last answer space if there is no mistake.

Sample A
- A After we ate, Lucy
- B and I helped my father
- *C wash and dry the dishes
- D (No mistakes)

Sample B
- *J It is almost 915.
- K I hope that Bernie and
- L Carolyn get here soon.
- M (No mistakes)

1
- A The roof leaked.
- B Now Betty needed
- C to get it repaired.
- *D (No mistakes)

2
- J The weather reporter said the
- K skies would be clear. Who could
- L have guessed it would rain?
- *M (No mistakes)

3
- *A It was June 14 1998. Marcus
- B Franklin was about to find
- C out if his rocket would fly.
- D (No mistakes)

4
- J Did you try the ice cream
- *K made with green tea It
- L was strange but tasty.
- M (No mistakes)

5
- A A balloon festival was being
- *B held nearby. I wanted my sister?
- C to take me and my brother to it.
- D (No mistakes)

6
- J Our new puppy went through
- K every room in the house, sniffing
- *L everywhere for the cat
- M (No mistakes)

7
- A My best friend is moving.
- *B Shes leaving with her family
- C at the end of the summer.
- D (No mistakes)

8
- J Pia takes ballet lessons, but
- K she wants to quit. She'd rather
- *L study piano with Mrs Roycko.
- M (No mistakes)

STOP

128

Check to see that the students have filled in the correct answer circle.

Say Now you will do more items. Look for an answer that has a punctuation mistake. If none of the answers has a mistake, choose the last answer. Work by yourself until you come to the STOP sign at the bottom of the page. When you have finished, you can check over your answers to this test. Then wait for the rest of the group to finish. Any questions?

Answer any questions that the students have.

Say Start working now. You will have 10 minutes.

Allow 10 minutes.

Say It's time to stop. You have completed Test 5. Check to see that you have completely filled in your answer circles with dark marks. Make sure that any marks for answers that you changed have been completely erased. Now you may close your books.

Review the items with the students. Have them indicate completion of the lesson by entering their score for this activity on the progress chart at the beginning of the book. Then collect the students' books and answer sheets if this is the end of the testing session.

Unit 11 Test Practice

Test 5 **Punctuation**

Directions: Fill in the space for the answer that has a mistake in punctuation. Fill in the last answer space if there is no mistake.

Sample A
A After we ate, Lucy
B and I helped my father
* C wash and dry the dishes
D (No mistakes)

Sample B
*J It is almost 915.
K I hope that Bernie and
L Carolyn get here soon.
M (No mistakes)

1 A The roof leaked.
   B Now Betty needed
   C to get it repaired.
* D (No mistakes)

2 J The weather reporter said the
   K skies would be clear. Who could
   L have guessed it would rain?
* M (No mistakes)

3 *A It was June 14 1998. Marcus
   B Franklin was about to find
   C out if his rocket would fly.
   D (No mistakes)

4 J Did you try the ice cream
* K made with green tea It
   L was strange but tasty.
   M (No mistakes)

5 A A balloon festival was being
* B held nearby. I wanted my sister?
   C to take me and my brother to it.
   D (No mistakes)

6 J Our new puppy went through
   K every room in the house, sniffing
* L everywhere for the cat
   M (No mistakes)

7 A My best friend is moving.
* B Shes leaving with her family
   C at the end of the summer.
   D (No mistakes)

8 J Pia takes ballet lessons, but
   K she wants to quit. She'd rather
* L study piano with Mrs Roycko.
   M (No mistakes)

STOP

128

Administration Time: 20 minutes

Say Turn to Test 6, Part 1 on page 129.

Check to see that the students have found page 129.

Say Look at your answer sheet. Find the part called Test 6, Part 1, Usage. All your answers for this test should be marked on your answer sheet, not in your book.

Check to see that the students have found the correct part of the answer sheet.

Say This test will check how well you can find mistakes in English usage. Remember to make sure that the circles for your answer choices are completely filled in. Press your pencil firmly so that your marks come out dark. Completely erase any marks for answers that you change.

Look at Sample A. Read the answer choices. Find the answer that has a mistake in usage. If there is no mistake, choose the last answer. Mark the circle for your answer on the answer sheet.

Allow time for the students to mark their answers.

Say Answer circle C should have been marked because the word *her* should be *she*. If you chose another answer, erase yours and fill in answer circle C now.

Check to see that the students have filled in the correct answer circle.

Say Look at Sample B. Find the answer that has a usage mistake. If there is no mistake, choose the last answer. Mark the circle for your answer.

Allow time for the students to mark their answers.

Say You should have marked answer circle M because none of the answers has a mistake in English usage. If you chose another answer, erase yours and fill in answer circle M now.

Unit
11

Test Practice
Test 6 Part 1 **Usage**

Directions: Fill in the space for the answer that has a mistake in usage. Fill in the last answer space if there is no mistake.

Sample A	A	Do you know
	B	where my sister is?
*	C	Her isn't at home?
	D	(No mistakes)

Sample B	J	The cook put the
	K	potatoes in the oven. They
	L	will have to cook for an hour.
*	M	(No mistakes)

1 A Yolanda served strawberries
 * B for dessert. Her bought them
   C at the market on Lyle Street.
   D (No mistakes)

2 *J The leafs of the trees fell
   K early this year. It was because
   L of the dry weather we had.
   M (No mistakes)

3 A Alexander Murai is my
 * B most oldest friend. I've
   C known him for years.
   D (No mistakes)

4 J When we go on a long hike,
 * K Frieda and I makes sack
   L lunches to take with us.
   M (No mistakes)

5 A It snowed much harder than
   B we thought it would. We decided
   C to cancel our trip to Denver.
 * D (No mistakes)

6 *J Dad built my sister
   K and me a tree house in the
   L oak tree behind the garage.
   M (No mistakes)

7 *A I and Melissa slept late on
   B Saturday morning. We were tired
   C after talking most of the night.
   D (No mistakes)

8 J I have always liked drawing
   K things. One day, I hope to
   L go to art school.
 * M (No mistakes)

STOP

129

Check to see that the students have filled in the correct answer circle.

Say Now you will do more items. Look for an answer that has a mistake in usage. If none of the answers has a mistake, choose the last answer. Work until you come to the STOP sign at the bottom of the page. When you have finished, you can check over your answers to this test. Then wait for the rest of the group to finish. Do you have any questions?

Answer any questions that the students have.

Say Start working now. You will have 15 minutes.

Allow 15 minutes.

Say It's time to stop. You have completed Test 6, Part 1. Check to see that you have completely filled in your answer circles with dark marks. Make sure that any marks for answers that you changed have been completely erased. Now you may close your books.

Review the items with the students. Have them indicate completion of the lesson by entering their score for this activity on the progress chart at the beginning of the book. Then collect the students' books and answer sheets if this is the end of the testing session.

Test Practice

Test 6 Part 1 **Usage**

Directions: Fill in the space for the answer that has a mistake in usage. Fill in the last answer space if there is no mistake.

Sample A			Sample B		
	A	Do you know		J	The cook put the
	B	where my sister is?		K	potatoes in the oven. They
*	C	Her isn't at home?		L	will have to cook for an hour.
	D	(No mistakes)	*	M	(No mistakes)

1   A   Yolanda served strawberries
 * B   for dessert. Her bought them
   C   at the market on Lyle Street.
   D   (No mistakes)

2 *J   The leafs of the trees fell
   K   early this year. It was because
   L   of the dry weather we had.
   M   (No mistakes)

3   A   Alexander Murai is my
 * B   most oldest friend. I've
   C   known him for years.
   D   (No mistakes)

4   J   When we go on a long hike,
 * K   Frieda and I makes sack
   L   lunches to take with us.
   M   (No mistakes)

5   A   It snowed much harder than
   B   we thought it would. We decided
   C   to cancel our trip to Denver.
 * D   (No mistakes)

6 *J   Dad built my sister
   K   and me a tree house in the
   L   oak tree behind the garage.
   M   (No mistakes)

7 *A   I and Melissa slept late on
   B   Saturday morning. We were tired
   C   after talking most of the night.
   D   (No mistakes)

8   J   I have always liked drawing
   K   things. One day, I hope to
   L   go to art school.
 * M   (No mistakes)

STOP

129

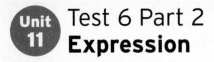
Administration Time: 15 minutes

Say Turn to Test 6, Part 2 on page 130.

Check to see that the students have found page 130.

Say Look at your answer sheet. Find the part called Test 6, Part 2, Expression. All your answers for this test should be marked on your answer sheet, not in your book.

Check to see that the students have found the correct part of the answer sheet.

Say This test will check how well you can find mistakes in English expression. There are different kinds of items in this test, so be sure to read each set of directions carefully.

Look at Sample A. Read the sentence with the underlined part and the answer choices. Find the answer that fits best in the sentence. If the underlined part is correct, choose the last answer. Mark the circle for your answer on the answer sheet.

Allow time for the students to mark their answers.

Say Answer circle A should have been marked because the word *collects* fits best in the sentence. If you chose another answer, erase yours and fill in answer circle A now.

Check to see that the students have filled in the correct answer circle.

Say Now you will do more items. Read the directions for each section before choosing an answer. Remember to make sure that the circles for your answer choices are completely filled in. Press your pencil firmly so that your marks come out dark. Completely erase any marks for answers that you change. Work until you come to the STOP sign at the bottom of the page. When you have finished, you can

check over your answers to this test. Then wait for the rest of the group to finish. Do you have any questions?

Answer any questions that the students have.

Say Start working now. You will have 10 minutes.

Allow 10 minutes.

Test Practice
Unit 11 · Test 6 Part 2 **Expression**

Directions: Choose the best answer.

> **Sample** Vera **collected** postcards from all the cities she visits.
> **A** * A collects   B had collected   C collecting   D (No change)

Directions: For questions 9 and 10, choose the best way to write the underlined part of the sentence.

9 Neither Geri **and** I have been to the Atlantic shore.
   A yet   B but   * C nor   D (No change)

10 Our class **to visit** the science museum next month.
   J visiting   K visited   * L will visit   M (No change)

Directions: For questions 11 and 12, choose the best way of writing the idea.

11 A Vegetables can be stored in refrigerators or in freezers. Fruit, too.
   B Vegetables and fruit can be stored they're put in refrigerators and freezers.
   C Either in a refrigerator or in a freezer, vegetables and fruit being stored.
   * D Vegetables and fruit can be stored in a refrigerator or in a freezer.

12 *J I build model airplanes.
   K I build and put together model airplanes.
   L I build airplanes that I put together.
   M I build put together airplanes.

STOP

130

Say It's time to stop. You have completed Test 6, Part 2. Check to see that you have completely filled in your answer circles with dark marks. Make sure that any marks for answers that you changed have been completely erased. Now you may close your books.

Review the items with the students. Have them indicate completion of the lesson by entering their score for this activity on the progress chart at the beginning of the book. Then collect the students' books and answer sheets if this is the end of the testing session.

Test Practice

Test 6 Part 2 **Expression**

Directions: Choose the best answer.

Sample Vera **collected** postcards from all the cities she visits.

A * A collects   B had collected   C collecting   D (No change)

Directions: For questions 9 and 10, choose the best way to write the underlined part of the sentence.

9 Neither Geri **and** I have been to the Atlantic shore.
A yet   B but   * C nor   D (No change)

10 Our class **to visit** the science museum next month.
J visiting   K visited   * L will visit   M (No change)

Directions: For questions 11 and 12, choose the best way of writing the idea.

11 A Vegetables can be stored in refrigerators or in freezers. Fruit, too.
B Vegetables and fruit can be stored they're put in refrigerators and freezers.
C Either in a refrigerator or in a freezer, vegetables and fruit being stored.
* D Vegetables and fruit can be stored in a refrigerator or in a freezer.

12 *J I build model airplanes.
K I build and put together model airplanes.
L I build airplanes that I put together.
M I build put together airplanes.

STOP

130

Administration Time: 25 minutes

Distribute scratch paper to the students.

Say Turn to Test 7, Part 1 on page 131.

Check to see that the students have found page 131.

Say Look at your answer sheet. Find the part called Test 7, Part 1, Math Concepts. If you need to, you may work on scratch paper, but be sure to mark all your answers for this test on your answer sheet.

Check to see that the students have found the correct part of the answer sheet.

Say This test will check how well you understand and solve mathematics problems. Remember to make sure that the circles for your answer choices are completely filled in. Press your pencil firmly so that your marks come out dark. Completely erase any marks for answers that you change.

Look at Sample A. Read the problem and the four answer choices. Then solve the problem. On your answer sheet, find the answer circles for Sample A. Mark the circle for the answer to the problem.

Allow time for the students to mark their answers.

Say Answer circle A should have been filled in. If you chose another answer, erase yours and fill in circle A now.

Check to see that the students have filled in the correct answer circle.

Say Now do Sample B. Solve the problem and mark the circle for the answer you find.

Allow time for the students to mark their answers.

Say Answer circle M should have been filled in because it contains only even numbers. If you chose another answer, erase yours and fill in circle M now.

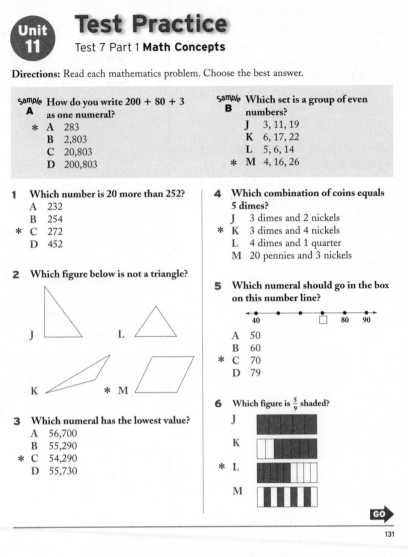

Check to see that the students have filled in the correct answer circle.

Say Now you will solve more mathematics problems. Work by yourself. Remember that you may use scratch paper to solve the problems. When you come to the GO sign at the bottom of a page, turn to the next page and continue working. Work until you come to the STOP sign at the bottom of page 133. When you have finished, you can check over your answers to this test. Then wait for the rest of the group to finish. Any questions?

Answer any questions that the students have.

Say Start working now. You will have 20 minutes.

Allow 20 minutes.

Unit 11 Test 7 Part 1 **Math Concepts**

7 **Which operation sign should be placed in the box to get the smallest answer?**

20 □ 4 =

A +
B −
C ×
* D ÷

8 **Which of these shows what the paper at the right would look like when it is unfolded?**

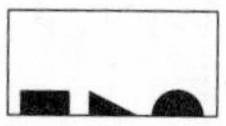

J * L

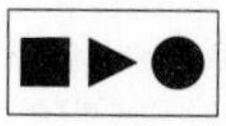

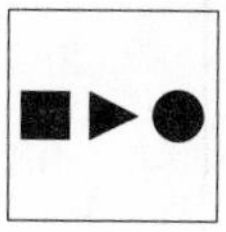

K M

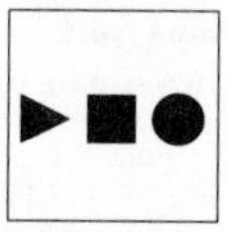

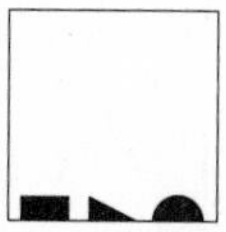

9 **How can 2000 + 400 + 8 be written as one numeral?**

A 248
B 2,048
* C 2,408
D 2,480

10 **Which clock shows 8 minutes before 10 o'clock?**

J

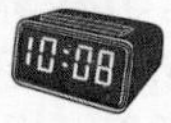

L

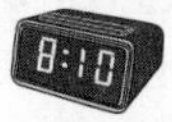

* K

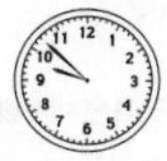

M

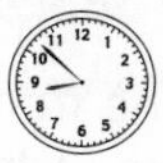

11 **What is the missing factor in the number sentence below?**

32 ÷ □ = 8

* A 4
B 34
C 50
D 336

12 **The length of a regular toothbrush is between**

J 2 and 3 inches.
* K 6 and 8 inches.
L 2 and 3 feet.
M 5 and 7 feet.

GO

132

Say It's time to stop. You have completed Test 7, Part 1. Check to see that you have completely filled in your answer circles with dark marks. Make sure that any marks for answers that you changed have been completely erased. Now you may close your books.

Review the items with the students. Have them indicate completion of the lesson by entering their score for this activity on the progress chart at the beginning of the book. Then collect the students' books and answer sheets if this is the end of the testing session.

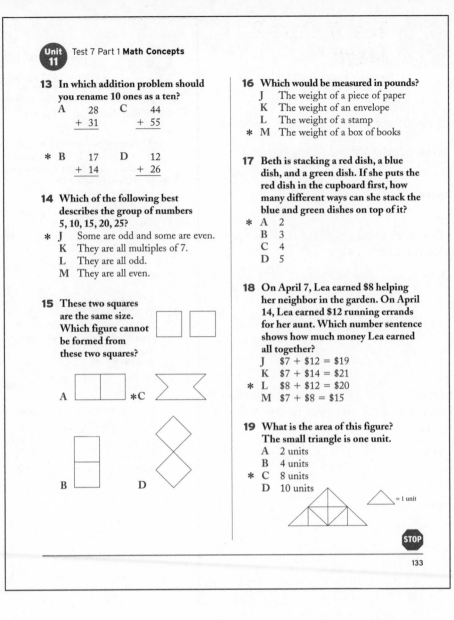

13 In which addition problem should you rename 10 ones as a ten?

A	28	C	44
	+ 31		+ 55
* B	17	D	12
	+ 14		+ 26

14 Which of the following best describes the group of numbers 5, 10, 15, 20, 25?

* J   Some are odd and some are even.
  K   They are all multiples of 7.
  L   They are all odd.
  M   They are all even.

15 These two squares are the same size. Which figure cannot be formed from these two squares?

A   *C

B   D

16 Which would be measured in pounds?

  J   The weight of a piece of paper
  K   The weight of an envelope
  L   The weight of a stamp
* M   The weight of a box of books

17 Beth is stacking a red dish, a blue dish, and a green dish. If she puts the red dish in the cupboard first, how many different ways can she stack the blue and green dishes on top of it?

* A   2
  B   3
  C   4
  D   5

18 On April 7, Lea earned $8 helping her neighbor in the garden. On April 14, Lea earned $12 running errands for her aunt. Which number sentence shows how much money Lea earned all together?

  J $7 + $12 = $19
  K $7 + $14 = $21
* L $8 + $12 = $20
  M $7 + $8 = $15

19 What is the area of this figure? The small triangle is one unit.

  A   2 units
  B   4 units
* C   8 units
  D   10 units   = 1 unit

STOP

133

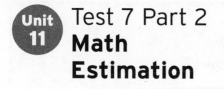
Administration Time: 15 minutes

Distribute scratch paper to the students.

Say Turn to Test 7, Part 2 on page 134.

Check to see that the students have found page 134.

Say Look at your answer sheet. Find the part called Test 7, Part 2, Math Estimation. If you need to, you may work on scratch paper, but be sure to mark all your answers for this test on your answer sheet.

Check to see that the students have found the correct part of the answer sheet.

Say This test will check how well you understand and solve estimation problems. Remember to make sure that the circles for your answer choices are completely filled in. Press your pencil firmly so that your marks come out dark. Completely erase any marks for answers that you change.

Look at Sample A. Read the problem and the four answer choices. Then solve the problem. On your answer sheet, find the answer circles for Sample A. Mark the circle for the answer to the problem.

Allow time for the students to mark their answers.

Say Answer circle B should have been filled in because it is the best estimate to the solution of 48 mittens minus 21 mittens. If you chose another answer, erase yours and fill in circle B now.

Check to see that the students have filled in the correct answer circle.

Say Now do Sample B. Solve the problem and mark the circle for the answer you think is best.

Allow time for the students to mark their answers.

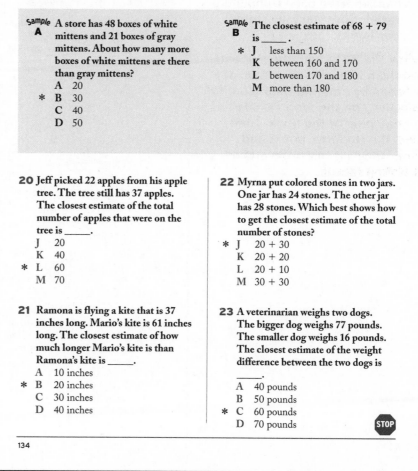

Test Practice

Test 7 Part 2 **Math Estimation**

Directions: Choose the best answer.

Sample A A store has 48 boxes of white mittens and 21 boxes of gray mittens. About how many more boxes of white mittens are there than gray mittens?
  A 20
* B 30
  C 40
  D 50

Sample B The closest estimate of 68 + 79 is _____ .
* J less than 150
  K between 160 and 170
  L between 170 and 180
  M more than 180

20 Jeff picked 22 apples from his apple tree. The tree still has 37 apples. The closest estimate of the total number of apples that were on the tree is _____ .
  J 20
  K 40
* L 60
  M 70

21 Ramona is flying a kite that is 37 inches long. Mario's kite is 61 inches long. The closest estimate of how much longer Mario's kite is than Ramona's kite is _____ .
  A 10 inches
* B 20 inches
  C 30 inches
  D 40 inches

22 Myrna put colored stones in two jars. One jar has 24 stones. The other jar has 28 stones. Which best shows how to get the closest estimate of the total number of stones?
* J 20 + 30
  K 20 + 20
  L 20 + 10
  M 30 + 30

23 A veterinarian weighs two dogs. The bigger dog weighs 77 pounds. The smaller dog weighs 16 pounds. The closest estimate of the weight difference between the two dogs is _____ .
  A 40 pounds
  B 50 pounds
* C 60 pounds
  D 70 pounds

134

Say Answer circle J should have been filled in because the solution to the problem is less than 150. If you chose another answer, erase yours and fill in circle J now.

Check to see that the students have filled in the correct answer circle.

Say Now you will solve more mathematics problems. Work by yourself. Remember that you may use scratch paper to solve the problems. Work until you come to the STOP sign at the bottom of the page. When you have finished, you can check over your answers to this test. Then wait for the rest of the group to finish. Any questions?

Answer any questions that the students have.

Say Start working now. You will have 10 minutes.

Allow 10 minutes.

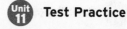

Say It's time to stop. You have completed Test 7, Part 2. Check to see that you have completely filled in your answer circles with dark marks. Make sure that any marks for answers that you changed have been completely erased. Now you may close your books.

Review the items with the students. Have them indicate completion of the lesson by entering their score for this activity on the progress chart at the beginning of the book. Then collect the students' books and answer sheets if this is the end of the testing session.

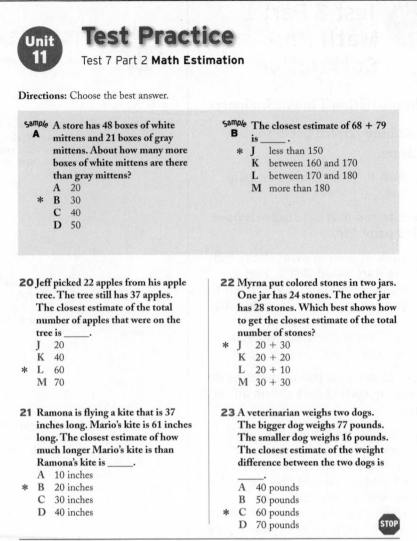

Unit 11

Test Practice
Test 7 Part 2 **Math Estimation**

Directions: Choose the best answer.

Sample A A store has 48 boxes of white mittens and 21 boxes of gray mittens. About how many more boxes of white mittens are there than gray mittens?
- A 20
- * B 30
- C 40
- D 50

Sample B The closest estimate of 68 + 79 is _____ .
- * J less than 150
- K between 160 and 170
- L between 170 and 180
- M more than 180

20 Jeff picked 22 apples from his apple tree. The tree still has 37 apples. The closest estimate of the total number of apples that were on the tree is _____ .
- J 20
- K 40
- * L 60
- M 70

21 Ramona is flying a kite that is 37 inches long. Mario's kite is 61 inches long. The closest estimate of how much longer Mario's kite is than Ramona's kite is _____ .
- A 10 inches
- * B 20 inches
- C 30 inches
- D 40 inches

22 Myrna put colored stones in two jars. One jar has 24 stones. The other jar has 28 stones. Which best shows how to get the closest estimate of the total number of stones?
- * J 20 + 30
- K 20 + 20
- L 20 + 10
- M 30 + 30

23 A veterinarian weighs two dogs. The bigger dog weighs 77 pounds. The smaller dog weighs 16 pounds. The closest estimate of the weight difference between the two dogs is _____ .
- A 40 pounds
- B 50 pounds
- * C 60 pounds
- D 70 pounds

STOP

134

Test 8 Part 1 Math Problem Solving

Administration Time: 15 minutes

Distribute scratch paper to the students.

Say Turn to Test 8, Part 1 on page 135.

Check to see that the students have found page 135.

Say Look at your answer sheet. Find the part called Test 8, Part 1, Math Problem Solving. If you need to, you may work on scratch paper, but be sure to mark all your answers for this test on your answer sheet.

Check to see that the students have found the correct part of the answer sheet.

Say This test will check how well you understand and solve word problems. Remember to make sure that the circles for your answer choices are completely filled in. Press your pencil firmly so that your marks come out dark. Completely erase any marks for answers that you change.

Look at Sample A. Read the problem and the four answer choices. Then solve the problem. On your answer sheet, find the answer circles for Sample A. Mark the circle for the answer to the problem.

Allow time for the students to mark their answers.

Say Answer circle A should have been filled in because the correct answer to the problem is 4. If you chose another answer, erase yours and fill in circle A now.

Check to see that the students have filled in the correct answer circle.

Say Now do Sample B. Read the problem and the four answer choices. Then solve the problem. Mark the circle for the answer to the problem. If the correct answer is not given, choose answer M, Not given.

Test Practice

Test 8 Part 1 **Math Problem Solving**

Directions: Read each mathematics problem. Choose the best answer.

Sample A Hattie is helping her father tile the kitchen. She carried 24 tiles from the garage to the kitchen. It took her 6 trips. How many tiles did she carry on each trip?
* **A** 4
B 5
C 18
D 30

Sample B A bird built a nest 15 feet up in a tree. The top of the tree is 25 feet from the ground. How far from the top of the tree is the bird's nest?
J 9 feet
K 20 feet
L 40 feet
* **M** Not given

1 Jamie and Matthew were playing marbles. Jamie knocked out 33 marbles, and Matthew knocked out 41 marbles. How many more marbles did Matthew knock out than Jamie?
* **A** 8
B 12
C 74
D Not given

2 Jamie and Matthew shot their marbles to see how far they could go. Matthew shot his marble 70 inches. Jamie shot her marble 7 inches farther than Matthew did. How can they find out how far Jamie shot her marble?
J Multiply 70 by 7
K Divide 70 by 7
* **L** Add 7 and 70
M Subtract 7 from 70

3 Matthew has 30 green marbles. Jamie has half as many green marbles as Matthew has. How many green marbles does Jamie have?
* **A** 15
B 20
C 45
D 60

4 Jamie's mother told them that they could score 5 points for each white marble they knocked out. How many white marbles did Jamie knock out if she scored 25 points?
* **J** 5
K 20
L 30
M 125

STOP

135

Allow time for the students to mark their answers.

Say Answer circle M should have been filled in because the correct answer, 10 feet, is not given. If you chose another answer, erase yours and fill in circle M now.

Say Now you will solve more mathematics problems. Remember that you may use scratch paper to solve the problems. Work until you come to the STOP sign at the bottom of the page. When you have finished, you can check over your answers to this test. Then wait for the rest of the group to finish. Any questions?

Answer any questions that the students have.

Say Start working now. You will have 10 minutes.

Allow 10 minutes.

Say It's time to stop. You have completed Test 8, Part 1. Check to see that you have completely filled in your answer circles with dark marks. Make sure that any marks for answers that you changed have been completely erased. Now you may close your books.

Review the items with the students. Have them indicate completion of the lesson by entering their score for this activity on the progress chart at the beginning of the book. Then collect the students' books and answer sheets if this is the end of the testing session.

Test Practice

Test 8 Part 1 **Math Problem Solving**

Directions: Read each mathematics problem. Choose the best answer.

Sample A Hattie is helping her father tile the kitchen. She carried 24 tiles from the garage to the kitchen. It took her 6 trips. How many tiles did she carry on each trip?

  * **A** 4
     B 5
     C 18
     D 30

Sample B A bird built a nest 15 feet up in a tree. The top of the tree is 25 feet from the ground. How far from the top of the tree is the bird's nest?

     J 9 feet
     K 20 feet
     L 40 feet
  * **M** Not given

---

1 Jamie and Matthew were playing marbles. Jamie knocked out 33 marbles, and Matthew knocked out 41 marbles. How many more marbles did Matthew knock out than Jamie?

  * **A** 8
     B 12
     C 74
     D Not given

2 Jamie and Matthew shot their marbles to see how far they could go. Matthew shot his marble 70 inches. Jamie shot her marble 7 inches farther than Matthew did. How can they find out how far Jamie shot her marble?

     J Multiply 70 by 7
     K Divide 70 by 7
  * **L** Add 7 and 70
     M Subtract 7 from 70

3 Matthew has 30 green marbles. Jamie has half as many green marbles as Matthew has. How many green marbles does Jamie have?

  * **A** 15
     B 20
     C 45
     D 60

4 Jamie's mother told them that they could score 5 points for each white marble they knocked out. How many white marbles did Jamie knock out if she scored 25 points?

  * **J** 5
     K 20
     L 30
     M 125

STOP

135

Test 8 Part 2
Data Interpretation

Administration Time: 15 minutes

Distribute scratch paper to the students.

Say Turn to Test 8, Part 2 on page 136.

Check to see that the students have found page 136.

Say Look at your answer sheet. Find the part called Test 8, Part 2, Data Interpretation. If you need to, you may work on scratch paper, but be sure to mark all your answers for this test on your answer sheet.

Check to see that the students have found the correct part of the answer sheet.

Say This test will check how well you understand a graph. Remember to make sure that the circles for your answer choices are completely filled in. Press your pencil firmly so that your marks come out dark. Completely erase any marks for answers that you change.

Find Sample A. Look at the table and the sentences below the samples. Read the problem for Sample A and the four answer choices. Then solve the problem. On your answer sheet, find the answer circles for Sample A. Mark the circle for the answer to the problem.

Allow time for the students to mark their answers.

Say Answer circle A should have been filled in. If you chose another answer, erase yours and fill in circle A now.

Check to see that the students have filled in the correct answer circle.

Say Now do Sample B. Use the table to find the answer. Mark the circle for the answer to the problem.

Allow time for the students to mark their answers.

Test Practice

Unit 11

Test 8 Part 2 **Data Interpretation**

Directions: Use the information in the table to answer the questions.

Sample A In the afternoon Jane picked 9 more pounds of peaches. At the end of the day, how many pounds of peaches had Jane picked?
* A   28
  B   29
  C   38
  D   48

Sample B In the morning, the girls picked the most pounds of which fruit?
* J   Peaches
  K   Cherries
  L   Plums
  M   There is not enough information to tell.

Student	Cherries	Peaches	Plums
Jane	6	19	11
Kim	7	20	8
Saraliene	10	24	15

Jane, Kim, and Saraliene picked fruit at an orchard. The girls picked cherries, plums, and peaches. The table shows the number of pounds of fruit they picked in the morning.

5 How many pounds of cherries were picked?
* A   23
  B   33
  C   49
  D   Not given

6 How many more pounds of peaches than cherries did Kim pick?
* J   13
  K   15
  L   27
  M   Not given

7 Saraliene knew that last time she picked fruit, she picked twice as many pounds of plums as she did this trip. Which of the following could she use to help find the number of pounds of plums she picked last time?
  A   How many pounds of plums Kim picked today
  B   How many pounds of cherries and peaches she picked today
* C   The total pounds of plums she picked today
  D   The total pounds of plums picked by all three girls

STOP

136

Say Answer circle J should have been filled in. If you chose another answer, erase yours and fill in circle J now.

Check to see that the students have filled in the correct answer circle.

Say Now you will solve more mathematics problems. Remember that you may use scratch paper to solve the problems. Work until you come to the STOP sign at the bottom of the page. When you have finished, you can check over your answers to this test. Then wait for the rest of the group to finish. Any questions?

Answer any questions that the students have.

Say Start working now. You will have 10 minutes.

Allow 10 minutes.

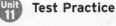

Say It's time to stop. You have completed Test 8, Part 2. Check to see that you have completely filled in your answer circles with dark marks. Make sure that any marks for answers that you changed have been completely erased. Now you may close your books.

Review the items with the students. Have them indicate completion of the lesson by entering their score for this activity on the progress chart at the beginning of the book. Then collect the students' books and answer sheets if this is the end of the testing session.

Test Practice

Test 8 Part 2 **Data Interpretation**

Directions: Use the information in the table to answer the questions.

^{Sample} **A** In the afternoon Jane picked 9 more pounds of peaches. At the end of the day, how many pounds of peaches had Jane picked?
* A 28
  B 29
  C 38
  D 48

^{Sample} **B** In the morning, the girls picked the most pounds of which fruit?
* J Peaches
  K Cherries
  L Plums
  M There is not enough information to tell.

Student	Cherries	Peaches	Plums
Jane	6	19	11
Kim	7	20	8
Saraliene	10	24	15

Jane, Kim, and Saraliene picked fruit at an orchard. The girls picked cherries, plums, and peaches. The table shows the number of pounds of fruit they picked in the morning.

5 How many pounds of cherries were picked?
* A 23
  B 33
  C 49
  D Not given

6 How many more pounds of peaches than cherries did Kim pick?
* J 13
  K 15
  L 27
  M Not given

7 Saraliene knew that last time she picked fruit, she picked twice as many pounds of plums as she did this trip. Which of the following could she use to help find the number of pounds of plums she picked last time?
  A How many pounds of plums Kim picked today
  B How many pounds of cherries and peaches she picked today
* C The total pounds of plums she picked today
  D The total pounds of plums picked by all three girls

STOP

136

170 **Unit 11** **Test Practice**

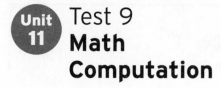

Administration Time: 15 minutes

Distribute scratch paper to the students.

Say Turn to Test 9 on page 137.

Check to see that the students have found page 137.

Say Look at your answer sheet. Find the part called Test 9, Math Computation. If you need to, you may work on scratch paper, but be sure to mark all your answers for this test on your answer sheet.

Check to see that the students have found the correct part of the answer sheet.

Say This test will check how well you can solve computation problems. Remember to make sure that the circles for your answer choices are completely filled in. Press your pencil firmly so that your marks come out dark. Completely erase any marks for answers that you change.

Look at Sample A. Read the problem and the four answer choices. Then solve the problem. On your answer sheet, find the answer circles for Sample A. Mark the circle for the answer to the problem. If the correct answer is not given, choose answer D.

Allow time for the students to mark their answers.

Say Answer circle B should have been filled in because the correct answer to the problem is 257. If you chose another answer, erase yours and fill in circle B now.

Check to see that the students have filled in the correct answer circle.

Say Now do Sample B. Solve the problem and mark the circle for the answer you think is best.

Allow time for the students to mark their answers.

Test Practice
Test 9 Math Computation

Directions: Solve each problem. Choose the answer you think is correct. If the correct answer is not given, fill in the space for the last answer, N.

Sample A	227 + 30 =		A	217		Sample B	36 + 28 =		J	13
		*	B	257					K	14
			C	250					L	54
			D	N				*	M	N

1	6 + 8 =		A	13		5	4 × 522 =		A	524
		*	B	14					B	4,022
			C	54					C	4,084
			D	N				*	D	N

2	17 − 9		J	9		6	564 + 18		J	572
			K	12				*	K	582
			L	26					L	682
		*	M	N					M	N

3	459 − 5 =		A	104		7	21 ÷ 3 =		A	6
			B	444					B	78
		*	C	454					C	24
			D	N				*	D	N

4	37 + 2	*	J	39		8	54 ÷ 9 =		J	5
			K	49				*	K	6
			L	59					L	7
			M	N					M	N

STOP

137

Say Answer circle M should have been filled in because the solution to the problem, 64, is not one of the choices. If you chose another answer, erase yours and fill in circle M now.

Check to see that the students have filled in the correct answer circle.

Say Now you will solve more computation problems. Remember that you may use scratch paper to solve the problems. Work until you come to the STOP sign at the bottom of the page. When you have finished, you can check over your answers to this test. Then wait for the rest of the group to finish. Any questions?

Answer any questions that the students have.

Say Start working now. You will have 10 minutes.

Allow 10 minutes.

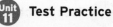

Say It's time to stop. You have completed Test 9. Check to see that you have completely filled in your answer circles with dark marks. Make sure that any marks for answers that you changed have been completely erased. Now you may close your books.

Review the items with the students. Have them indicate completion of the lesson by entering their score for this activity on the progress chart at the beginning of the book. Then collect the students' books and answer sheets if this is the end of the testing session.

Test Practice

Unit 11

Test 9 **Math Computation**

Directions: Solve each problem. Choose the answer you think is correct. If the correct answer is not given, fill in the space for the last answer, N.

Sample A $227 + 30 =$	A 217 * B 257 C 250 D N	**Sample B** $36 + 28 =$ J 13 K 14 L 54 * M N

1 $6 + 8 =$
    A 13
* B 14
    C 54
    D N

2   17
    − 9
    J 9
    K 12
    L 26
* M N

3 $459 − 5 =$
    A 104
    B 444
* C 454
    D N

4   37
   + 2
* J 39
    K 49
    L 59
    M N

5 $4 × 522 =$
    A 524
    B 4,022
    C 4,084
* D N

6   564
   + 18
    J 572
* K 582
    L 682
    M N

7 $21 ÷ 3 =$
    A 6
    B 78
    C 24
* D N

8 $54 ÷ 9 =$
    J 5
* K 6
    L 7
    M N

STOP

137

Test 10
Maps and Diagrams

Administration Time: 25 minutes

Say Turn to Test 10 on page 138.

Check to see that the students have found page 138.

Say Look at your answer sheet. Find the part called Test 10, Maps and Diagrams. Mark all your answers for this test on your answer sheet.

Check to see that the students have found the correct part of the answer sheet.

Say This test will check how well you can use maps and diagrams. Remember to make sure that the circles for your answer choices are completely filled in. Press your pencil firmly so that your marks come out dark. Completely erase any marks for answers that you change.

Look at the map for Sample A and the question. On your answer sheet, find the answer circles for Sample A. Mark the circle for the answer to the question.

Allow time for the students to mark their answers.

Say Answer circle D should have been filled in because the town of Lane is located where Rt. 17 and Highway 32 come together. If you chose another answer, erase yours and fill in circle D now.

Check to see that the students have filled in the correct answer circle.

Say Now you will answer more questions. Mark your answers on the answer sheet. When you come to a GO sign, turn the page and continue working. Work until you come to the STOP sign at the bottom of page 140. When you have finished, you can check over your answers to this test. Then wait for the rest of the group to finish. Any questions?

Test Practice
Test 10 **Maps and Diagrams**

Directions: Read each question. Choose the best answer.

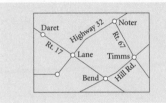

Sample A Which town is found where Rt. 17 and Highway 32 come together?
  A Noter
  B Bend
  C Daret
  * D Lane

Directions: Use this calendar to answer questions 1–3.

May						
Sun	Mon	Tue	Wed	Thu	Fri	Sat
		1	2	3	4	5
6	7	8	9	10	11	12
13	14	15	16	17	18	19
20	21	22	23	24	25	26
27	28	29	30	31		

1 What date is the second Friday in May?
  A The 3rd
  B The 4th
  C The 10th
  * D The 11th

2 At the Willard School, soccer practice takes place on Tuesday afternoon. How many times will soccer practice take place during May?
  J Two
  K Three
  L Four
  * M Five

3 On May 24, Jeff sent a letter to his cousin, Sara. It arrived the following Wednesday. How many days did it take the letter to arrive?
  A Five
  * B Six
  C Seven
  D Eight

GO

138

Answer any questions that the students have.

Say Start working now. You will have 20 minutes.

Allow 20 minutes.

Mascot	First	Second	Third	Fourth	Fifth	Sixth
			Grade			
Tigers			3		1	2
Leopards		1		2		3
Lions	3		1		3	
Cheetahs		2				
Wolves	1	3		1		1
Bears	2		2	3	2	

Directions: The students in each grade of a school voted for a school mascot. This chart shows the first, second, and third choices of each grade. Use the chart to answer questions 4–6.

4 Which animal name received the most first-place votes?
  J   Tigers
* K   Wolves
  L   Leopards
  M   Cheetahs

5 Which animal name received the fewest votes?
  A   Lions
  B   Bears
* C   Cheetahs
  D   Tigers

6 How many classes chose the name "Bears"?
* J   4
  K   3
  L   2
  M   1

GO

Say It's time to stop. You have completed Test 10. Check to see that you have completely filled in your answer circles with dark marks. Make sure that any marks for answers that you changed have been completely erased. Now you may close your books.

Review the items with the students. Have them indicate completion of the lesson by entering their score for this activity on the progress chart at the beginning of the book. Then collect the students' books and answer sheets if this is the end of the testing session.

Directions: Below is a map of a state park. Use the map to answer questions 7–12.

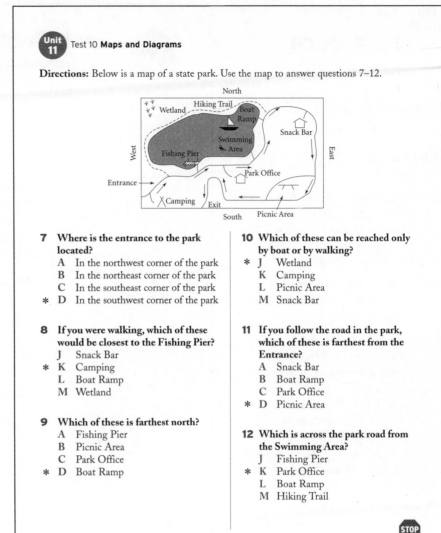

7 Where is the entrance to the park located?
  A   In the northwest corner of the park
  B   In the northeast corner of the park
  C   In the southeast corner of the park
  * D   In the southwest corner of the park

8 If you were walking, which of these would be closest to the Fishing Pier?
  J   Snack Bar
  * K   Camping
  L   Boat Ramp
  M   Wetland

9 Which of these is farthest north?
  A   Fishing Pier
  B   Picnic Area
  C   Park Office
  * D   Boat Ramp

10 Which of these can be reached only by boat or by walking?
  * J   Wetland
  K   Camping
  L   Picnic Area
  M   Snack Bar

11 If you follow the road in the park, which of these is farthest from the Entrance?
  A   Snack Bar
  B   Boat Ramp
  C   Park Office
  * D   Picnic Area

12 Which is across the park road from the Swimming Area?
  J   Fishing Pier
  * K   Park Office
  L   Boat Ramp
  M   Hiking Trail

STOP

140

Administration Time: 30 minutes

Say Turn to Test 11 on page 141.

Check to see that the students have found page 141.

Say Look at your answer sheet. Find the part called Test 11, Reference Materials. Mark all your answers for this test on your answer sheet.

Check to see that the students have found the correct part of the answer sheet.

Say This test will check how well you understand reference materials. Remember to make sure that the circles for your answer choices are completely filled in. Press your pencil firmly so that your marks come out dark. Completely erase any marks for answers that you change.

Look at the words for Sample A. If you put these words in alphabetical order, which one would come first? On your answer sheet, find the answer circles for Sample A. Mark the circle for your answer.

Allow time for the students to mark their answers.

Say Answer circle B should have been filled in because *race* comes first if you put the words in alphabetical order. If you chose another answer, erase yours and fill in circle B now.

Check to see that the students have filled in the correct answer circle.

Say Now do Sample B. Read the question and decide which answer is correct. Mark the circle for the answer you think is best.

Allow time for the students to mark their answers.

Say Answer circle M should have been filled in because the table of contents tells you about the chapters of a book. If you chose another answer, erase yours and fill in circle M now.

 Unit 11

Test Practice
Test 11 **Reference Materials**

Directions: Choose the best answer.

Sample A		Sample B
A team		Where in a book should you look to find out what is contained in each chapter?
* B race		
C slow		J On the title page
D under		K In the index
		L In the glossary
		* M In the table of contents

Directions: For questions 1–6, choose the word or name that would appear first if the words or names were arranged in alphabetical order.

1
A gentle
B field
C home
* D edge

2
J noise
* K meal
L pearl
M office

3
A Reagan, Robert
B Pavarotti, Louis
* C Nielson, Lester
D Olivier, Larry

4
J brush
K break
L brick
* M braid

5
A daytime
B daylight
* C daybreak
D daydream

6
J King, Peggy
* K King, Nancy Ann
L King, Omar
M King, Samuel

GO

141

Check to see that the students have filled in the correct answer circle.

Say Now you will answer more questions. There are different kinds of questions in this test, so be sure to read the directions for each part carefully. Mark your answers on the answer sheet. When you come to a GO sign, turn the page and continue working. Work until you come to the STOP sign at the bottom of page 144. When you have finished, you can check over your answers to this test. Then wait for the rest of the group to finish. Any questions?

Answer any questions that the students have.

Say Start working now. You will have 25 minutes.

Allow 25 minutes.

Directions: Use this table of contents to answer questions 7–12.

Pirates Aplenty	
Chapter	**Page**
1 Treasure Chest of Pirate Facts	6
2 An Assortment of Pirate Ships	10
3 Life Aboard a Pirate Ship	16
4 The History of Pirates	18
5 Legendary Pirates of Seas	20
6 Popular Pirate Hideouts	27
7 Today's Treasure Hunters	30

7 Which of these would Chapter 5 tell you the most about?
  A   How pirates spent their time
* B   Pirates who were well known
  C   The time period when pirates existed
  D   Which seas pirates sailed in

8 Which chapter would tell you lots of different information about pirates?
* J   Chapter 1
  K   Chapter 2
  L   Chapter 3
  M   Chapter 4

9 Which chapter would tell you what it was like to be a pirate?
  A   Chapter 1
  B   Chapter 2
* C   Chapter 3
  D   Chapter 7

10 Which chapter would tell you about the first pirate and how piracy grew after that?
  J   Chapter 2
  K   Chapter 3
* L   Chapter 4
  M   Chapter 6

11 Where should you start reading if you wanted to learn more about the ships in which pirates sailed?
  A   Chapter 6
* B   Chapter 2
  C   Chapter 3
  D   Chapter 4

12 Where should you start reading to find out where buried treasure has been found lately?
  J   Page 6
  K   Page 20
  L   Page 27
* M   Page 30

GO

142

Directions: For questions 13–16, imagine that you are using a library card catalog or computer to look up information.

13 To find books about holidays from around the world, it would be best to look under

* **A** "holidays" as a subject.
 B "from around the world" as a subject.
 C "world" as a subject.
 D "holidays from" as a subject.

14 To find books with games that can be played in a swimming pool, it would be best to look under

 J "games that can be played."
 K "swimming pool."
 L "swimming."
* **M** "games."

15 To find children's books written by Gerald T. Hesslink, look under

 A "T. Hesslink, Gerald" as an author.
 B "children's books" as a subject.
* **C** "Hesslink, Gerald T." as an author.
 D "Gerald" as an author.

16 To find books of poems by Shel Silverstein, look under

 J "books of poems" as a subject.
* **K** "Silverstein, Shel" as an author.
 L "poems" as a subject.
 M "Shel" as an author.

GO

143

Say It's time to stop. You have completed Test 11. Check to see that you have completely filled in your answer circles with dark marks. Make sure that any marks for answers that you changed have been completely erased. Now you may close your books.

Review the items with the students. Have them indicate completion of the lesson by entering their score for this activity on the progress chart at the beginning of the book.

 Unit 11 Test 11 **Reference Materials**

Directions: Use this dictionary and pronunciation guide to answer questions 17–21.

C • c

car•i•bou (**kar'**ə boo') *n.* A kind of North American deer

ca•tas•tro•phe (kə **tas'**trə fē) *n.* A terrible event; disaster

clar•i•fy (**klar'**ə fī') *v.* To make something clear

clas•si•fy (**klas'** ə fī') *v.* To organize into groups

clenched (klencht) *v.* Tightly closed

coax (kōks) *v.* To persuade

con•ceal (kən' **sēl'**) *v.* To hide

coun•cil (**koun'** səl) *n.* A group that makes decisions

cun•ning (**kŭn'** ĭng) *adj.* Clever in a sneaky, dishonest way

cy•clone (**sī'** klōn') *n.* A powerful wind that moves in a circular motion

---

Pronunciation Guide for this dictionary:

ă rat	ĭ bit	ŭ nut	ə stands for
ā lay	ī tie	û burn	a in metal
ĕ net	ŏ not		o in lemon
ē me	ō so		

---

17 How should you spell the word that describes a group of decision makers?
- A counsel
- * B council
- C cownsl
- D councel

18 How should you spell the name of a weather condition?
- J cyclaon
- K cycloan
- * L cyclone
- M cycloon

19 The word *coax* rhymes with
- A joys.
- B jobs.
- C joins.
- * D jokes.

20 Which word fits best in this sentence? "Before you agree to do something for a client, you should have the client _____ what needs to be done."
- J conceal
- * K clarify
- L coax
- M classified

21 Which word best describes a person who cheats when playing games?
- * A cunning
- B complex
- C clenched
- D classified

STOP

144

Administration Time: 45 minutes

Say Turn to Test 12 on page 145.

Check to see that the students have found page 145.

Say Look at your answer sheet. Find the part called Test 12, Science. Mark all your answers for this test on your answer sheet.

Check to see that the students have found the correct part of the answer sheet.

Say This test will check how well you understand science. Remember to make sure that the circles for your answer choices are completely filled in. Press your pencil firmly so that your marks come out dark. Completely erase any marks for answers that you change.

Read Sample A to yourself. Think about the question and look at the answer choices. On your answer sheet, find the answer circles for Sample A. Mark the circle for your answer.

Allow time for the students to mark their answers.

Say Answer circle C should have been filled in because only plants make food using the sun. If you chose another answer, erase yours and fill in circle C now.

Check to see that the students have filled in the correct answer circle.

Say Now do Sample B. Read the question and decide which answer is correct. Mark the circle for the answer you think is best.

Allow time for the students to mark their answers.

Say Answer circle L should have been filled in because Earth is a planet. If you chose another answer, erase yours and fill in circle L now.

Check to see that the students have filled in the correct answer circle.

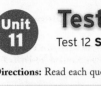

Unit 11 Test Practice
Test 12 **Science**

Directions: Read each question and the answer choices. Choose the best answer.

Sample A One way that plants are different from animals is that
- A only plants reproduce and make more of themselves.
- B only plants have cells.
- *C only plants make food using the sun.
- D only plants have a life cycle.

Sample B Which of these is a planet?
- J The sun
- K The moon
- *L Earth
- M America

1 Fossils are formed when
- A strong rivers wash patterns into rocks.
- B unusual stones are cracked open.
- *C parts of plants or animals are preserved.
- D wind makes unusual shapes on sand.

2 How does a battery work?
- *J Chemical energy is changed to electrical energy.
- K Light energy is changed to electrical energy.
- L Heat energy is converted to light energy.
- M Mechanical energy is converted to light energy.

3 Which complete set of items would a magnet pick up?
- A Toothpicks, napkins, and straws
- *B Nails, pins, and paperclips
- C Tin foil, plastic, and pennies
- D Glass, wax, and silverware

4 To help prevent colds, what is the best thing you can do?
- *J Wash your hands with warm, soapy water.
- K Stay home from school.
- L Turn the heat up higher at night.
- M Get regular checkups at the doctor.

GO

145

Say Now you will answer more questions. Mark your answers on the answer sheet. When you come to a GO sign, turn the page and continue working. Work until you come to the STOP sign at the bottom of page 154. When you have finished, you can check over your answers to this test. Then wait for the rest of the group to finish. Any questions?

Answer any questions that the students have.

Say Start working now. You will have 40 minutes.

Allow 40 minutes.

5 If clouds are dark and heavy, what is the weather probably like?

   A Cold and sunny

   B Warm and bright

   C Sunny and humid

* D Rainy or snowy

6 When did dinosaurs live?

   J Hundreds of years ago

   K Thousands of years ago

* L Millions of years ago

   M Dozens of years ago

7 The moon has many

* A craters.

   B plants.

   C animals.

   D lakes.

8 Bird beaks come in many different shapes. Which of the following is not a real beak shape?

   J A sharp, hooked beak for eating flesh

   K A pointed beak to poke into fruits or berries

   L A lower beak that strains water

* M A beak that has fingers like a hand

9 Every 24 hours, Earth has day and night because

   A Earth revolves around the sun.

   B the sun revolves around Earth.

* C Earth rotates on its axis.

   D the moon makes the tides rise and fall.

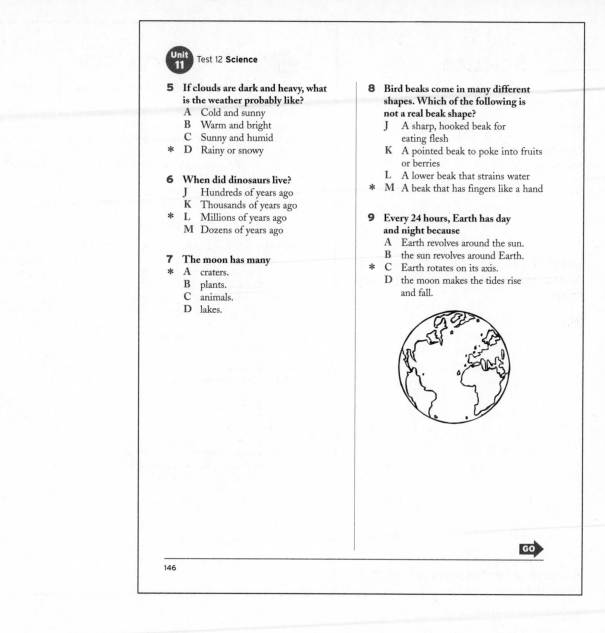

GO

146

Directions: Use the information below to answer questions 10–13.

Asia dropped a golf ball from four different heights to see how high it bounced. Her friend, Tyrell, made a chalk mark on a nearby brick wall at the highest point of each bounce. Then they made a chart to show what happened.

Test	Height of Drop	Height of Bounce
Q	1 foot	8 inches
R	2 feet	1 foot 6 inches
S	3 feet	2 feet 5 inches
T	4 feet	3 feet 9 inches

10 What would make Asia's results inaccurate?

    J Taking turns dropping the ball

    K Using a tape measure rather than a ruler

    L Talking to Tyrell when she drops the ball

* M Measuring the height of the drop incorrectly

11 During which drop did the ball bounce the highest?

    A Q

    B R

    C S

* D T

12 If Asia does this test again, what can she do to get more accurate results?

    J Use different kinds of balls for each bounce

* K Drop the ball several times from each height

    L Make the chalk marks herself

    M Do the test indoors

13 What can Asia conclude about bouncing balls from her experiment?

* A The higher above ground a ball is dropped, the higher it will bounce.

    B Small balls do not bounce as high as large balls.

    C Balls travel higher if they are bounced when it is very cold.

    D Balls bounce better closer to the ground.

GO

147

14 An animal species is extinct when
   J   it has no living relatives.
   K   there are few places for it to live.
   L   it doesn't live where people can see it easily.
* M   not one animal of that species is alive.

15 Conserving water and electricity means
   A   never sharing these things with other people.
   B   drinking only sodas and turning off the television.
* C   using what you need and no more.
   D   building large power plants.

16 Jon plans to weigh a lead cube that measures about two inches on each side and an empty cereal box. He thinks that the cereal box will weigh more because it is bigger. Is he right?
   J   Yes, because the larger the object the more it will weigh.
* K   No, because the lead cube has a greater mass.
   L   No, because the air in the box will help it to float like a balloon.
   M   Yes, because larger objects always have more mass.

17 Water that evaporates from oceans and other bodies of water forms
   A   steam.
   B   oxygen.
* C   clouds.
   D   lightning.

18 How can scientists tell the difference between meat-eating dinosaurs and plant-eating dinosaurs?
   J   Plant-eaters had darker green skin.
   K   Meat-eaters had longer tails.
   L   Plant-eaters were much smaller.
* M   Meat-eaters had sharp, pointed teeth.

 GO

Directions: Use the chart below to answer questions 19 and 20.

Life Stages of Insects

Insect	Egg	Larva	Pupa	Adult
Fly	1 day	8 days	9 days	35 days
Ladybug	4 days	18 days	15 days	9 months
Butterfly	14 days	1 month	6 months	2 months

19 How long does it take for a butterfly to change from the beginning of the egg stage to the completion of the pupa stage?

   A 6 months and 35 days

   B 2 months

* C 7 months and 14 days

   D 9 months

20 Which insect stage lasts for the longest period of time?

   J The ladybug's larva stage

   K The fly's adult stage

   L The butterfly's pupa stage

* M The ladybug's adult stage

21 Why do seeds have an outer coat?

   A Because the ground is cold in winter

   B To keep the seed dry

* C To protect the plant inside and keep it moist

   D So animals cannot eat them

22 Dirt and rocks sometimes come down a mountain as a landslide. The major cause of a landslide is

   J electricity.

* K gravity.

   L light.

   M thunder.

GO

Directions: Use the information below to answer questions 23–26.

Erin filled two pots with dirt and planted a lima bean seed in each one. She put one in a dark closet and the other on a sunny windowsill. She watered both of them twice a week. A few weeks later, the plant on the windowsill stood six inches high and had five large green leaves. The one in the closet drooped over the edge of the pot. It measured two inches long and had one brownish, yellow leaf.

23 What did Erin want to find out?
  A Does watering make seeds grow?
* B Do seeds need sunlight to grow well?
  C Do different seeds grow at different rates?
  D What color leaves do lima bean plants have?

24 Why did Erin put one pot in the closet?
  J To keep it warm
  K So her cat wouldn't spill it
* L So it would not get sunlight
  M To keep wind away from the plant

25 What can Erin conclude from her experiment?
  A The same kind of seed can grow different plants.
* B Sunlight is necessary for proper plant growth.
  C Watering plants causes them to have yellow leaves.
  D All plants will have five leaves if they have sunlight.

26 If Erin repeated the experiment, how could she have more confidence in her results?
  J Measure the height of the plants every day.
  K Put a growing light in the closet.
* L Use seeds from a different kind of plant.
  M Use bottled water rather than tap water.

27 Soil that is made mostly of decayed plants and animals is called
* A loam topsoil.
   B beach sand.
   C gravel.
   D limestone.

28 Which organs are most involved when you exercise?
   J Stomach and liver
   K Brain and kidneys
   L Heart and stomach
* M Lungs and heart

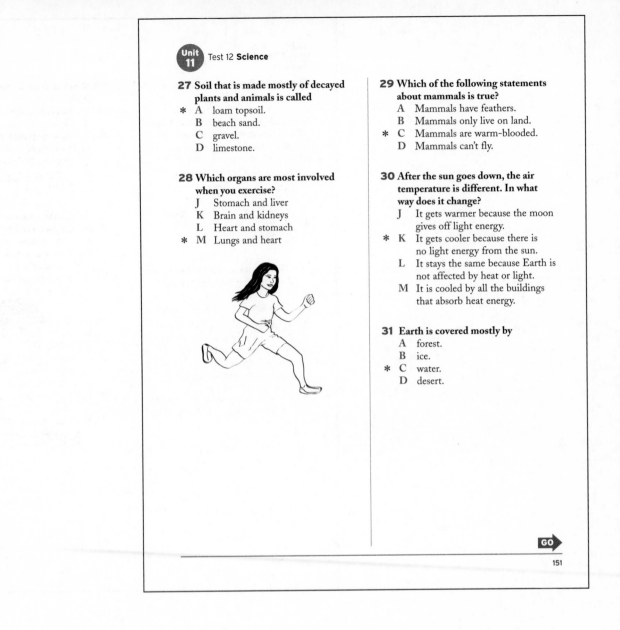

29 Which of the following statements about mammals is true?
   A Mammals have feathers.
   B Mammals only live on land.
* C Mammals are warm-blooded.
   D Mammals can't fly.

30 After the sun goes down, the air temperature is different. In what way does it change?
   J It gets warmer because the moon gives off light energy.
* K It gets cooler because there is no light energy from the sun.
   L It stays the same because Earth is not affected by heat or light.
   M It is cooled by all the buildings that absorb heat energy.

31 Earth is covered mostly by
   A forest.
   B ice.
* C water.
   D desert.

GO

32 **Which of these is true about a magnet?**

* J A magnet has two poles.
  K A magnet is always very heavy.
  L A magnet causes gravity.
  M A magnet floats on water.

33 **Which of these is most likely to become a fossil?**

  A The skin of an animal
  B The footprint of an animal
* C The bone of an animal
  D The hair of an animal

34 **Which of these uses a change from electric energy into heat energy?**

* J A toaster
  K A kite
  L A radio
  M A window

35 **Which of these is true about a magnet?**

  A Magnets can pick up all kinds of metals.
* B Some magnets are stronger than others.
  C Magnets don't work under water.
  D Some magnets can pick up paper and wood.

36 **What is the most important reason to wash your hands?**

  J To have strong skin
  K To have nice nails
  L To look neat
* M To remove germs

GO

152

37 Fog is most like

* A   a cloud.
  B   a storm.
  C   smoke.
  D   fire.

38 You might find all of these things on the surface of the moon except

  J   dust.
  K   rocks.
* L   plants.
  M   craters.

39 A bird's feathers are most like

  A   a human's hands.
  B   a snake's tongue.
  C   a bear's growl.
* D   a fish's scales.

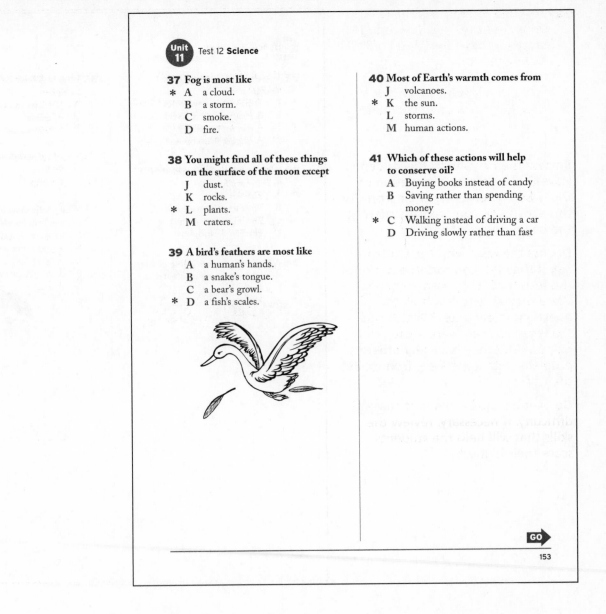

40 Most of Earth's warmth comes from

  J   volcanoes.
* K   the sun.
  L   storms.
  M   human actions.

41 Which of these actions will help to conserve oil?

  A   Buying books instead of candy
  B   Saving rather than spending money
* C   Walking instead of driving a car
  D   Driving slowly rather than fast

GO

Say It's time to stop. You have completed Test 12. Check to see that you have completely filled in your answer circles with dark marks. Make sure that any marks for answers that you changed have been completely erased. Now you may close your books.

Review the items with the students. Have them indicate completion of the lesson by entering their score for this activity on the progress chart at the beginning of the book.

Discuss the tests with the students. Ask if they felt comfortable during the tests, or if they were nervous. Were they able to finish all the questions in each test? Which tips that they learned were most helpful? Did they have any other problems that kept them from doing their best?

Go over any questions that caused difficulty. If necessary, review the skills that will help the students score their highest.

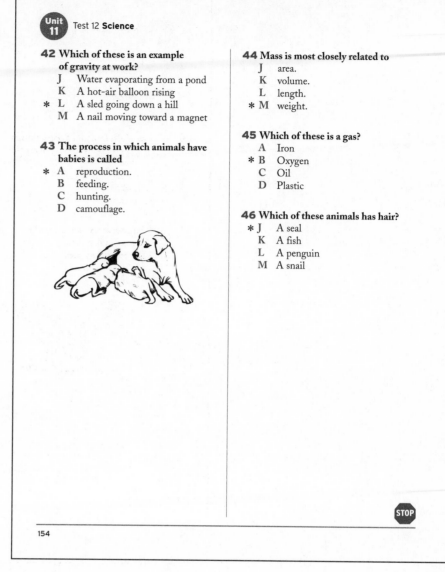

Unit 11 Test 12 **Science**

42 Which of these is an example of gravity at work?
  J   Water evaporating from a pond
  K   A hot-air balloon rising
* L   A sled going down a hill
  M   A nail moving toward a magnet

43 The process in which animals have babies is called
* A   reproduction.
  B   feeding.
  C   hunting.
  D   camouflage.

44 Mass is most closely related to
  J   area.
  K   volume.
  L   length.
* M   weight.

45 Which of these is a gas?
  A   Iron
* B   Oxygen
  C   Oil
  D   Plastic

46 Which of these animals has hair?
* J   A seal
  K   A fish
  L   A penguin
  M   A snail

STOP

154

Page 50
Sample A: B
1. A
2. G
3. D
4. F
5. C
6. directions

Test, pages 51–53
Sample A: D
1. D
2. F
3. B
4. F
5. A
6. J
7. B
8. J
9. cut
Sample B: C
10. B
11. H
12. A
13. J
14. D
Sample C: C
15. F
16. C
17. H
18. C
19. G
20. B
21. fix

Unit 5: Page 55
Step 1: What is the greatest number of toys Jackie can buy with $5.00?

Step 2:
Bears cost $1.98
Dogs cost $1.50
Cats cost $1.45
Birds cost $1.10
Snakes cost $.88
Jackie has $5.00
Jackie can buy no more than one of each animal.

Step 3: Buy toys one at a time, starting with the least expensive, until there isn't enough money left to buy another toy.

Step 4: Buy the first toy
$5.00
$\underline{-.88}$
$4.12

Buy the second toy
$4.12
$\underline{-1.10}$
$3.02

Buy the third toy
$3.02
$\underline{-1.45}$
$1.57

Buy the fourth toy
$1.57
$\underline{-1.50}$
$.07

Step 5: Yes, because there were only 7 cents left after the 4 least expensive toys were purchased.

Page 56
Step 1: Describe the 4 outfits Eduardo can make.

Step 2:

Shirts	Pants
1 striped	1 black
1 solid	1 blue

Step 3: Make a list of combinations of shirts and pants.

Step 4: Outfit 1 Striped shirt & black pants

Outfit 2 Striped shirt & blue pants

Outfit 3 Solid shirt & black pants

Outfit 4 Solid shirt & blue pants

Step 5: Yes, because it lists 4 different outfits.

Unit 6: Page 57
Sample A: B
1. A
2. Mike
3. G
4. A

Page 58
Sample A: B
1. $\frac{4}{5}$
2. D
3. H
4. C
5. F

Page 59
Sample A: A
1. C
2. H
3. C
4. 24

Pages 60–61
Sample A: D
1. B
2. F
3. blue
4. D
5. H
6. D
7. G

Page 62
Sample A: C
1. A
2. 2 and 3
3. H
4. B

Pages 63–64
Sample A: D
1. 4 centimeters
2. A
3. G
4. B
5. J
6. C
7. H

Page 65
Sample A: C
1. how many fish Michelle put into the water
2. D
3. J
4. D

Page 66
Sample A: D
1. A
2. J
3. E
4. H
5. B
6. F
7. B
8. K

Page 67
Sample A: B
1. C
2. 18
3. J
4. B

Test, pages 68–69
Sample A: D
Sample B: G
1. B
2. J
3. C
4. G
5. A
6. H
7. 8
8. A
9. J
10. B
11. $3.75
12. J
13. C
14. G

Test, pages 70–77
Sample A: D
1. B
2. J
3. A
4. G
5. A
6. H
7. 210
8. D
9. H
10. B
11. J
12. A
13. G
14. B
15. J
16. D
17. J
18. C
19. G
20. 2
21. C
22. G
23. C
24. F
25. 3
26. B
27. G
28. B
29. G
30. C
31. G
32. football and basketball
33. A
34. G
35. D
36. H
37. B
38. F
39. D
40. G

Core Skills: Test Preparation, Grade 3

Answer Key

Unit 2: Pages 7–8
1. A
2. G
3. There was no light in the room.
4. C
5. H
6. to sell again

Pages 9–10
1. C
2. J
3. baby ducks
4. C
5. G
6. A person who is social is someone who spends a lot of time with his family and friends.

Pages 11–12
1. B
2. H
3. Saliva is something that is found in your throat. It helps you swallow food, softens your food so your tongue can taste it and helps your body to break the food down.
4. B
5. J
6. An animal's or person's bones.

Pages 13–14
1. C
2. H
3. Her dream was to study law.
4. D
5. F
6. B
7. 9 years

Pages 15–16
1. A.D. 393
2. C
3. H
4. C
5. 1896

Pages 17–18
1. D
2. get out a flashlight
3. H
4. C
5. Take the cake out of the oven and let it cool.

Pages 19–20
1. C
2. J
3. He was rescued in August.
4. C
5. in Missouri
6. F

Pages 21–22
1. A chameleon's ability to change colors can save its life.
2. C
3. G
4. A
5. J

Pages 23–24
1. D
2. F
3. C
4. how cats are very much like lions and tigers
5. what makes a tree a conifer

Pages 25–26
1. Gabriela let Jodi borrow her blue dress.
2. B
3. H
4. A
5. Vince was friends with everyone at camp.
6. H
7. D

Pages 27–28
1. C
2. The man will fall off the bicycle.
3. G
4. C
5. H
6. A

Pages 29–30
1. C
2. angry because she had to do all the work
3. H
4. He was happy because the man did not want to keep the coin.

Pages 31–32
1. The computer helps him speak.
2. C
3. H
4. A
5. H

Unit 3: Pages 33–40
Sample A: B
1. hide-and-seek
2. C
3. H
4. A
5. they were worried
6. J
7. B
8. J
9. D
10. to keep moisture in the pot for a while
11. H
12. A
13. H
14. July 4, 1998
15. A
16. H
17. A
18. H
19. B
20. to plant for food
21. J
22. A
23. J
24. A
25. F
26. A

27. J
28. to make beds
29. A
30. G

Test, pages 41–47
Sample A: C
1. A
2. by using special chemicals to keep it from crumbling
3. J
4. C
5. G
6. A
7. H
8. They fell out of Gabriel's jacket.
9. B
10. F
11. chop it
12. B
13. J
14. B
15. H
16. B
17. to become an astronaut
18. G
19. B
20. H
21. D
22. F
23. B
24. A gust of wind blew him into the water.
25. G
26. D
27. J
28. C

Unit 4: Page 48
Sample A: D
1. C
2. pain
3. G
4. C
5. G
6. B

Page 49
Sample A: D
1. B
2. J
3. C
4. H